PELICAN HISTORY OF THE UNITED STATES
General Editor: Robert A. Divine

Volume 8

RISE TO GLOBALISM

Stephen E. Ambrose was born in Decatur, Illinois, in 1936. In 1956 he was graduated from the University of Wisconsin. He continued his education at Louisiana State University and, again, at the University of Wisconsin, receiving his Ph.D. in 1963. Formerly Eisenhower Professor of War and Peace at Kansas State University, he is currently Professor of History at the University of New Orleans. He has written twelve books, including a history of West Point and studies of Lincoln and Eisenhower. His most recently published volume is *Crazy Horse and Custer*. Among his hobbies Professor Ambrose counts organic gardening, duck hunting, and woodworking.

Stephen E. Ambrose

Rise to Globalism

American Foreign Policy, 1938–1976

Revised Edition

Penguin Books

Penguin Books Ltd, Harmondsworth,
Middlesex, England
Penguin Books, 625 Madison Avenue,
New York, New York 10022, U.S.A.
Penguin Books Australia Ltd, Ringwood,
Victoria, Australia
Penguin Books Canada Limited, 2801 John Street,
Markham, Ontario, Canada L3R 1B4
Penguin Books (N.Z.) Ltd, 182–190 Wairau Road,
Auckland 10, New Zealand

First published with subtitle *American Foreign Policy, 1938–1970*, 1971
Reprinted 1972, 1973, 1975
Revised edition, with subtitle *American Foreign Policy, 1938–1976*,
published 1976
Reprinted 1977, 1978

ISBN 0 14 02.1247 7

Library of Congress catalog card number: 76-350

Printed in the United States of America by
George Banta Company, Inc., Menasha, Wisconsin
Set in Linotype Baskerville

For Missy

Contents

I returned and saw under the sun that the race is not to the swift, nor the battle to the strong, neither yet bread to the wise nor riches to men of understanding, but time and chance happeneth to them all.

ECCLESIASTES

We are willing to help people who believe the way we do, to continue to live the way they want to live.

DEAN ACHESON

Introduction

As Franklin Roosevelt began his sixth year as President, the United States had an Army of 185,000 officers and men with an annual budget of less than $500 million. America had no military alliances and no American troops were stationed in any foreign country. Except on the high seas and within North America, the nation had no offensive capability at all. The overwhelming sentiment within the country was isolationist. Most Americans felt that their country had been cheated by the European powers at the Versailles Conference at the conclusion of World War I and they were determined that never again would the United States be dragged into European disputes. America was willing, even anxious, to trade with foreign powers, but that was all. The single most important fact about American foreign policy in early 1939 was that the great bulk of the American people felt little obligation to become involved in foreign wars, much less that their nation should establish a hegemony over Western Europe or Southeast Asia. American security, the *sine qua non* of foreign policy, seemed assured, not because of American alliances or military might but because of the distance between America and any potential enemy.

One generation later the United States had a standing Army of well over one million men, with an Air Force and a Navy almost as large. The budget of the Department of Defense was almost $80 billion. The United States had military alliances with 48 nations, had 1,517,000 soldiers and sailors stationed in 119 countries, and had an offensive capability sufficient to destroy the world many times over. It had been deeply involved in a bloody conflict in Indochina for over a decade, used military force to intervene in Lebanon and the Dominican Republic, supported an invasion of Cuba, distributed enormous quantities of arms to friendly governments around the world, and fought an undeclared, but costly, war in Korea. Foreign trade and investments abroad had reached unprecedented levels.

After 1945 most Americans felt that the Soviet Union had cheated their country at the Yalta Conference and they were determined that never again would the United States be guilty of taking a soft line with the communists. American policy sought to stop Russian or communist expansion, an attitude that allowed American leaders to assume the role of world policemen. But no matter how far overseas America extended her power, the technological revolution had overcome distance and, despite anything America could do, national security was constantly in jeopardy.

Taken as a whole, the differences between 1938 and 1976 constituted a revolution in means and methods. Although visible elsewhere, this revolution was seen most clearly in the organization, size, techniques, doctrine, and purposes of the American Armed Services. In every significant way, the Armed Services of 1976 were radically different from the Army and Navy of 1938. Before World War II, the military existed to defend the United States from attack; after 1945 its major function was to defend American hegemony outside North America.

The revolution came about in part because of the rise of other nations able to attack the United States or its outposts, now greatly extended, and the demonstration of their willingness to do so. All of the winners of World War II participated in the arms race, generally for the same reasons, so that by the sixties Russia and Great Britain, as well as the United States, were far more armed than they had been in the thirties. The failure of the United Nations to keep the peace, a result of the inability of the great powers to trust each other, combined with awesome military might to create an insecure world order.

America led the way. By 1976 it was capable of intervening almost anywhere almost immediately, and had done
so frequently. This did not constitute a total shift in method,
to be sure, for in the nineteenth century and the first two
decades of the twentieth century the United States had
intervened when it was technologically feasible for it to do
so, pushing its borders to the Pacific Ocean and on to Hawaii
and the Philippines, which was logistically about as far as it
could go. In the nineteen-twenties and the thirties, however,
intervention had receded as the country concentrated on
domestic policies.

A shift in attitudes accompanied the change in policy
after World War II. Before the war most Americans had a
rather curious view of the world scene. They believed in a
natural harmony of interests between nations, assumed
there was a common commitment to peace, and argued that
no nation or people could profit from a war. These beliefs
implied that peace was the normal condition between
states, and that war, if it came, was an aberration resulting
from the irrational acts of evil or psychotic men. It was
strange indeed that a nation that had come into existence
through a victorious war, gained large portions of its territory through war, established its industrial revolution and
national unity through a bloody civil war, and won a
colonial empire through war, could believe that war profited
no one. It was equally strange that a nation that had had
one major war per generation of its existence, plus almost
continuous warfare on its frontier, could assume that peace
was the natural condition of states. Yet Americans did so
believe. They seemed to feel that Germans, like all Europeans, recognized that World War I had demanded ghastly
sacrifices for no gain and that therefore only Hitler and a
few ranking Nazis, not the German people, wanted war.
What Americans did not see was that Hitler was an
authentic expression of a general German desire to set
things right and establish German dominance over
Europe. What had gone wrong in 1914-18, most Germans

reasoned, was not that they had fought, but that they had lost.

The American analysis of the basis of international relations made it difficult, perhaps impossible, for the United States to react effectively to the world crisis of the late thirties. America, England, and France wished to maintain the *status quo* without having to fight for it – thus they wished for peace. Germany, Italy, and Japan wished to change the *status quo* without having to fight in order to do so – thus they too wished for peace. But there was a basic difference in the wishing, and the American assumption that there was a world interest in peace was utopian. As the British soldier Spenser Wilkinson put it, 'It is not peace but preponderance that is in each case the real object. The truth cannot be too often repeated that peace is never the object of policy; you cannot define peace except by reference to war, which is a means and never an end.' By making peace the object of their foreign policy, and by assuming that it represented rationality and the general good, Americans found it difficult to influence events on the eve of World War II.

By 1968 Americans had changed their attitudes. They may not have come to relish war, but they had learned to accept it as a normal condition. They had also come to have an awareness of their vulnerability, which led to the belief, so popular after World War II, that 'if we don't fight them there we'll have to fight them in San Francisco'. The threat had to be met early and overseas. Certainly not all Americans accepted this analysis, but enough did to give the administration support for overseas adventures, at almost any cost.

A historic change of this magnitude cannot be brought about by one man, or even by powerful groups of men. The forces at work are complex and difficult to describe separately, much less in their interaction. But if any one man had to be singled out as the most responsible individual in creating the shape of the world of 1968, and America's role in it, that man would be Adolf Hitler. It was Hitler who forced Roosevelt, his successors, and the American people generally to adopt a new foreign policy, Hitler who upset such balance as had been attained at Versailles, Hitler who threatened to create a world-power in Europe that potentially could make a successful military challenge to the United States, Hitler who opened East Europe to the Soviet Union, previously hemmed in by capitalistic nations, Hitler who created a vacuum in Western Europe in 1945. Most of all, Hitler was the personification of irrational evil, the madman who would, if he could, destroy the world.

Having accepted this image of Hitler, the American people and their leaders found it relatively easy to transfer the image to the man they regarded as Hitler's successor, Joseph Stalin. Technological change, especially in military weapons, gave added impetus to the process. For the first time in its history, the United States could be threatened from abroad. High-speed ships, long-range bombers, jet aircraft, atomic weapons, and eventually intercontinental missiles all combined to endanger the actual physical security of the United States. Previously, those who tried to unite Europe by force, such as Napoleon or the Kaiser, indirectly threatened the economy of the United States, but not its basic security. By the late thirties, however, this situation was changing, and by the early fifties the process was complete. The combination of the new weaponry and irrational, evil rulers like Hitler or Stalin terrified many Americans.

The process of transference of attitudes towards Hitler onto others gained in popularity as time went on, until by the mid-sixties it could be applied even to those who did not have modern, sophisticated weapons. Secretary of State Dean Rusk could use, with apparent success, an analogy that linked the leaders of tiny North Vietnam with Hitler. Whatever the historical faults of Rusk's comparison of any move toward peace in Vietnam to the appeasement of Hitler at Munich, it had the virtue of triggering an automatic reaction among large segments of the population. Hitler's legacy cannot be ignored. Much of the modern world and American foreign policy testifies to his lasting influence.

Everything that the United States has done in the generation since 1938, obviously, could not be traced to the reaction to Hitler. There were other forces at work. At the conclusion of World War II, America was in an enviable position. Her power was such that it invited comparison with Imperial Rome. In all the world, only America had a healthy economy, an intact physical plant capable of mass production of both heavy and consumer goods, and excess capital. It seemed obvious that America would finance the reconstruction of a war-torn world, which carried with it the implication that American leaders would decide what form the reconstruction would take, even to the point of influencing the nature of the governments rising from the smouldering ashes. American troops occupied Japan, the only important industrial power in the Pacific, while American influence was dominant in France, Britain, and western Germany, the industrial heart of Europe. The Pacific and the Mediterranean had become American lakes. Most of all, the United States had a monopoly on the atomic bomb.

Yet despite the nation's preeminent position in the world, America's leaders in the summer of 1945 feared the future. There were three fundamental reasons. The first was the possibility of the emergence of another Hitler − a role Stalin seemed already to have assumed. The second was technological. The atomic secret could not be kept forever (scientists estimated Russia would have the bomb within five to fifteen years) and the German development of rocket weapons clearly illustrated that once missile technology was more mature, the United States would never again be invulnerable. The third fear was economic.

The shadow of the depression loomed as ominously over the decision-makers' shoulders as did the shadow of Munich. There was an almost universal feeling in Washington that in the post-war era America might slip – or plunge – into another depression, which would lead to a revolution at home. Whether the political right or left triumphed made little difference, as leading figures in the Administration saw it, for the result would be the same either way – an end to the American system.

American foreign policy in the crucial years from 1945 to 1950 can be understood only in reference to the widespread fear of another depression. To oversimplify, most men at most times expect the future to resemble the past and, just as the Truman Administration (and its successors) used the increasingly irrelevant example of Hitler and Munich as the touchstone for American relations with Stalin and the rest of the non-capitalist world, so did the Administration believe that the return to pre-war economic conditions might spell a return to depression.

How to avoid depression became the great concern. Government spending could help, but not much – the New Deal had obviously treated only symptoms and had not provided a cure. In 1945, almost no one believed that in peace-time Washington could spend anything like enough money to keep the economy booming, unless the nation adopted some form of central economic dictation. The trouble with extensive central planning and control, however, as the men of 1945 saw it, was that it would evolve into either a government of the right or one of the left, each of which was repugnant.

The solution to the problem of another depression, as most of the policy-makers in the Truman Administration saw it, was a continuation of the New Deal (renamed Fair Deal) and, far more important, greatly expanded foreign trade. What America needed above all, according to the analysis, was foreign markets in which she could sell the products pouring out of her factories – and, as some realized, access to raw materials to feed the factories.

The trouble with expanded foreign trade as a preferred solution to America's economic dilemma was that much of the proposed market place was closed. This was almost as true of the British Commonwealth as it was of the Soviet Union and its satellites, and at the time of the lend-lease agreements in 1941, and again during the negotiations for the British loan in 1945, the Americans had used their heaviest financial weapons to force the British to break down the imperial preference system and open their markets. They met with only limited success, but what really worried Truman and his advisers was the trend throughout the world. In the non-white colonies, the determination to be free both politically and economically created an objective revolutionary situation almost everywhere in the Third World, which carried with it the threat of nationalization of raw material sources, basic industry, and markets. From the American point of view, it made little difference if the nationalization was carried out by governments of the right or of the left – Hitler's National Socialism had made it nearly as difficult for American corporations to compete in Germany as Stalin's communism did in Russia. In Europe, in 1945, the trend was strongly in the direction of further nationalization, with the Labour Party in Britain moving in the same direction as the Russian puppet governments in East Europe.

To generalize (as did the Administration leaders as they looked to the future), what Americans feared was that their manufacturers would be unable to compete with foreign industries that had all the resources of the state behind them. If the rest of the world nationalized its basic industries and/or closed its markets, America could avoid over-production and a resultant depression only by nationalizing the means of production and distribution itself. American foreign policy after 1945 had as one of its guiding stars, therefore, the prevention of these evils – or, put positively, the creation of an open door everywhere. To insure these conditions the nation prepared to use her economic might (as in the British loan and the Marshall Plan) or her military muscle (as in Greece, Korea, and elsewhere). The leaders believed that free, private enterprise was essential to a free, open, democratic society, and they would save it at home by imposing it abroad.

The program had some failures, many successes. The enormous expansion in American production and financial predominance became the central factor in world economics. American corporate investment abroad increased astronomically and the government assumed the obligation of protecting – indeed, encouraging – those investments. But one of the tragedies of American foreign policy was that the United States reached the imperialistic stage at a time when the peoples of the exploited nations were increasingly determined that they would no longer be ruled by others, especially white men. After World War II the United States generally regarded the Third World as a source of raw material and labor, or various parts of it as sites for potential or actual military bases, but even where the Americans were genuinely trying to create a better life they were regarded with suspicion.

Even had the American economy not required foreign markets, outlets for investment, or access to raw materials, the ideological differences between the Soviet Union and the United States would have fed an arms race, which neither country 'began' but from which neither shrank. With good reason, each was deeply suspicious of the other. Nuclear weapons and the missiles to deliver them became the pivot around which much of the Cold War revolved. Each time one side developed a new bomb or built additional missiles, the other side followed. The growth of the Armed Services and their suppliers – the military-industrial complex – gave generals and admirals and industrialists new sources of power, leading to a situation in which Americans tended to find military answers to political problems. The President and his chief advisers frequently were tempted to accept the military solution precisely

because the United States did have so much power. No
people or nation, it seemed, could stand against the American Armed Services, and one of the best things about
inaugurating military action was that when the shooting
was over the Americans could make the political decisions
unilaterally — assuming they won. Not until the mid-
seventies did large numbers of Americans learn the painful
lesson that the power to destroy is not the power to control.

The United States of the Cold War period, like ancient
Rome, was concerned with all political problems in the
world. The loss of this or that country to communism,
therefore, while not in itself a threat to American physical
security, carried with it implications that officials in
Washington found highly disturbing. They became greatly
concerned with trends, with the appearance as well as the
reality of events, and there was much talk of dominoes. Who
ruled the Dominican Republic, for example, was of concern to one or two American corporations only, and clearly
nothing that happened on the island posed the slightest
threat to American security. But the State Department, the
White House, and the C.I.A. were certain that if the
communists won in the Dominican Republic, they would
soon win elsewhere. In the early sixties, few important
officials argued that South Vietnam was essential to the
defense of the United States, but the attitude that 'we have
to prove that wars of national liberation don't work' (a
curious attitude for the children of the American Revolution to hold) did carry the day, aided in no small measure
by the argument that if Vietnam went communist, all
Southeast Asia would soon follow. Then would come the
Pacific islands, and finally the fight would be on America's
West Coast.

The attitude that what happened anywhere in the world
was important to the United States differed radically from
the American outlook of 1938. One reason for the change
was the astonishing growth of America's overseas military
bases. The American Armed Services flowed into many

vacuums at the end of the war and once American troops were stationed on foreign soil, that soil was included in the list of America's 'vital interests'. But America's rise to globalism was by no means mindless, just as it was not exclusively a reaction to the supposed communist challenge During World War II Henry Luce of *Life* magazine spoke for most political leaders as well as American businessmen and soldiers when he said that the twentieth century would be the American century. The politicians looked for areas in which American influence could dominate; the businessmen looked for profitable markets and new sources of raw materials; the military looked for overseas bases. All found what they wanted as America after World War II inaugurated a program of expansion that had no inherent limits.

Americans who wanted to bring the blessings of democracy, capitalism, and stability to everyone meant just what they said – the whole world, in their view, should be a reflection of the United States. Americans launched a crusade for freedom that would be complete only when freedom – as they defined it – reigned everywhere. Conservatives like Senator Robert Taft doubted that such a goal was obtainable, and old New Dealers like Henry Wallace argued that it could be achieved only at the cost of domestic reform. But most politicians and nearly all businessmen and soldiers signed on as crusaders.

While America was creating her empire, while her businessmen and soldiers and politicians moved into Latin America, Europe, Southeast Asia and nearly everywhere else, her leaders scarcely wondered if there were limits to American power. The disorderly expansion and the astronomical growth of areas defined as constituting a vital interest seemed to Washington and Wall Street and the Pentagon as entirely normal and natural. Almost no important public figure argued that the nation was overextended, just as none could suggest any attitude towards communism other than that of unrelieved hostility. The idea that the Third World would resent, and eventually

struggle against, American domination was hardly considered.

Only the ultimate military reality put limits on American
expansion. At no time after 1950 was the United States
capable of destroying Russia or her allies without taking on
totally unacceptable risks herself. The crusade against
communism, therefore, soon took the form of containment
rather than overt attack. Containment, with its implication
of an acceptance of a permanently divided world and thus
of a limit to American expansion, led to almost intolerable
frustration. But hardly anyone seriously considered an
alternative to containment. By the mid-seventies, America,
despite defeat in Indochina, remained determined to hold
to her empire, whatever the cost. The revolution in attitudes, policies, and methods that began in 1939 had gone
too far to be easily reversed

[1]

The Twisting Path to War

THE United States was fairly well satisfied with the world of 1938. The depression was the chief fact of life, and it had not yet been licked, but there was no overpowering sentiment to overcome it through foreign adventures. Secretary of State Cordell Hull believed that the ultimate solution to the Depression would come through increased foreign trade, which led him to advocate policies designed to hold onto current markets and to open new ones, but he never advocated force to accomplish these ends and in any case the President and the Congress were more inclined to search for economic solutions at home. In Europe, anti-communism was triumphing in Spain, while in central and eastern Europe governments hostile to the Soviet Union continued to hem in the Russians. Germany was a threat, especially after Hitler's victory at Munich, but it seemed possible that he would now be satisfied to consolidate his gains in Austria and Czechoslovakia. Certainly as long as Britain and France continued to stand against Hitler the United States had nothing to fear militarily from Germany and trade with Europe could continue at a normal pace.

On the other side of the world, the United States felt that in combination with the British, French, and Dutch it still held the upper hand. The Pacific was not an American lake, but neither did it belong to anyone else, and American outposts in Hawaii and the Philippines gave the United States a powerful position. The raw materials of the Netherlands East Indies (N.E.I.) and the Malayan Peninsula were available to the West, while the French continued to control the other key positions in Southeast Asia.

The Open Door policy in China had been battered almost beyond recognition, but still the Japanese were unable to conquer that vast land. Japan was aggressive, determined to end white man's rule in Asia, and thus a threat to the American position in the Pacific, but she lacked crucial natural resources and was, hopefully, tied down for a long time to come in China.

On the great land mass connecting Europe and Asia, Russia remained an enigma, but a fairly quiet, non-expansive one. In the Mid-East and Africa, European colonialism seemed to work, and Americans, although they verbally disapproved of the more repressive aspects of the exploitation, were nevertheless not inclined to do anything about it. In Latin America, American economic imperialism, although tempered politically by Roosevelt's Good Neighbor policy, guaranteed raw materials for American industries.

The United States in 1938 saw no pressing need for any great change in the world and indeed little justification for even minor modifications. The attitude inside the country towards war reinforced this belief. Unlike Winston Churchill or Hitler or some of the Japanese leaders, and unlike his cousin Theodore Roosevelt, Franklin Roosevelt saw neither glory nor romance in war, nor did he feel that it strengthened the national fiber. If not a pacifist, the President was certainly no militarist.

Isolationism reigned in the Congress, reflecting a national mood. The Nye Committee, conducting a Senate investigation, had 'proved' that Wall Street had dragged the United States into World War I in order to protect banker's loans to the Allies and showed that corporations had enjoyed exorbitant wartime profits while evading taxation. The idea that World War I had been fought for the benefit of big business was easily accepted by a Depression generation that blamed its current economic ills on the same businessmen.

American foreign policy in 1938, then, was to support the

status quo, but only through vaguely worded statements. Roosevelt, Hull, and a majority of the American people did not want a German domination of Europe or a Japanese domination of Asia, but neither were they ready to do much to stop it. Least of all were they ready to improve the Armed Services so that the United States could threaten to punish aggression.

In mid-March 1939, Hitler's armies overran Czechoslovakia. Britain and France tried to make it clear to Germany that they were finished with appeasement; if Hitler struck again in eastern Europe, there would be war. One key question was what the United States would do. The answer, in the end, was nothing. Senator Key Pittman introduced a resolution that would repeal the arms embargo and permit American industries to sell war goods on a cash-and-carry basis, a resolution that would obviously favor England and France, for they alone had the financial resources and sea power to buy and transport arms from the United States. But Roosevelt gave the resolution no public support and it failed. Although the President and a majority of the people had declared that their sympathies lay with the democracies, they had also demonstrated to Hitler that in the immediate future he had little to fear from the United States.

On 23 August 1939, as Hitler's pressure on Poland mounted, Roosevelt sent offers to act as a conciliator to the King of Italy, the President of Poland, and Hitler. An Assistant Secretary of State who helped draft the messages said they would 'have about the same effect as a valentine sent to somebody's mother-in-law out of season'. The messages constituted Roosevelt's major effort to stop war in Europe. That same day, 23 August, Hitler announced the Nazi–Soviet Pact, which provided for the division of Poland between Russia and Germany and relieved Germany of the nightmare of a two-front war. On 1 September, the Nazis struck at Poland; two days later Britain and France declared war.

The failure to prevent war had widespread repercussions on the American domestic scene. Before the conflict began there had been general agreement on the need to prevent it; when the shooting started, Americans began to split sharply over the question of what to do about it. Although most wished to stay out, the isolationists resisted any steps that might lead to aid to the democracies, fearing that the United States would thereby become so committed to an Allied victory that, as in 1917, she would be drawn into the war against her will. Those who would later be interventionists wanted to abandon all pretense at neutrality and give material aid to Britain and France. Roosevelt took a middle-ground, one which was not only politically expedient but which probably accurately indicated his own sentiments. As was often the case, he was reflecting the national mood. Sixty per cent of the people queried by pollsters in October 1939 said they felt it had been a mistake to enter the last war, and Roosevelt himself had been impressed by the revelations of the Nye Committee. On 21 September, after first carefully canvassing leading Congressmen to make certain that he would not offend by what he said, Roosevelt spoke to a special session of Congress in his first major address on the war. Four times he declared that his policy was aimed at keeping the United States out of the war. He then asked for repeal of the embargo on arms and approval of a cash-and-carry system. Although this would obviously aid the democracies, Roosevelt insisted that it was merely a return to traditional international law and would insure peace for America. The isolationists were furious, but in November the bill carried.

Cash-and-carry symbolized much that was to follow. It did align the United States with the democracies, reiterate American concern and friendship for Western Europe, and make it clear that the country would resist any attempt to upset the balance of power in Europe. But it also indicated that the United States was unwilling to pay a high price to stop Hitler. America would sell arms to the democracies, as long as they picked them up and carried them off. No American sailors would risk their lives in delivering the equipment. Roosevelt made no effort to force American industry to retool in order to provide Britain and France with arms, gave no indication that any sacrifice at all would be required of the American people to defeat Hitler (in fact said explicitly that the exact opposite was his intention), and did practically nothing to beef-up the Armed Services. Later, when the threat from Germany loomed larger, Roosevelt went farther, but never, even after Pearl Harbor, was he willing to cut deeply into the civilian economy in order to provide material to America's allies. Nor would he ever be willing to pay a high cost in lives or goods to defeat Hitler. The theme of America's participation in World War II was victory at the lowest possible cost.

Most nations at war fight with what they have at hand, more particularly with what they have more of than their opponents or their allies. This rule of thumb also applies to tactics. After World War II Russian generals were amazed to hear that Americans often cleared a path through mine-fields by setting off the mines through the use of artillery. This seemed to the Russians an irresponsible waste of valuable shells. The Americans were equally astonished to learn that the Russian method was to march troops through the minefields. Each side used what it had in abundance. The great advantages enjoyed by Americans in the war were that they had more material and money than anyone else, and they were physically separated from the aggressors. Therefore, like Great Britain in the nineteenth century, it was obviously a wise American policy to pay others to do the fighting that had to be done, especially since the United States did not have to devote an excessive share of her production to war goods to provide the tools necessary to defeat the Axis, nor was her homeland threatened. Geography had played a great role in Britain's domination in the nineteenth century; geography was central to America's rise in the twentieth century. All the nations involved in

World War II wanted victory at the lowest possible cost, but America was the lucky one.

The irony was that the United States, after paying the least of all the Allies in lives or (in relative terms) in material expended for the war, gained the most from victory. Roosevelt's policy of limited mobilization, which continued through the war, left the United States at the war's conclusion in by far the most powerful position of all the Allies. The American economy was intact and booming, the Pacific had become an American lake, with U.S. Navy bases scattered throughout the ocean and with U.S. Army troops in occupation of the leading industrial power of Asia. America was the leader of a rapidly emerging West European union. There was another aspect to the ironic outcome of the war; millions of Americans came to believe that their country had been tricked by the Soviet Union during the wartime conferences, that the United States had made enormous sacrifices for no purpose, and that the only winner was Russia – which had lost nearly half its productive capacity and 20 million people. The important point, nevertheless, was that the United States had taken Britain's place and played her nineteenth-century role by avoiding huge battles on the Continent, paying others to do the fighting, and thereby being the only power at the conclusion strong enough to assume a predominant position. Whether this was a brilliant application of a policy of following national self-interest, or just geographical luck, or a combination of both, did not really matter. America did as much as was necessary, although during the early stages of the war it appeared that she was taking uncommonly large risks by not doing more.

The limitation on American commitment was obvious from the beginning. After Hitler's armies overran Poland, a period of stagnation set in on the Western Front. Americans called it a 'phony war' and saw no reason to strain themselves to shore up the democracies, or even to build up their own strength. Roosevelt increased the Regular Army from

210,000 to 217,000 and asked for an Army budget of $853 million, which the House of Representatives cut by nearly 10 per cent. These paltry figures constituted an announcement to the world that the United States did not intend to fight in Europe in the near future. Army Chief of Staff George Marshall had warned Congress, 'If Europe blazes in the late spring or early summer, we must put our house in order before the sparks reach the Western Hemisphere,' but it did no good. Even had Roosevelt wished to inaugurate a vigorous foreign policy, he had nothing but the potential of the United States with which to operate, and given the Congressional and public mood even the potential was none too frightening.

The German spring offensive of 1940, from the beginning successful beyond the wildest dreams of the German General Staff, brought forth a tough verbal but a limited practical response from the United States. The isolationists were supposedly strongest in Congress, but Congress proved more willing than Roosevelt to begin preparing America for war. The President asked for a supplemental appropriation of $732 million for the Army, which would raise the Regular Army to 255,000; Congress, after hearing General Marshall's desperate appeals, raised the force level to 375,000 and the total appropriation for the War Department to $3 billion. The Nazis, meanwhile, rolled on. On 15 May the new British Prime Minister, Winston Churchill, urgently requested forty or fifty American destroyers to protect the Atlantic supply line. Churchill called it a matter of 'life or death'. Roosevelt was reluctant to act. On 5 June, with the fall of France imminent and Britain about to be left standing alone, he told a Cabinet official it would require an act of Congress to transfer the destroyers to England and implied that he was not ready to ask for such a bill.

He was ready to speak out, if only to test the nation's mood. On 10 June 1940, the President told the graduating class of the University of Virginia that the United States would follow 'two obvious and simultaneous courses', extending to France and Britain 'the material resources of this nation' and speeding up the development of these resources so that the American Armed Services could be improved. The speech was hailed by interventionists in the United States as setting a new course, but the French quickly discovered it was not to be. On 14 June French Premier Paul Reynaud appealed to Roosevelt to send American troops to Europe in France's hour of need. Roosevelt refused. He informed Reynaud that only Congress could declare war, leaving the inference that Congress would not do so even if the President asked for such a declaration. Perhaps more important, even had Roosevelt wanted to act, he had no troops available to send overseas. The next day Churchill made an eloquent appeal. 'A declaration that the United States will if necessary enter the war might save France,' he pointed out. 'Failing that, in a few days French resistance may have crumpled and we shall be left alone.' Roosevelt could or would do nothing and within the week France surrendered.

The fall of France was a shattering blow. No one, not even the Germans and least of all American Army experts, had expected it. The United States now faced an entirely new situation. No longer could the nation comfortably expect that, as in 1914–17, British and French blood would stop the Germans. Britain, alone, might survive, although even that was questionable, but never would she be able to roll back the Nazis by herself. The best-disciplined and most highly educated, motivated, and productive nation in Europe now dominated the Continent. The balance of power was gone. America had been shut out of the European market, perhaps permanently. Hitler posed no immediate military threat, but if he could conquer England and get control of the British fleet, then overrun Russia – suddenly real possibilities – he would command the greatest military might the world had ever known. What could happen then was anyone's guess, but it was becoming increasingly apparent that it behooved Americans to do something more than sit by and watch. Hitler could be stopped, and some kind of balance restored in Europe, only if others came to Britain's aid.

Roosevelt is generally given credit for having sensed these truths. He did not move quickly or dramatically, however, because of public opinion. Certainly the polls taken at the time indicated that his gestures and policies carried America forward as fast and as far as the majority wanted to go. In July of 1940, although 40 per cent queried said it was more important to help England than to keep out of the war, less than 5 per cent thought that the United States should declare war on Germany. In November 1941, 65 per cent were ready to help England whatever the consequences. Still less than 25 per cent were ready to declare war. These figures have been often cited to prove that Roosevelt could have done no more than he did. But what the figures do not show is the absence of Presidential leadership. If Roosevelt did believe that America had to enter the war to protect Western civilization, not to mention the territorial integrity of the United States, he certainly never made this clear to the American people. The truth is he probably had an inner conflict that reflected the public confusion. He was very much of his time and place, sharing general attitudes on the mistake of entering World War I. In a famous election speech in Boston on 30 October 1940, he declared: 'And while I am talking to you mothers and fathers, I give you óne more assurance. I have said this before, but I shall say it again and again and again: Your boys are not going to be sent into any foreign wars.'

Neither, it seemed, was a great deal of American equipment. The British still obtained supplies only on a cash-and-carry basis and they still lacked the destroyers necessary to protect the convoys transporting the goods they could afford to purchase. Even when Lord Lothian, the British ambassador, and the pro-British Committee to Defend America by Aiding the Allies suggested that the United States trade over-age destroyers for naval and air bases on British islands in the Western Hemisphere, Roose-velt did nothing. He also failed to respond to a Churchill plea for the destroyers on 21 July: 'Mr President, with great respect I must tell you that in the long history of the world this is a thing to do NOW.' The British were losing merchant shipping at sea in appalling numbers, the Battle of Britain was reaching its peak, and the German General Staff was preparing plans for a final invasion of the home isles. In the United States, the Presidential election campaign began and the President took no part in a national debate on a peace-time conscription bill.

The President's caution knew few bounds. He allowed private groups to work out the details of the destroyers-for-bases deal, which eventually (2 September) gave the British fifty over-age destroyers in return for rent-free bases on British possessions from Bermuda to British Guiana. 'What is most striking about the . . . deal,' Robert Divine has noted, 'is the caution and reluctance with which the President acted,' a reflection of Roosevelt's own doubts about a proper policy. 'In June he announced a policy of all-out aid to Britain, yet he delayed for nearly four months after receiving Churchill's desperate plea for destroyers. He acted only after interventionists had created strong public support, only after the transfer could be disguised as an act in support of the American defense program, only after the leader of the opposition party had agreed not to challenge him politically on this issue, and only after his legal advisers found a way to bypass Congress.' Divine concludes, 'What may have appeared on the surface to be a bold and cour-ageous act by the President was in reality a carefully cal-culated and virtually foolproof maneuver.'

There was, meanwhile, a growing tension between the War Department and the White House. General Marshall took it as established policy that the United States looked forward to Hitler's defeat and wanted to make a contri-bution to it. He reasoned that the only way to do so was to meet and defeat the German army on the plains of Northwest Europe, a proposition that never had Roosevelt's full backing. If Marshall wanted to take on the Wehrmacht he needed a mass army, and to get that he needed conscription. But given the tenor of Roosevelt's third-term campaign, there was no possibility that the President could give public support to a conscription bill. This put Marshall in a seemingly insoluble dilemma, for he could hardly carry out an openly anti-Hitler policy without the President's support, especially in the crucial task of getting millions of men into uniform, equipped, and trained. Congress proved more willing to act than the President. Private groups, led by Republicans Henry L. Stimson and Elihu Root, Jr, persuaded friendly Congressmen to introduce a selective service bill in both houses of Congress. Roosevelt kept his hands off, but he did give Marshall permission to support the bill; the President also helped by appointing Stimson the Secretary of War. In late August 1940, Congress authorized the President to call the National Guard and other reserves to active duty for one year, and on 16 September it provided for selective service for one year. Both measures limited the employment of troops raised under them to the Western Hemisphere, but they were a start.

There was a widespread assumption in the United States, later shared by many historians, that Roosevelt was hiding his true intentions until after the election campaign. Even though the Republican nominee, Wendell Willkie, made an issue of foreign policy only at the climax of the 1940 campaign, it was generally true that interventionists voted for Roosevelt, isolationists for Willkie. By December, with the triumph of the election victory behind him, Roosevelt was free to move swiftly and boldly to bolster the British. His actions, however, while important, were not decisive, probably because he still thought it possible simultaneously to keep the civilian economy rolling within the United States, to give aid to Britain, and to defeat Hitler without an American involvement in the war. Roosevelt's later shift to a more active policy, such as it was, seems to have come more as a result of German success in Russia than as a result of his election victory.

Churchill was one of those who felt the re-elected Roosevelt would be a different man from the third-term candidate. Shortly after the election, he sent the President a lengthy and bleak description of the British situation, emphasizing that his nation was running out of money. Cash-and-carry would no longer suffice, for 'the moment approaches when we shall no longer be able to pay cash for shipping and other supplies'. Roosevelt responded sympathetically. On 7 December 1940, he called in the press, outlined the British dilemma, and said he believed that 'the best defense of Great Britain is the best defense of the United States'. Seeking to avoid the mistakes of Woodrow Wilson and the whole muddle of World War I war debts, Roosevelt said he wanted to get rid of the dollar sign by simply lending or leasing to England the supplies she needed. He compared his scheme to the idea of lending a garden hose to a neighbor whose house was on fire.

In a radio address to the nation a few days later, Roosevelt justified lend-lease as essential to national security. If England fell, 'all of us in the Americas would be living at the point of a gun'. Continuing the theme inherent in his Presidential campaign, he said the best way to keep the United States out of the war was to 'do all we can now to support the nations defending themselves against attack by the Axis'. He declared again that he had no intention of sending American boys to Europe; his sole purpose was to 'keep war away from our country and our people'. He would do this by making America the 'great arsenal of democracy'.

It took three months, but in early March 1941 lend-lease went through Congress, with an appropriation of $7 billion. It was a most unneutral act, placing the United States squarely on the British side in the conflict and constituting, in Secretary Stimson's words, 'a declaration of economic war'. Bold as lend-lease was in its conception, however, the practice was something less. For a variety of reasons, Roosevelt refused to provide strongly centralized control, lend-lease administration was confused, some American officials tried to use the new system as a wedge to get American firms into the British Commonwealth market and to force the British to sell their holdings on the American Continents, the Army held back on sending arms to Britain that were needed within the United States, and most important of all the total amount of goods shipped, in comparison with the need, was small. Lend-lease may have been the most unsordid act in human history, as Churchill called it, but there was much that was petty about it and in any event by itself it was hardly sufficient to do the job.

What was needed was a far more extensive American involvement. Still, although a majority in the Cabinet felt the time for vacillation was over and urged the President to ask for a declaration of war against Germany, Roosevelt moved slowly. He declared an Atlantic neutrality zone that extended almost to Iceland, ordering the Navy to patrol the area and give warning of aggressors, which meant in practice reporting the location of German submarines to the British. In July, following Hitler's invasion of Russia, with its early successes which made Germany appear a greater threat than ever, Roosevelt began to step up the number and extent of his acts. American troops occupied Iceland (they had moved onto Greenland in April), and the Navy began escorting convoys as far as Iceland. In September, when a German submarine fired a torpedo at an American destroyer, Roosevelt delivered a strong speech denouncing the 'rattlesnakes of the Atlantic' and implying that American ships would shoot German submarines on sight. He also decided that henceforth the Navy would escort British merchant ships half-way across the Atlantic. In October 1941, Roosevelt asked for and got from Congress a removal of nearly all restrictions on American commerce from the Neutrality Acts. Henceforth, American merchant vessels could carry equipment to British ports.

Roosevelt's tone, in public and private, was now one of unrestrained belligerency. German advances to the gates of Moscow made it impossible to underestimate the threat. Roosevelt therefore created a situation which, he believed, made it only a matter of time before the Germans would give him a chance to ask Congress for a declaration of war. He seems to have reasoned that Hitler could not long permit American ships to transport goods to Britain. The Germans would have to order their submarine captains to sink the American vessels. Roosevelt could then overcome isolationist opposition in Congress and get a declaration of war.

Whether he was right or not will never be known. A few weeks later Germany declared war on the United States, but for reasons that had little to do with the shipping issue. Had it not been for the Japanese attack on America's Pacific outposts, however, and Hitler's honoring of his pledge to join the Japanese if war came between them and the United States, it is doubtful that the Germans would have taken the last step of a formal declaration. Certainly they would have met Roosevelt's expectations and started sinking American ships, but they had nothing to gain from declaring war. This would have left Roosevelt at the end of his rope. He would have had to ask Congress for war on the basis of an attack on the American merchant marine, but unlike Wilson in 1917 he could not have pretended that neutrality had been violated, since the United States had long since ceased to be neutral. Surely the isolationists would have resisted a request for war by arguing that the American ships should not have been sailing for Britain, carrying war material, in the first place. Even had a Presidential request for war carried in the Congress, Roosevelt would have been leading a bitterly divided country.

By December 1941, American foreign policy in Europe had failed to make any significant contribution to stopping, much less overcoming, Hitler. In retrospect, the steps the

President and the Congress took to protect American interests in Europe (which, if difficult to define precisely, included at a minimum the defeat of the Nazis) were halting and limited. Roosevelt had not provided the leadership the situation required. Hesitant to make a final commitment himself, reluctant even after his re-election to lead a public debate on the issues involved, cautious to an extreme in his efforts to keep Britain going, unwilling to interfere with the domestic economy, he had become a prisoner of events. Everything hinged on Russia and Britain. If they kept going, America could – eventually – supply them with the tools and enough fighting divisions to do the job. The United States stood to profit enormously from such an outcome, but in the meantime it was taking great risks.

The American ship of state was drifting, without a rudder or power, in a storm. When the Germans invaded Russia in June 1941, with successes that promised to give them quickly total control of the Eurasian heartland, the United States was unable to help. Roosevelt did extend lend-lease to the Soviets, but the trickle of supplies made no significant contribution to the Russian defense. The world's greatest industrial nation could not stem the tide of Fascism. Roosevelt's caution was so great that in September 1941, when the original selective service bill ran out and had to be repassed if the soldiers already partly trained were to be retained in the Army, he refused to pressure Congress, either privately or publicly. Working behind the scenes, General Marshall was able to get the draft bill passed – by one vote. Even this left the United States Army ridiculously small (1,600,000) if the nation ever intended to play a role in the outcome of the conflict raging in Europe.

Fortunately for the United States, the British and Russians held out, making it possible for America to later exert her power to influence the development and shape of Europe. Fortunately, also, the Japanese solved Roosevelt's dilemma for him.

In 1938 American policy towards Europe was to maintain the *status quo*, but, much as most American leaders feared a German domination of the Continent, they were unwilling or unable to do much in a practical way to prevent it. In the Far East, although American actions were sharper, there was still hesitation. In part this was because policy towards Japan was always subordinate to the need to contain Germany, by far the more powerful and dangerous enemy. The Armed Services did not want to become involved in a Pacific war until the European conflict had been settled. The Europe-first policy, however, represented the attitudes of the military and the Cabinet more than it did a general sentiment. The American people were badly divided on the question of the proper response to Hitler; the divisions almost disappeared when the question was Japanese aggression. The racist nature of the conflict in the Pacific, the fact that the Pacific war was unencumbered by embarrassing allies such as the British imperialists (who confined their Pacific fighting to the Burma theater) or the Russian communists, and America's self-imposed mission to maintain an Open Door in China combined to make all but the most extreme isolationists willing to defend American interests in the Far East.

The Japanese program aimed at making Japan the great power of the Pacific, with control of China, French Indo-china, the Malayan Peninsula, and the N.E.I. It was essential to the Japanese that they should have these areas if Japan were to be a great power, for despite her human resources Japan was almost devoid of critical raw materials, especially oil. The place to get the oil was Southeast Asia. This fact dictated Japanese policy and the American response.

The American colony of the Philippines lay directly athwart the Japanese proposed line of advance. Although not crucial economically, the Philippines were of prime strategic importance. Whether correctly or not, the Japanese were convinced that the United States would never allow them to advance into Malaya or the N.E.I. without striking against the flanks of their lines of communications. More fundamentally, they realized that the United States would never willingly allow them to become a great power and would consistently oppose, certainly diplomatically and possibly militarily, their advance southward. Thus although the Japanese realized that if they goaded the United States into war, and the United States chose to fight it to a finish, they were doomed, they felt they were doomed even without war if they accepted the American program for the Far East. They were convinced that the United States was determined to reduce Japan to a position of secondary importance, which left Japan with no alternative but to go to war while she still had the power to do so. She might lose, but defeat was better than submission. 'Japan entered the war,' a prince of the Japanese Imperial family wrote, 'with a tragic determination and in desperate self-abandonment.' If she lost, 'there will be nothing to regret because she is doomed to collapse even without war.'

The United States, for its part, could not look with favor on a situation in which the oil, tin, rubber, bauxite, and other resources that abound in Southeast Asia were in the hands of an unfriendly power. Japanese control of the region, although it would present little or no immediate military threat to the United States, would shut Americans out of a potentially rich trading market while denying to the United States the natural resources of the area. There was in addition the threat inherent to the Philippines in a Japanese advance, which as a colony Americans had promised to defend. Most of all, perhaps, although this would be difficult to document and certainly did not appear in position papers at the time, was the inherent logic of the Japanese thrust. As a part of their demand for great-power status, the Japanese wanted the white man out of Asia, with the Continent and its off-shore islands run by Asians, although not necessarily for the benefit of all Asians. Americans, along with the British, French, and Dutch, could never agree, not only because of the practical effects in their immediately threatened colonies but also because of the example it would set for the colored peoples throughout the world. In practice, then, the United States soon became the defender of white man's rule in Asia.

The decision to turn to war came from the Japanese, for anxious as the Americans were to stop the Japanese in China the United States did not have the military muscle to fight even a one-front war. Americans were certain that when the time came they would be able to end Japanese pretensions in the Far East, but they wanted to postpone the time as long as possible. In the period 1938–41 America undertook to slow the Japanese advance, but it simultaneously did all that it could – within the framework of a policy of hostility to Japan – to prevent the outbreak of war. In the end, the policy of trying to stop the Japanese without having to fight failed.

The fall of France in 1940, and Britain's total preoccupation with Germany, opened the door to Southeast Asia to Japan. Bogged down in her war with China, Japan decided to overcome her crippling shortage of oil through a program of expansion southward. Only the Soviet Union and the United States were potentially strong enough in the Pacific to interfere; Japan moved politically to immobilize these threats. In the late summer of 1940 she signed a five-year non-aggression pact with the Soviets, a pact that Stalin, fearing Hitler, was happy to negotiate.

Japan also signed the Tripartite Pact with the Germans and Italians, which pledged the three nations to support each other if any became involved in a war with the United States. Since this would present the United States with a two-front war if it resisted by force the upsetting of the *status quo* in Asia, the Japanese hoped it would tie America's hands.

Still Japan moved cautiously, since her leaders hoped to end the Chinese war before embarking on more dangerous ventures. The German invasion of Russia in June 1941 suddenly opened new possibilities, and a great debate ensued. Should Japan take advantage of Russia's desperate position *vis-a-vis* Germany and attack the Soviets through Siberia? Some military leaders thought so. Others argued that because of Hitler's involvement in the east, Germany no longer posed a real threat to England, which would have the effect of strengthening the Anglo-American position in the Pacific. Japan, therefore, should seek to reach an agreement with the United States, making such concessions as necessary. Still others held out for the long-planned conquest of Southeast Asia.

Roosevelt listened in on the debate through the medium of MAGIC, the code name applied to intercepted and decoded Japanese messages, and characterized it as 'a real drag-down and knock-out fight . . . to decide which way they were going to jump – attack Russia, attack the South Seas [or] sit on the fence and be more friendly with us'. The decision was to reject the first course, since Japan would not gain much by conquering easternmost Russia, and to try to combine the two latter courses. Japan would move south immediately, meanwhile trying to avoid war with the United States by carrying on negotiations. If it came to it, however, the Imperial Conference that made the decision decreed, 'we shall not be deterred by the possibility of becoming involved in a war with England and America.' The first step was the unresisted occupation of French Indochina, which gave Japan possession of air and naval bases from which she could launch attacks on Singapore, the Philippines, and the N.E.I.

American strategy in the summer of 1941 was embodied in a paper entitled RAINBOW 5. Never specific on implementation, it called for a holding action in the Pacific with an all-out offensive in Europe. The basic idea was that while it would be easy to deal with the Japanese once Hitler was eliminated, if the United States put its major effort into defeating Japan it might win in the Pacific and still lose in Europe. American military weakness supported the conclusion, for although the American fleet was stationed in Pearl Harbor (put there by Roosevelt in 1940, against naval advice, as a deterrent to the Japanese), it was by no means capable of dealing an effective blow to the Japanese. It was not even capable of carrying out the minimum requirement of RAINBOW 5, which envisioned the garrison in the Philippines holding out against Japanese attack until the fleet could get through to save the colony.

Given this situation the U.S. Navy, then in the process of rebuilding, did not wish to provoke the Japanese. It wanted time, not only to bring about Hitler's defeat but also to build a first-class striking force. The Chief of Naval Operations, Admiral Harold R. Stark, advised the President to do nothing when the Japanese moved into French Indochina. But whatever the military realities, Roosevelt had political realities to deal with, too. Unable or unwilling to take a stronger stand against Hitler, he found that the polls indicated nearly 70 per cent of the people were willing to risk war in the Pacific rather than let Japan continue her expansion. To slow the aggressor, he froze all Japanese assets in the United States. Since Japan no longer had the dollars with which to purchase materials of war, and since Roosevelt persuaded the British and Dutch to support his move, the effect of the freezing was to create an economic blockade of Japan.

The freezing made it clear to the Japanese that they either had to pull back from Indochina and even China itself, thereby reaching an agreement with the United States which would provide them with oil, or go to war. The one slim hope remaining was that America's fear of a two-ocean war would impel Roosevelt to compromise. From August until November 1941, the Japanese sought some form of acceptable political compromise, all the while sharpening their military plans and preparations. If the diplomatic offensive worked, the military one could be called off, including the planned surprise attack on the U.S. fleet at Pearl Harbor.

In essence, the Japanese demanded from the United

States a free hand in Asia in return for a guarantee of the neutrality of the Philippines and no war in the Far East. There were variations through a series of proposals, but the central points always included an end to Western aid to China, an Anglo-American promise not to 'meddle in nor interrupt' a settlement between Japan and China, a Western recognition of Japan's 'special position' in French Indochina, an Anglo-American agreement not to reinforce their bases in the Far East, and a resumption of commercial relations with Japan, which included selling oil.

Although the Americans were willing to go part way to compromise, they would not even consider giving the Japanese a free hand in China. Since it was precisely on this point that the Japanese were most adamant, conflict seemed inevitable. Neither side wanted war, in the sense that each would have preferred to gain its objectives without fighting for them, but both were willing to move on to a showdown. In Japan, it was the military who pressed for action, over the protests of the civilians, while in America the situation was reversed. Prime Minister Konoye of Japan resigned in October when he was unable to secure military approval of a partial withdrawal from China in order to 'save ourselves from the crisis of a Japanese–American war'. His successor, General Tojo, was willing to continue negotiations with the United States, but only until late November. If nothing came of them by then, Japan would strike.

In the United States Roosevelt, sure that the national interest, if not its security, was at stake, stood firm, even though his military advisers strongly urged him to avoid a crisis with Japan until he had dealt with Germany. Secretary Hull made one last effort, suggesting on 21 November that the United States offer a *modus vivendi* that would have involved a three months' truce. Japan might have accepted it, but Chiang Kai-shek, the Chinese leader, protested so vehemently that Hull never made the offer. 'I have washed my hands of the Japanese situation,' Hull told Stimson on

27 November, 'and it is now in the hands of . . . the Army and Navy.'

A little over a week later, on Sunday, 7 December, the Japanese launched their attack, hitting Pearl Harbor, the Philippines, Malaya, and Thailand. They soon added the N.E.I. to the list. On 8 December the Anglo-Americans declared war on Japan, but the United States still had no more excuse to go to war with Germany than it had on 6 December. Even in the excitement created by Pearl Harbor, Roosevelt had not dared ask Congress for a declaration of war against Germany. All war plans had assumed that the United States and the United Kingdom would concentrate their efforts against Germany; suddenly it seemed that the war would take an entirely unexpected course, with the Americans fighting only the Japanese. On 11 December Hitler ended the growing uncertainty by honoring the Tripartite Pact and declaring war on the United States. The Axis had rescued Roosevelt from his dilemma.

The Japanese decision to initiate a war with the United States was based on a faulty assumption. Although they fully appreciated the industrial potential of the United States and recognized that it would be able to fight a major war on two fronts eventually, the Japanese believed that by eliminating the U.S. Pacific Fleet they would gain a free hand in the Pacific for a year-and-a-half or two years, during which time they could set up a defensive perimeter that would force the United States to fight a long and costly war. The Americans, Japan's leaders believed, would shrink from the task and in the end would agree to a negotiated peace that would allow Japan to retain its gains in Southeast Asia.

The fallacies in the Japanese concepts were numerous. As de Tocqueville pointed out 106 years earlier, Americans are slow to rise to war but vicious once it begins. His observation had special application when the Americans were involved in a war with one of the world's colored peoples.

There was never the slightest possibility that the Americans would quit until the 'little yellow bastards' had been humbled. The sneak attack on Pearl Harbor fed this sentiment.

A second Japanese assumption may have been more reasonable. The Japanese felt they had to eliminate the Pacific Fleet and the American base in the Philippines to have a chance of winning. This belief rested on their conviction that the United States would not allow them to make any further gains in Southeast Asia and would use the fleet to stop them. Although there was no American territory in the Pacific essential to Japanese economic plans, they were sure that an attack on Malaya and the N.E.I. would bring America into the war, with the U.S. forces on the Philippines striking at the flanks of their lines of communication south. A number of Americans, both then and since, argued that the Japanese were wrong. They contended that had the enemy limited his attacks to Malaya and the N.E.I., Roosevelt would have been in the embarrassing position of having to ask Congress for a declaration of war to defend British and Dutch colonial possessions, and argue that nothing in Roosevelt's record indicates that he would have done so.

No one will ever know, but had the Japanese ignored the Philippines they would have been taking an even graver risk than they had already accepted. Roosevelt consistently took a harder line with Japan than with Germany, possibly because he was personally more outraged by Japanese aggression, certainly because he had the public behind him. Whatever the military logic of avoiding war in the Pacific until Germany was defeated, the political and psychological pressures for war with Japan were overriding. It is possible that had Japan ignored the Philippines and Pearl Harbor on 7 December, Roosevelt still would have asked for, and might have received, a declaration of war against the Japanese Empire.

All of which is speculation. The fact was that by 11 Dec-

ember 1941 the United States was at war with the Axis.
The *status quo* in Europe and in Asia had been challenged
and was being upset. America had been unable to preserve
it short of war. The task, it now seemed, was to restore the
status quo by defeating those who wished to change it. This
pointed towards a policy of the defeat of the Axis, quickly
and at the least possible cost. It also implied a blindness on
the part of America's leaders to the possibility of change other
than that represented by Germany and Japan – especially
the anti-colonial movement in the Third World. The United
States was committed to preserving the *status quo* as a result
of its determination to put down the German and Japanese
challenges, which would later leave it relatively unprepared
to meet the new challenges of Third World revolution. Still,
nothing loomed so large in 1941 as the need to defeat the
Axis, a task of staggering proportions but one that carried
with it great opportunities for the extension of American
power and influence. The United States was quick to grasp
them.

2

The War in Europe

ONE of the more striking aspects of American foreign policy during the war was the almost complete failure to use any formal structure within the government to set national policy. Roosevelt generally ignored the State Department and Hull contented himself and his agency with relatively minor matters. The Cabinet seldom met in full session. The War, Navy, and Treasury Departments concerned themselves with this or that aspect of the war, there was little co-ordination between them and they frequently were not aware of each other's views. There was nothing comparable to the British War Cabinet, which contained the heads of the ministries most intimately involved in the war effort and which met constantly. For the most part Roosevelt operated informally, checking here and there as the mood hit him. His most important adviser, especially in the later stages of the war, was General Marshall. Harry Hopkins, Secretary Stimson, and Admiral Ernest King, who became Chief of Naval Operations in 1942, also played key roles; like Marshall, however, this was as much a result of the power of their personalities as of the positions they held.

The result of the absence of structure was confusion and drift in policy. Although there was agreement on the principle of defeating Germany first, no agency or individual was responsible for long-term planning. No one seems to have been charged with asking, 'What kind of a world do we want when the war is over?', at least not in a formal sense or in such a way as to influence the development of military plans. Individuals did concern themselves with such problems as what leaders the United States should promote in the nations it helped liberate, or even where United States troops should be and what areas they should be occupying when hostilities ended, but they did so on their own, usually without encouragement, and there was no certainty that they would be able to get their views before the President.

The absence of a consistent policy was evident throughout the war. The Americans did not gear their policy single-mindedly to opposition to left-wing political forces in Europe, nor to the quick defeat of Germany, nor to the post-war position of America in Europe. There were operations that embraced one or another of these goals, but there was no single guiding star to which America hitched her foreign policy throughout the war. It was hardly possible that there could have been consistency, given Roosevelt's haphazard administrative system and given the need to co-operate with the British, who had differing aims and whose views had to be taken into account.

What consistency there was came from the military. After 1942 military considerations dominated and the generals and admirals enjoyed unprecedented power. This was increased because they did have an agency that could set common policies, the Joint Chiefs of Staff (J.C.S.), but the J.C.S. did not get its power instantly. It did not even exist at the beginning of the war and throughout 1942 Roosevelt ignored or went counter to much of its advice. It came into being in December 1941, when the British came to Washington for a conference on the conduct of the war. The British already had a formal military structure, the Chiefs of Staff Committee (C.O.S.). To provide a parallel organization, the Americans established the J.C.S. Composed of Marshall, King, General Henry Arnold of the Army Air Forces, and Admiral William Leahy, Roosevelt's personal Chief of Staff, the J.C.S. had a wide range of committees and agencies under it, providing the Chiefs with information, position papers, and recommendations. The J.C.S. was interested in, and had influence over, nearly every aspect of the American war effort. Its unity and prestige were such that it was the closest thing the United States had to the British War Cabinet. The two co-equal bodies, J.C.S. and C.O.S., then merged into the Combined Chiefs of Staff (C.C.S.), which became the agency responsible for the direction of the Allied military effort.

The C.C.S. reported to and took its directions from the two heads of government. When the military chiefs agreed, the tendency was to inform Churchill and Roosevelt about what would be done; often, however, the C.C.S. could not agree, at which point the political leaders had to break the deadlock and make the decision. In practice, much to Marshall's chagrin, this meant that Churchill had a large influence on the development of American policy, for he was proficient at swinging Roosevelt around to his point of view.

Basic strategic and political differences between the Allies were apparent at the initial meeting of the C.C.S. Churchill presented the British view, which called for closing and tightening the ring against Germany, then stabbing in the knife when the enemy was exhausted. He advocated a series of land operations around the periphery of Hitler's European fortress, combined with bombing raids against Germany itself and encouragement to resistance forces in the occupied countries. This represented traditional British policy, abandoned only once, from 1914 to 1918, an aberration Churchill was determined not to repeat. He would let the Continentals do their own fighting, just as the great British statesmen of the past had done. What he had forgotten, however, was that in the past British friends on the Continent shared general British political and economic concepts. In 1941, those who were willing to fight Hitler, whether they were Russians, Frenchmen in the Resistance, Yugoslavs, or Greeks, were all on the political left. Churchill's policy, to the extent that it was carried out, meant in practice that he was giving a tremend-

ous boost to the forces of the left in Europe, for they would
be the ones with the guns when the end came.

The American military opposed Churchill's policy,
although not because they had taken a firm position on
either helping or hindering the forces of the left. Marshall
felt that the closing and tightening the ring concept was
risky rather than safe, that it would waste lives and material
rather than save them, and that it was politically unwise
rather than shrewd. To leave the Red Army to face the
bulk of the Wehrmacht, Marshall believed, was to court
disaster. He was not at all sure that the Russians could
survive unaided and he thought it would be the greatest
military blunder of all history to allow an army of 8,000,000
men to go down to defeat without doing anything to prevent
it. For the Allies to avoid a confrontation with the Germans
on the Continent in 1942 or 1943 might save Anglo-
American lives in the short run, but it might also lead to a
complete victory for Hitler in the end. Even if Churchill was
right in supposing that the Red Army would hold out and
eventually take care of the primary job – breaking the
Wehrmacht's back – Marshall believed that the effect
would be to let the war drag on into 1944 or even 1945. The
end result would be higher, not lower, Anglo-American
casualties. Finally, Marshall feared that he would not be
able to hold the President and the American people to the
Germany-first commitment, with its implication of a
passive defense in the Pacific, if nothing decisive were being
done in Europe. The Asia-firsters, with their already
impressive political base in the United States, would be
able to switch priorities and force the administration to
concentrate on the Japanese.

Marshall therefore proposed that the C.C.S. set as a goal
for 1942 a build-up of American ground, air, and naval
forces in the United Kingdom, with the aim of launching a
massive cross-Channel invasion in the spring of 1943. He
argued that only thus could the Americans bring their
strength to bear in a decisive manner, only thus could the

Allies give significant help to the Russians, only thus could the final aim of victory be quickly achieved.

There were two specific problems with Marshall's program of a 1942 build-up and a 1943 invasion. First, it would be of little help to the Russians in 1942, and second it would mean that the United States would spend a year without engaging in any ground fighting with the Germans. The second point worried Roosevelt, for he wanted to get the American people to feel a sense of commitment in the struggle for Europe (well into 1942 public opinion polls revealed that Americans remained passive about the German threat, eager to strike back at the Japanese). The fastest way to do it was to get involved in the European fighting. The President therefore insisted that Americans engage Germans somewhere in 1942, preferably before the Congressional elections in November. But Roosevelt was also drawn to Churchill's concept of closing the ring, with its implication that the Russians would take the bulk of the casualties, and he was determined that the first American offensive should be successful, all of which made the periphery more tempting as a target than Northwest Europe.

Marshall proposed, as an addition to his program for a 1943 invasion, an emergency landing on the French coast in September 1942. The operation, code name SLEDGE-HAMMER, would be in the nature of a suicide mission, designed to take pressure off the Russians. It would go forward only if an immediate Russian collapse seemed inevitable. But although Marshall had no intention of starting SLEDGEHAMMER except as a last resort, he could and did hold it out to Roosevelt as an operation that would satisfy the President's demand for action in 1942. The obvious difficulty was the risk, and Churchill countered with a proposal to invade French North Africa, code name TORCH, as a beginning in the program of closing the ring. This was certainly much safer than a cross-Channel attack in either 1942 or 1943, especially since it would be a surprise assault on the territory of a neutral nation (the

French armistice government at Vichy controlled the French colonies). TORCH dovetailed nicely with British political aims, since it would help the British re-establish their position in the Mediterranean, currently reduced to Gibraltar, Malta, and Egypt.

Marshall's and Churchill's proposals were mutually exclusive. In July 1942, Roosevelt sent Marshall, Harry Hopkins, and Admiral King to London to reach agreement with the British. But the C.C.S. could not agree. The British refused to commit themselves to SLEDGE-HAMMER, said they were willing to study a 1943 cross-Channel invasion further, and insisted that something be done in 1942. Marshall and King refused to be sucked into North Africa, which they feared would tie down the Allies for a year or more, thus making a 1943 invasion impossible and leaving the Red Army to its own devices. When they could not move the British, Marshall and King reported a deadlock to Roosevelt.

Roosevelt had to decide. The pressures on him, from all sides, were enormous. Soviet Foreign Minister Molotov had visited him in the spring, and in a burst of enthusiasm Roosevelt had promised a Second Front in 1942. Although the President had tried to be non-specific about where the front would be opened. Molotov, like all the rest of the world, thought of a Second Front only in terms of the plains of Northwest Europe. Roosevelt also knew that the hard-pressed Russians – facing nearly 200 Nazi divisions on a front that extended from Leningrad to the Caucasus, with huge areas, including their prime industrial and agricultural lands, under occupation, with millions of dead already and with a desperate need for time in which to rebuild their industry and their army – regarded a Second Front as absolutely essential and as a clear test of the Western democracies' good faith. If the Anglo-Americans did nothing to draw off some German divisions, and soon, the Russians could only believe that it meant the Allies were willing to see Hitler win, in the east at least.

Roosevelt was never foolish enough to believe that any-one but the Nazis would benefit from a German victory over Russia, nor did he want Stalin to think that he hoped that would happen, but he did have other concerns and pressures. America was nowhere near full mobilization. Whatever Marshall's plans, the U.S. Army could not by itself invade France. Even in combination with the British, the United States would have taken heavy casualties. Churchill and the C.O.S. were insistent about not going back onto the Continent in 1942, or indeed until every-thing had been well prepared, and they made North Africa sound attractive to the President. Churchill was willing to go himself to Moscow to explain TORCH to Stalin and said he could convince the Soviets that TORCH did constitute a second front. Given British intransigence, it seemed to Roosevelt that for 1942 it was TORCH or nothing. He picked TORCH.

On 28 July Roosevelt gave his orders to Marshall, still in London. General Dwight Eisenhower, commander of the American forces in Britain, commented that 22 July could well go down as the 'blackest day in history'. Eisenhower and Marshall were convinced that the decision to launch a major invasion of French North Africa in November 1942 would have repercussions that would shape the whole course of the war, with implications that would stretch out far into the post-war period. They were right. Once TORCH was successful, the temptation to build up the already existing base in Algeria and Tunisia and use it as a springboard for further operations was overwhelming. By far the greater part of the Anglo-American effort in 1942–3 went into the Mediterranean, first in North Africa, then Sicily (July 1943), and finally Italy (September 1943). Impressive gains were made on the map, but there was no decisive or even significant destruction of German power.

The Russians, alone, stemmed the Nazi tide, then began to roll it back. Victory was coming, and the Anglo-American casualty lists were short, but nevertheless the price was high.

Because the end in Europe was delayed, the switch-over to the full offensive in the Pacific had to be delayed, too. Russian suspicions of the Western democracies, already great, increased. The Anglo-Americans, because they refused to participate in the liberation of East Europe, forfeited all right to a say in the post-war situation in the area. They had already done so at Munich, leaving the organization, politics, social structure, and loyalties of the area in Hitler's hands. They did so again in 1942–3 by agreeing, in effect, that whoever won the Russo-German war could control the area, since the Western allies would not involve themselves in the fighting.

It was not a conscious decision, certainly not in the terms outlined above. The practical problems involved in launching a 1942 or even a 1943 invasion were enormous, perhaps insurmountable. It is quite possible that the British were right in arguing that a cross-Channel attack begun before everything was ready would simply result in a blood bath, leaving the Anglo-Americans in an even worse position *vis-à-vis* the sources of power in East Europe than where they ended up. And in any case the policy did work for the United States, for it meant no defeats and control of Western Europe. But the point was that the political considerations taken into account did not include the post-war organization of East Europe, where after the war the United States would try to force its views on the Soviets. Political motives were paramount in the TORCH decision, but they had nothing to do with control of the Eurasian heartland. Churchill wanted a strong British presence in the Mediterranean, while Roosevelt wanted a quick and relatively safe American involvement to boost morale at home. Both got what they needed from TORCH.

Relations between nations during war are highly complex, whether they are friendly, allied, neutral, or enemies; the ordinary stresses and strains are heightened when one country has troops on the soil of another. Sovereignty then becomes, in certain respects, meaningless, especially when the occupying power has a preponderance of force. This was the case in French North Africa after 8 November 1942, but it was even more complicated because the occupying force was an allied one, and the Anglo-Americans could not agree on a policy. The Allies were in a position, or so it appeared, to dictate who would govern not only French Morocco, Algeria, and Tunisia, but also Metropolitan France itself, for obviously whoever was in control in Algiers when France was liberated would have the inside track to take power in Paris.

The trouble was that the Allies could not agree on a candidate. Anglo-American policies towards France had followed divergent paths ever since the armistice in the summer of 1940, with the British throwing their weight behind Charles de Gaulle's Free French movement while the Americans tried to make a deal with Marshal Pétain's collaborationist Vichy government. For Churchill, Vichy stood for everything he and his friends had denounced at Munich and again when the French quit in 1940. Pétain and his associates had accepted the armistice and were eager to join Hitler in building a New Order in Europe. They had always mistrusted the British and their feelings were even stronger after the British sank part of the French fleet in Oran. To Churchill, therefore, the Free French movement, which had refused to accept the armistice and denounced Pétain as a traitor, 'was the core of French resistance and the flame of French honour'. Post-war France, the Prime Minister held, would have to be purged of all the Vichy officials and reconstituted under de Gaulle's leadership. Churchill had his problems with de Gaulle throughout the war, as the two egotists often rubbed each other wrong, but the alternative of the hated Vichy, with its supine creatures who had left England in the lurch in 1940 and accepted surrender and dishonor, made Churchill gag.

The United States took the view that one could do business with Vichy. Much in Pétain's program appeared to

Roosevelt and Hull to represent the best hope for France, especially those parts that stood for work, patriotism, and stability. De Gaulle represented a new, unknown France, while Vichy stood for the old. De Gaulle believed that France had to be reconstituted from top to bottom. All the Vichy scum – the police chiefs and their brutality, the clerks and their petty graft, the generals and their lust for glory and position – had to be flushed out. 'It is not our fault,' he declared, 'if France is undergoing a virtual revolution at the same time as being at war.' The United States wished to deny the revolution and its consequences, having already signed an economic accord with the Vichy rulers of North Africa that benefitted both sides and avoiding the dangers inherent in dealing with de Gaulle.

Roosevelt's policy towards de Gaulle, which had a strong element of personal bitterness, has mystified many observers. One thing is clear – something more than personal pique was involved. The President did everything in his power to stop de Gaulle's rise, primarily because of his fear that the French people upon liberation would, as they had in the past, run to an extreme. Either the weak, inefficient radical governments of the Popular Front type would take over, or there would be a man on a white horse, a Boulanger or even a Napoleon. De Gaulle was dangerous either way. He had the aura of the man on the white horse about him. Without any mandate whatsoever from the French people, he had set himself up as head of the French state. He carried himself like a dictator, deliberately insulted foreigners and Frenchmen who did not agree with him, was totally ruthless in his relations, and used personal loyalty rather than efficiency as a criterion for advancement within his organization. What made him even more dangerous was the way that he flirted with the forces of the left, especially the communists in the Resistance. 'France faces a revolution when the Germans have been driven out,' the President once said, and he feared that the man most likely to profit from it would be de Gaulle.

Roosevelt spent much time searching for an alternative to de Gaulle. He might have wanted to turn to Vichy, but Pétain was too thoroughly brushed with the tar of the collaborationist. Roosevelt's best hope was the French Army, which represented the forces of stability and conservatism without appearing to be pro-Nazi. For a year the President supported General Henri Giraud, a World War I hero who had escaped German captivity in 1941 and who tried to stand between de Gaulle and Pétain. In 1942 he was living in retirement in unoccupied France. Giraud had Fascist sympathies, had no place in the hierarchy of the French Army, no popular following, no organization, no social imagination, no interest in politics (except to maintain the *status quo*), no program, and no administrative experience or abilities. Nevertheless, Roosevelt made him the American candidate for the leadership of French North Africa. He came into Algiers on the heels of Eisenhower's armies to attempt to assume command of the French North African Army.

The American effort to by-pass de Gaulle and shake the French Army loose from Vichy through the device of using Giraud failed. The French officers could see no reason at all to obey the orders of a man, whatever his background, who had no connection with their government, and to the best of its ability the French Army ignored Giraud's call to lay down its arms and instead resisted the invasion. The situation forced the U.S. Army to take the lead in formulating a policy. There was never the slightest chance that the French officers would obey de Gaulle, who after all had denounced them as traitors for following Vichy's orders, so the alternatives for the Allies were to fight and conquer the French Army, then institute a military occupation of North Africa, thereby tying up thousands of troops on occupation duties, or to find a senior officer in the Vichy hierarchy with whom the Allies could do business.

The men on the spot in Algiers, General Mark Clark and State Department representative Robert Murphy, never hesitated. To Clark, the military requirements were paramount and he was ready to deal with anyone who could get the French Army to switch over to the Allied side. To Murphy, a conservative Catholic with highly placed friends in Vichy, anything was preferable to creating a chaotic situation from which only de Gaulle could profit.

By accident, Admiral Jean Darlan was in Algiers when the invasion hit. Darlan was bitterly anti-British, author of Vichy's anti-semitic laws, and a willing collaborationist, but he was also the Commander-in-Chief of Vichy's armed forces and he was ready to double-cross Pétain. He agreed to a deal proposed by Clark and Murphy, which required him to order the French to lay down their arms, in return for which the Allies made him the Governor General of all French North Africa. Giraud would be the head of the North African Army. Within a few days the French officers obeyed Darlan's order to cease fire, and a week after the invasion Eisenhower flew to Algiers and approved the deal.

Roosevelt, who had not expected to have to go so far in cooperating with Vichy, was taken aback. For some days he withheld approval, telling reporters that Eisenhower's deal with Darlan was simply an arrangement, temporary in nature, which by no means constituted a recognition of Darlan as head of the French North African government. But the logic of his own policy worked against Roosevelt. If not Darlan, then some other Vichy official would have to control, since the President would not support de Gaulle and the American military would go to any length to avoid a fight with the French. Eventually Roosevelt caved in, giving his approval to the Darlan deal.

The result was that in its first major foreign-policy venture in World War II, the United States gave its support to a man who stood for everything Roosevelt and Churchill had spoken out against in the Atlantic Charter. As much as Goering or Goebbels, Darlan was the antithesis of the principles the Allies said they were struggling to establish. It was quickly apparent that Darlan would ignore Eisenhower's rather tepid pressure to liberalize the administration of the area; American and British presence in North Africa made no practical difference in day-to-day life. Jews were still persecuted, unable to practice professions, attend schools, or own property; Arabs continued to be beaten and exploited; the French generals who had co-operated with the Nazis and fought the Americans lived in splendor amid the squalor that surrounded them.

The Darlan deal raised a storm of protest in liberal circles in the United States and Britain. 'What the hell are we fighting for?' radio commentator Edward Murrow demanded. Churchill's friends were aghast, Churchill himself hardly less so. Grudgingly, he went along, mainly because – as he later explained to the indignant de Gaulle – 'Each time we must choose between Europe and the open sea, we shall always choose the open sea. Each time I must choose between you and Roosevelt, I shall always choose Roosevelt.' De Gaulle and other critics of the Darlan deal raised serious questions: Did it mean that when the Allies got into Italy they would make a deal with Mussolini? If the opportunity presented itself, would they deal with Hitler or, more likely, the German generals? Roosevelt rode out the storm by stressing the temporary nature of the deal. Darlan, increasingly indignant, complained that the Americans regarded him as a lemon to be squeezed dry, then thrown away when its usefulness was over.

A happy solution came on Christmas Eve, 1942, when an anti-Nazi young Frenchman in Algiers assassinated Darlan. The embarrassment of dealing with Darlan was finished. Eisenhower saw to it that Giraud replaced the admiral at the head of the Imperial Council that ran North Africa and it pleased Roosevelt to have Giraud finally on top. The British, always more sensitive to the moral stigma of dealing with Darlan, were delighted to be rid of him; besides, their candidate, de Gaulle, had hated Darlan but was merely contemptuous of Giraud and could work with him. As Clark put it, 'Admiral Darlan's death was . . . an act of Providence . . . . His removal from the scene was like the lancing of a troublesome boil. He had served his purpose, and his death solved what could have been the very difficult problem of what to do with him in the future.'

Still, deep-rooted suspicions about American intentions towards liberated Europe remained. Stalin was hardly alone in wondering if Roosevelt would promote the forces of law, order, stability, and the *status quo* – in short, the forces of the right – in Italy, Belgium, Denmark, Norway, and the rest of occupied Europe as well as in France. At the conclusion of the Casablanca Conference, in January 1943, Roosevelt tried to allay the suspicions. He announced that the Anglo-American policy toward Germany and Japan, and by implication towards Italy, was to demand unconditional surrender. Churchill, after some hesitation, supported the policy.

What did it mean? Roosevelt did not give out any details. Presumably unconditional surrender meant the Allies would fight until such time as the Axis governments put themselves unconditionally into the hands of the Allies, but beyond that nothing was known. What kind of governments would replace those of Mussolini, Tojo, and Hitler? Obviously there would be a period of military occupation, with control invested in an Allied military governor, but then what? Roosevelt did not say.

He did not because, in all probability, he did not know himself. Always the self-confident pragmatist, he was sure that he could handle situations as they arose. He would play it by ear, continuing to make most of his decisions, as Eisenhower had done with Darlan, on the basis of military expediency. Meanwhile, he had assured Stalin and the world that there would be no deals with Hitler and his gang, that the Anglo-Americans would fight on until the Axis governments quit. Then he would settle everything to everyone's satisfaction. By keeping everything vague, meanwhile, he kept everyone happy. There was no bickering over war aims.

Roosevelt's self-confidence was hardly justified, as Franco-American relations soon demonstrated. At the beginning of 1943 Giraud was on top, but he would not stay there long. With British encouragement, de Gaulle came to Algiers, organized a French Committee of National Liberation, and along with Giraud became co-President. Giraud was a political innocent, however, and despite Roosevelt's strongest efforts – which included a grandiose reception at the White House, designed to give Giraud prestige, and orders to Eisenhower to keep real power out of de Gaulle's hands by any necessary means – de Gaulle soon squeezed Giraud out of the Committee of National Liberation altogether. By the end of 1943 Roosevelt's French policy was a shambles. De Gaulle was in power and his power rested on the liberal forces in Algiers and the left wing in France itself, for the Resistance was in the hands of the left and gave its loyalty to de Gaulle. All of Roosevelt's sarcastic remarks about de Gaulle, many of them downright insulting, availed the President nothing. By the time Paris was liberated, Franco-American relations were strained as they had never before been. Far from feeling gratitude towards the Americans for the liberation, de Gaulle was profoundly distrustful of Washington. The consequence of Roosevelt's French policy was that at the end of the war American influence in France was at its lowest ebb.

The major Anglo-American military operations in 1943 were directed against Italy. They began with the invasion of Sicily, where it took over a month to drive two German divisions from the island, and were followed by the assault on Salerno. Even though Italy quit the war, it was not until mid-1944 that the Allies reached Rome, and the spring of 1945 before they controlled the whole of Italy. Heavy military commitments had been made for results that were slim. The Allies had tied down twenty German divisions in

Italy, and they had obtained some additional airfields from which to send bombers against Germany, but that was all.

Political gains were more substantial. Italian surrender had been arranged well in advance of the Allied invasion of the mainland, on terms that suited both the Anglo-Americans and the existing Italian governing structure but which left out altogether the interests of the left opposition within Italy, not to mention the Soviet Union. Two weeks after the landings at Sicily, the Allies bombed Rome; as a result of the raid, and because of the deteriorating situation which the bombing symbolized, the Fascist Grand Council overthrew Mussolini. Marshal Pietro Badoglio, an old soldier who was in the King's favor, replaced Mussolini. Badoglio and his associates had no intention of changing anything within Italy; their sole motivation was to switch sides in the war so that they could stand with the winners when it ended. The Anglo-Americans were willing enough to oblige, although there were differences on details. Churchill was anxious to retain the monarchy while Roosevelt, citing the large Italian-American vote within the United States, favored a republic. But both sides were ready to proceed to make peace on the basis of the Badoglio government, and both were anxious to conclude a deal before the Russians could become involved.

There was, besides, the military situation. Eisenhower felt he was invading on a shoestring and many of his senior commanders thought landing as far north as Salerno too risky. The Allies were short of everything, most of all troops and landing craft. The Germans alone in Italy outnumbered the invading force nearly eight to one and the Germans and Italians combined had a twenty to one advantage. Eisenhower felt he had to have, at a minimum, a neutral Italian Army, and to get it he was willing to make extensive concessions.

The Italians were specific enough about the concessions they wanted. In August, Badoglio's representatives made secret contact with Eisenhower's staff. Italy wanted protection of the government in Rome from the Germans, to be allowed to declare war on Germany and join the Allies as a co-belligerent, thus completing the double-cross, and to be spared the humiliation of signing an unconditional surrender. Eisenhower was willing to grant the requests and urged his superiors in Washington and London to do so, but this was too much for Churchill, whose government had been fighting Italy since June 1940, or Roosevelt, whose Casablanca announcement about unconditional surrender had supposedly meant no more deals with Fascists, which Badoglio and his associates certainly were. The heads of government therefore delayed, the talks bogged down, and through August little was accomplished.

Churchill and Roosevelt were bending to the logic of their own desires, however, and gradually they gave Eisenhower permission to concede the central Italian demands. They wanted stability in Italy, a neutral Italian army, and a strong position on the peninsula that juts out into the Mediterranean. They could get these things with Badoglio; there was no indication that they could get them as easily by supporting the left opposition in Italy, which was clamoring for Anglo-American aid. The British and Americans were willing to concede much to Badoglio, for they wanted to avoid social upheaval and possibly chaos in Italy. When Eisenhower suggested that a general strike would hamper German movements in Italy and could be easily organized by co-operating with the left opposition, the heads of the Allied governments immediately discarded this idea. Instead they allowed the Italian government to surrender with conditions, to stay in power, to retain administrative control of non-battlefield areas in Italy, to keep the monarchy, and eventually to join the Allies as co-belligerent. It pained both Roosevelt and Churchill to make such broad concessions, but the military necessities seemed to them overwhelming.

The end result was that by 1945 the same groups that had run Italy before and during the war were still in power, backed by an Allied Control Council from which the Russians had been systematically excluded. Stalin had protested initially, but did not press the point, for he seems to have recognized the value of the precedent – those who liberated a country from the Nazis could decide what happened there. He was more than willing to allow the Allies to shape the future in Italy in return for the same right in Eastern Europe.

The implication of the Allied policy in Italy was that the liberating powers would be able to maintain occupation troops in the countries they overran and determine the nature of the post-war regime, but there were areas from which the Germans would pull back their forces without any direct pressure. The most important of these areas was Greece. The Germans certainly would not allow their troops in Greece to be cut off by the westward advance of the Red Army. When the Nazis left, there would be a vacuum in Greece; whoever moved into the vacuum first could expect to control the nation in the post-war period. There was a Greek government-in-exile in London, but it had no significant forces available; within Greece itself, the underground guerrilla forces belonged to the political left. Churchill feared that if nothing were done from the outside the communists would quickly seize power in Greece and throw that nation into the Soviet orbit. The British wanted to re-establish the old ruling classes, in part because of their general fear of the left and the rise of Soviet influence, more specifically because the right-wing forces in Greece had historically co-operated admirably with the British, granting them naval facilities in the eastern Mediterranean and investment opportunities. In order to put the government-in-exile and the monarchy back into power, Churchill was determined to have British troops in Greece as soon as the Germans pulled out.

The Americans had no serious objections, although Roosevelt did have some suspicions about the wisdom of reintroducing the monarchy, but Churchill's specific policies ran counter to the military requirements as the Americans saw them, which did lead to important differences. In September 1943, when the Italians surrendered and the Allies invaded Italy, Churchill wanted to put Allied troops onto Italian-controlled islands in the Aegean Sea, especially Kos and Leros, as a prelude to an invasion of Rhodes. The occupation of Rhodes, Churchill hoped, would bring Turkey into the war on the Allied side, provide a base for an Allied invasion of the Balkans, and most importantly allow the British to seize control in Greece.

The program raised fundamental questions for the United States. Not only did it mean that the United States would use its military power to insure the British post-war position in the Mediterranean, but it also meant that the Americans would have to delay the final defeat of the Nazis in support of a British political position. Beyond that, Churchill's policy would lead the United States into an anti-Soviet stance. To oversimplify, Americans faced a dilemma – did they want to fight the war in such a way as to forestall Russian gains, or did they want to gear their operations to the defeat of Germany? There was no unanimous answer. As will be seen there was strong anti-Soviet sentiment in the State Department and in the lower levels of the War Department, but Roosevelt himself wanted to try to get along with Stalin and the senior military officers generally were single-minded in their insistance on concentrating on Germany.

The J.C.S. position was decisive. By September 1943, when Churchill raised the question of extending operations into the eastern Mediterranean, the J.C.S. were coming into their own. Roosevelt had come to respect and follow the Chiefs' advice. The Chiefs were insistent that any operation aimed toward Rhodes and eventually the Balkans would dissipate Allied strength and delay the final victory. Eisenhower, in command in Italy, agreed. The military men feared that involvement in Rhodes, Greece, Turkey, and the Balkans would draw off so many men, planes, and landing craft that the 1944 invasion of France, which the British had agreed to at Casablanca, would have to be postponed again. Marshall and the other Chiefs would never agree to another postponement of the cross-Channel attack, partly because they thought it was the wrong strategy, mainly because it would mean in turn a post-ponement of the return to the offensive in the Pacific. To the Americans, a strong post-war position in Greece or even the Balkans was not worth the cost.

The British went into Greece alone when the Germans withdrew (late 1944), became involved in a civil war, and re-established the government-in-exile in Athens. The cost proved to be too high for the British, however, and in 1947 they had to withdraw. They had kept the communists out of power for two years, but they had gained little else. Eventually they had to turn the whole thing over to the Americans. By 1947 the Americans had a new set of assumptions about the world and they then made a different judgement about the importance of Greece.

American foreign policy in World War II was too com-plex and diverse to be encompassed by any generalization, no matter how sweeping. The closest thing to a policy was an effort at letting the military imperatives be decisive. If, for example, the Americans tried to promote a right-wing government in France and Italy and allowed the British to do the same in Greece, it was equally true that the United States dropped arms and equipment to the Resistance in France, which was decidedly left-wing, and to Tito in Yugoslavia, who was clearly leading a communist revolu-tion. Within occupied France, the Americans had to deal with the Resistance or pass up any opportunity to hurt the Germans, since there was no one else fighting the Nazis, but in Yugoslavia there was an alternative, in the form of a guerrilla force under General Mikhailovitch, who sup-ported the monarchy and the government-in-exile. Eisenhower and the Americans followed the British lead in giving aid to Tito, however, because he was more effective than Mikhailovitch in fighting the Nazis. Nor was it true that America concentrated single-mindedly on defeating the Nazis, since nearly every senior American officer warned the President that the 1942 North African invasion would delay the final victory. In that instance, and to a lesser extent in the invasion of Sicily and Italy, Roosevelt was responding more to domestic political pressures and Churchill's influence than to a desire to hasten Germany's defeat.

In January 1944, the confusion and drift that had characterized American policy came to an end. America was as mobilized as it would ever be. The Red Army had taken the sting out of the Wehrmacht. Eisenhower took command of the Allied Expeditionary Force (A.E.F.) in the United Kingdom and began the preparations for Operation OVERLORD, the cross-Channel assault. From that point on, a single question dominated American thought: 'Will this proposal help or hurt OVERLORD?' Marshall's view had triumphed. OVERLORD had top priority and subsidiary operations were geared to it, which was another way of saying that America was now concentrating, more or less exclusively, on the defeat of Germany. Post-war problems, for the most part, would be decided in the post-war period. In general, this was true until the very last day of the war.

Examples abound. Most involved the British, practically none the Russians, partly because the Americans had a close working relationship with the British and almost no contact with the Red Army, partly because the British were more concerned than the Americans with long-range questions. Three issues were especially important: what to do in the Mediterranean, what form the advance into Germany should take, and – in the final weeks of the war – whether the objective should be the political center of Berlin or the remaining military might of the

German Army. On all three issues, the Americans had their way. American preponderance in the Allied camp became so great that, if necessary, the J.C.S. could insist upon their judgement, while the British simply had to accept the decision in the best grace possible, for their contribution to Anglo-American resources was down to 25 per cent of the whole. The American domination of the Alliance reflected, in turn, a new era in the world's history. The United States had replaced Great Britain as the dominant power bordering on the Atlantic Ocean. By 1945 American production had reached levels that were scarcely believable. The United States was producing 45 per cent of the world's armament and nearly 50 per cent of the world's goods. Some two-thirds of all the ships afloat were American-built.

On the question of what to do in the Mediterranean, the Americans insisted on slowing down operations in Italy and invading the South of France in order to provide a covering force for Eisenhower's right flank and to open the port of Marseilles. The British objected, advocating instead operations into Austria and Yugoslavia, but they dared not argue their case on political grounds, for they realized that Roosevelt would turn a deaf ear to the political case and only by convincing the President could they hope to influence the final decision. But as Roosevelt told Churchill, 'My dear friend, I beg you to let us go ahead with our plan. For purely political reasons over here, I should never survive even a slight setback in OVERLORD if it were known that fairly large forces had been diverted to the Balkans.'

Churchill was interested in securing the British position in the Mediterranean by taking all of Italy and the Adriatic. He later declared that he was also interested in forestalling the Russians in central Europe, but he never used such an argument at the time. To the contrary, he repeatedly told Eisenhower – who bore the brunt of the argument on the American side – that he wanted to abandon the South of France attack and substitute for it an extended offensive in

Italy and the eastern Mediterranean strictly as a military proposition. Eisenhower was sure Churchill had Britain's post-war position in mind and told the Prime Minister that if he wished to change the orders (which directed Eisenhower to strike at the heart of Germany), he should talk to Roosevelt, not the Supreme Commander. On military grounds, Eisenhower insisted on landing in the South of France. Churchill could not persuade Roosevelt to intervene and the landings took place in August 1944, ending the Allies' opportunities to extend operations into central Europe or the Balkans. The Americans had been willing to go as far east in the Mediterranean as Italy, but no farther. The post-war expansion of the Soviet Union to the Balkans or central Europe did not seem to the Americans to be important enough to justify a diversion away from Germany; put another way, during the war East Europe in general did not rank very high on the American priority scale.

A second great issue, fought out in September 1944, was the nature of the advance into Germany. Eisenhower and his planners at Supreme Headquarters directed an offensive on a broad front, with the British and Canadian armies on the left (21st Army Group) and the American armies on the right (12th Army Group) moving forward more or less abreast. General Montgomery, commanding the British forces, argued for a single thrust as an alternative to Eisenhower's broad front. Montgomery wanted Eisenhower to give 21st Army Group all available supplies, stop the American armies where they were (near Paris), and allow the British and Canadian soldiers to thrust straight on through to Berlin. Montgomery realized that there was a certain amount of risk involved in the single thrust, not the least of which was that while 21st Army Group pushed forward along the north German coast it would have no protection for its right (south) flank. But he insisted that his plan was the only one that promised a quick end to the war. Churchill supported Montgomery, partly because he wanted the British to have the glory of capturing Berlin, mainly because he wanted the Anglo-Americans as far east as possible when they linked up with the Red Army.

Eisenhower insisted upon his own plan. Domestic politics played a large role in his decision, even though military considerations were uppermost in his mind. On a number of occasions he informed the British that under no circumstances could he afford to leave three American armies sitting in defensive positions while the British swept on to Berlin. Beyond the political factor, Eisenhower was absolutely convinced that the broad front was militarily correct. Whether he was right or wrong depended upon the priority one set. If the main goal, now that the Allies were fighting on the plains of Northwest Europe, was to insure a German defeat, Eisenhower's cautious approach was correct. But if the goal was to get the war over with as quickly as possible and in the process to forestall a Russian advance into central Europe by liberating Berlin, Prague, and the other important cities of the area, then Montgomery's audacious program was correct. Roles had been reversed. Eisenhower and Marshall, who in 1942 had been willing to accept any risk and go across the Channel, now adopted a dull, unimaginative, but thoroughly safe campaign. The British, who earlier had shuddered at the thought of confronting the Wehrmacht on the Continent, were now ready to take any chance to get the war over with and occupy Berlin.

One reason for the reversal in roles was that the British had become aware of the price they were going to have to pay for victory. Every day that the war continued there was a further drain on their limited resources. Next to Russia and possibly Japan, Britain was the most thoroughly mobilized nation in World War II. She was using up irreplaceable natural and human resources at an alarming rate. If she were to recover from victory she had to have something left with which to recover. As Montgomery put it, 'our "must" was different from the American must; a difference in urgency'. The Americans never felt this. Their economy had not been strained nor their manpower resources depleted. They saw no overwhelming reason to forestall the Russians in central Europe, for Roosevelt's policy remained one of trying to get along with Stalin after the war. The only urgency the Americans felt was to redeploy the troops in Europe to the Pacific for the final assault on the Japanese home islands, and there was no immediate hurry about that since the amphibious forces in the Pacific still had to obtain bases closer to Japan. More troops would not be needed in Asia until, at the earliest, the summer of 1945, and even Eisenhower's slow approach would bring victory in Europe by then.

The difference in approach, or sense of urgency, was well illustrated in December 1944 by the reaction to the German counter-offensive in the Ardennes. Eisenhower's armies, as a result of the broad-front advance, were fully committed and woefully short of reserves. Eisenhower sent an appeal to both London and Washington for additional manpower. Churchill, anxious to get the war over with, immediately ordered a new call-up from civilian life, one which reached deeply into Britain's remaining industrial force and provided Eisenhower with 250,000 more men. The American War Department, holding to its view that the greatest contribution the United States could make was through industrial production, refused to call up any additional manpower. Eisenhower's Chief of Staff, Walter B. Smith, was furious. Contrasting Washington and London, he told a staff meeting, 'When I was tossing on my bed last night, the thought came to me, "Should we not go on record to our Masters in Washington that if they want us to win the war over here they must find us another ten Divisions".' Look at Britain, about to produce another 250,000 men. If she can do that we should produce another 2,500,000.'

Smith missed the point, not only for the immediate situation but for the entire war. In comparison with Britain and Russia, Roosevelt was giving his nation victory at an extraordinarily low cost. This policy may have reflected only from Roosevelt's apprehension that the American people would not make sacrifices on the scale their allies did for a war that had never touched the United States directly, or it may have been deliberate calculation, but the result was the same nonetheless – when the war ended, America was incomparably more powerful than any other nation in the world. Britain and Russia, not to mention the defeated nations, had massive problems of reconstructing shattered economies; the major domestic problem in post-war America was how to absorb the veterans and avoid unemployment.

Even without the American reinforcements, the Allied armies overcame the crisis of the Battle of the Bulge and in the early spring of 1945 moved across the Rhine into Germany on a broad front. Eisenhower set as the immediate objectives the encirclement of the industrial Ruhr and a drive to Dresden to link up with the Red Army in central Germany, thus cutting Germany into two parts. Montgomery and Churchill objected. They wanted Eisenhower to give priority in supplies and air support to 21st Army Group for a drive to Berlin, which they wished to take before the Russians got there. During the opening stages of the controversy, in late March, the British advocated an offensive towards Berlin as a proper military move. Churchill later broadened his reasons, however, to include political factors.

There has been much confusion about Churchill's advocacy of Berlin as a target. It is commonly asserted that he wanted to keep the Russians out of eastern Germany, to retain a united Germany, and to maintain Berlin's status as the capital. There is an assumption that if the Allies had captured the city there would be no Berlin problem today. This is patent nonsense. Aside from the military factors (it is probable that Eisenhower could never have taken Berlin before the Red Army, even had he wanted to), it does not remotely reflect the policies Churchill was actually advocating. He never thought in terms of denying to the Russians their position in eastern Europe generally or east

Germany specifically, a position that had been agreed to much earlier and one that, in view of the relative contribution to the Nazi defeat made by the east and west, was much to the benefit of the Western democracies. Once the 1943 cross-Channel attack had been scuttled, there never was the slightest chance that the Russians could be kept out of eastern Europe. Churchill realized this; his agreement with Stalin during their Moscow meetings in the fall of 1944 signified his recognition of the inevitable. The Prime Minister also recognized that Roosevelt was not willing to join him in an anti-Soviet crusade.

What Churchill did want from Berlin was much less grandiose than a forestalling of communist influence in eastern and central Europe. His major concern was prestige, not so much for Britain as for the West. He told Roosevelt that the Russians were going to liberate Vienna. 'If they also take Berlin, will not their impression that they have been the overwhelming contributor to our common victory be unduly imprinted in their minds?' The idea that the Russians' feeling that they had done the most to defeat Hitler could be eradicated by an Allied capture of Berlin was really rather absurd, but it had great appeal to Churchill.

The Prime Minister had something more in mind. His country would be occupying the Ruhr, seemingly an ideal arrangement for the British since the Ruhr was the main prize, the industrial heart of Germany, and control of it would allow the British to shape the development of their chief European competitor. But there were problems, the most important of which was food. The Ruhr could not feed itself. Neither could Britain. Churchill did not want to be stuck with the responsibility of nourishing the Germans in the Ruhr, and he proposed to hold Berlin until the Russians, who would be occupying agricultural eastern Germany, made firm agreements on exchanging manufactured goods for food. He never proposed keeping the Russians out of Berlin altogether, but he did want to force them to trade before letting them in.

Roosevelt would have none of it. His own major concerns, in the weeks before his death on 12 April, were the
creation of the United Nations (the San Francisco Conference to draw up the Charter began shortly after Roosevelt's death), to insure the participation of the U.S.S.R. in
the U.N., and to maintain cordial relations with Stalin. He
refused to take a hard line with Stalin on the Russian
occupation of Poland or on Stalin's suspicions about the
surrender of the German forces in Italy to the Western
Allies. The President was not an experienced diplomat and
to the end he had no clear goals for the post-war world. His
sponsorship of the U.N. indicated that he had adopted
Woodrow Wilson's belief in collective security, but the
nature of the U.N. Roosevelt wanted, dominated as it was
by the Security Council, indicated that he retained a belief
in spheres of influence for the great powers. So did his
frequent remarks about the 'Four Policemen'. He was a
convinced opponent of colonialism, but without being
very specific about what would happen when independence came in Asia and Africa. Certainly he favored an
orderly transfer of power, which came to mean a transfer to
local elite groups that allowed the West to retain economic
control.

But if much of Roosevelt's policy was cloudy, mystifying
even his closest advisers, one thing was clear. To the
exasperation of some members of the State Department, not
to mention the Ambassador to Russia, W. Averell Harriman, the President refused to become a staunch anti-
Soviet. Harriman, Churchill, and later Truman assumed
that Russia would be unreasonable, grasping, probing,
power-hungry, and impossible to deal with except from a
position of great strength and unrelenting firmness.
Roosevelt rejected such assumptions. Furthermore, he seems
to have felt it was only reasonable for the Russians to be
uneasy about the nature of the governments on Russia's
western frontier – millions of the troops that attacked the
Soviet Union in 1941 came from the semi-Fascist and

Fascist societies in the area – and thus was willing to go a long way towards meeting Stalin's demands about East Europe. There was also an assumption, shared even by Churchill, that Stalin was stating the obvious when he remarked in early 1945, 'whoever occupies a territory also imposes on it his own social system.' Churchill, who had taken the lead in establishing this principle in Italy and Greece, later denounced Stalin for practicing it in East Europe, but the evidence indicates that Roosevelt was realistic enough to accept the *quid pro quo*.

The question of the nature of the alliance with Russia was a vexing one. In the public press, the Red Army was heroic, Stalin a wise and generous leader. Whether this had a deep or lasting effect on a people who mistrusted and feared communism at least as much as they did fascism is doubtful. Behind the scenes, meanwhile, and especially in the State Department, anti-Soviet feeling kept bubbling up. George Kennan, though a rather minor functionary in the State Department, expressed the mood best. Two days after the Nazis invaded Russia, Kennan wrote the deputy chief of the Department's Division of European Affairs 'that we should do nothing at home to make it appear that we are following the course Churchill seems to have entered upon in extending moral support to the Russian cause . . . . It seems to me that to welcome Russia as an associate in the defense of democracy would invite misunderstanding'. Kennan felt that throughout Europe 'Russia is generally more feared than Germany . . .' and implied that he agreed with this estimate of the relative dangers of communism and fascism.

The sentiment that Kennan represented may have been dominant in the State Department, but the Department was not setting policy. Roosevelt extended lend-lease to the Russians and gave moral support to Stalin. Bending to State Department pressure, he did refuse Stalin's request for an agreement that would recognize Russian territorial gains under the Nazi–Soviet pact in East Europe, remarking that territorial questions would be settled at the end of the war, but beyond that issue Roosevelt concentrated on working together with the Soviet Union against the common enemy. Kennan continued to protest. In 1944, when the Red Army had driven the Germans out of Russia and was preparing for the final offensive, Kennan argued that the time had come for a 'fullfledged and realistic political show-down with the Soviet leaders'. He wanted to confront them with 'the choice between changing their policy completely and agreeing to collaborate in the establishment of truly independent countries in Eastern Europe or of forfeiting Western-Allied support and sponsorship for the remaining phases of their war effort'. In practice, this meant returning to the *status quo ante bellum* outside the pre-1939 borders of the Soviet Union, with bitterly anti-Soviet governments in control of most of the nations from Poland to Greece.

By this time Kennan was the chief adviser to the American Ambassador in Moscow, Harriman, who accepted his views. Harriman advised Roosevelt to cut back on or even eliminate lend-lease shipments. In the War Department, too, there was great fear of the Soviets. In the summer of 1944 an agency of the J.C.S. warned the Secretary of State, 'While the war with Germany is well advanced towards final conclusion, the defeat of Germany will leave Russia in a position of assured military dominance in eastern Europe and in the Middle East.' The J.C.S. agency believed that the end of the war would 'find a world profoundly changed in respect of relative national military strengths, a change more comparable indeed with that occasioned by the fall of Rome than with any other change occurring during the succeeding fifteen hundred years. This is a fact of fundamental importance in its bearing upon future international political settlements and all discussions leading thereto.' After Japan was defeated, 'the United States and the Soviet Union will be the only military powers of the first magnitude.'

What would the Soviets do with all their new-found power? In August 1943, a colonel in the War Department prepared a position paper on the subject. 'The real objective of Russia is the Sovietization not only of Europe but of the world,' he declared. His recommendation was to try to get what we could from the Russians through agreement. 'As for Germany,' he continued, 'the mere threat of our alliance with her will suffice to give pause to Russia.'

Higher-ranking officers, while agreeing with the assumption that the Soviets aimed to take over the world, could not accept the idea of making an alliance with Hitler to stop Stalin. Marshall's chief assistant in the War Department made a different recommendation: 'Victory in the war will be meaningless unless we also win the peace. We must be strong enough militarily at the peace table to cause our demands to be respected. With this in view, we should give only such equipment to our Allies that they can put to better and quicker use than we can.' In short, cut down on lend-lease to the Russians.

From 1943 on, Roosevelt received numerous recommendations to cut back on lend-lease, but he always refused and the aid continued to flow. The reason was that the West needed the Red Army. Kennan and the War Department officers had failed to see this, but Marshall and Roosevelt were clear enough about who needed whom the most. Their greatest fear was precisely Kennan's greatest hope – that once the Red Army reached Russian borders it would stop. The Germans, in those circumstances, could have marched west and turned the full fury of the Wehrmacht against the Allies, and England and America had not mobilized anywhere near enough ground troops to batter their way into Berlin against such opposition. Further, there was the frightening possibility of new secret weapons. Germany had made rapid strides in military technology during the war, German propaganda continued to urge the people to hold on just a little longer until the new weapons were ready, and the Allies knew that the Germans were working on an atomic bomb. The V-weapons, jet-propelled airplanes and snorkel submarines were bad enough. To halt lend-lease to the Russians would slow the Red Army advance, giving the Germans more time to perfect their weapons. In addition, Marshall thought Russian aid in the war against Japan absolutely essential, for without it the Americans alone would have to take on the still intact Japanese Army, with frightfully high casualties. Better by far, Marshall reasoned, to remain friends with the Russians so that after Germany surrendered the Red Army could be turned against the Japanese, thereby saving hundreds of thousands of American lives.

The central dilemma of the war was embodied in these considerations. Until the very end almost no one in power in the West wanted Russia to stop advancing, but few Americans wanted them to dominate the political and economic structure of East Europe. It had to be one way or the other. Roosevelt decided the greater danger lay in an end to Russian offensives, and he continued to give Stalin what aid and encouragement he could in the Russian drive to the west.

In any case, the entire thrust of Roosevelt's posture on the shape of the world, whether it involved spheres of influence or collective security, universal principles of democracy and capitalism or the establishment of one's 'own social system', precluded any attempt on his part to race the Russians to Berlin or other critical places in central Europe. Roosevelt, knowing in advance Eisenhower's position on Berlin, agreed with Marshall that the Supreme Commander should have a free hand. Truman might have followed a different line, but by the time he was settled in the White House it was too late.

Eisenhower made his decision on military grounds. He thought it madness to send his forces dashing towards Berlin when there was little, if any, chance that they would get there before the Red Army, at a time when the bulk of the remaining German Army was far to the south. He also needed a clearly recognizable stop line, so that when his forces linked up with the Russians there would be no unfortunate incidents of the two allies shooting at each other by mistake. He therefore informed Stalin that he was going to halt when he reached the Elbe River and send his forces south. Churchill kept pestering him to push on eastwards; finally Eisenhower wired the C.C.S., 'I am the first to admit that a war is waged in pursuance of political aims, and if the Combined Chiefs of Staff should decide that the Allied effort to take Berlin outweighs purely military considerations in this theater, I would cheerfully readjust my plans and my thinking so as to carry out such an operation.' He was not, in other words, willing to risk the lives of 100,000 or more men for no military gain, but if his superiors were prepared to make Russia instead of Germany the enemy, he would change his plans, for then the military considerations would be much different. The C.C.S. made no reply, and for Eisenhower, Nazi Germany remained the enemy.

While Eisenhower's forces occupied southern Germany, the Russians battered their way into Berlin, suffering heavy casualties, probably in excess of 100,000. Herbert Feis points out that they gained 'the first somber sense of triumph, the first awesome sight of the ruins, the first parades under the pall of smoke'. Two months later they gave up to the West over half the city they had captured at such an enormous price. At the cost of not a single life, Great Britain and the United States had their sectors in Berlin. They have been there ever since.

More important, the war ended without any sharp break with the Russians. There had been innumerable strains in the strange alliance, but the United States and the U.S.S.R. were still allies and in May 1945 the possibility of continued co-operation was, if slim, alive. Much would depend on the attitude the United States took toward what the Soviets did in East Europe. It was as certain as the sun's rising that Stalin would insist on friendly governments there, which, translated, meant governments of the left. The landlords and factory owners, the generals and the aristocrats, would have to be thrown out. Along with them would go some of the most cherished concepts in the West, concepts to which the old ruling classes in East Europe had occasionally given lip-service – freedom of speech, elections, and enterprise. The men who ran the American government could not look with pleasure on the suppression of precisely those elements in East Europe with whom they identified. Neither Truman nor his advisers would ever be able to accept in good grace the communization of East Europe. There was also the economic question – a Soviet sphere might very well block American economic access to the area.

But the experience of World War II indicated that the United States still had alternatives, that hostility was not the only possible reaction to Stalin's probable moves. It was true that America had been content to leave the old rulers in power in Italy, tried to promote the forces of the right in France, and gone along with Churchill's program for Greece. But the United States had also demonstrated an ability to make realistic, pragmatic responses to developing situations. America had aided Tito and supported the French Resistance, had refused to get tough with the Russians, had made major decisions solely on the basis of what would most quickly bring about the fall of Fascist Germany.

In the spring of 1945 America had enormously more power, both absolutely and in relation to the rest of the world, than she had possessed in 1941. But to a lesser degree that had also been the situation in 1918, and after the First World War America disarmed and for the most part refused to intervene in affairs outside the North American Continent. She could do so again. America was the victor. Her decisions would go far towards shaping the structure of the post-war world. In May 1945, as had been the case throughout the war, she did not have a firm idea of what those decisions would be. It was still possible for the United States to travel down any one of several roads.

3

The War in Asia

One of the chief facts about the war in Asia was that with the exception of the return to the Philippines and some campaigns in the Netherlands East Indies (N.E.I.), the United States made its greatest military efforts in areas outside the productive and population centers. In contrast to the situation in Europe, when the war ended the Americans did not have troops occupying the major nations of mainland Asia and thus were unable to impose their will. America could and did have an influence in Indochina, Korea, Burma, India, and China, but she could not dictate developments. In general, this gave Asians a greater opportunity to work out their own destiny than that enjoyed by Europeans. Much of American foreign policy after the war was designed to compensate, to secure positions of power for American armed forces on mainland Asia in order to shape the future there. In China, North Korea, and Indochina the attempt failed. America could not do after 1945 what she had been unable to do during the war.

America failed to get onto mainland Asia because of military limitations. She had not mobilized enough of her manpower, and almost certainly could not have done so, to carry on a large-scale land war in both Europe and Asia. There were other limitations. It was approximately twice as far from the United States to Asia as it was to Europe, which meant that it took two ships going to Asia to do the work that one could do going from the United States to Europe, and until the very last months of the war merchant shipping was in short supply. Distance, both during and after the war, was a major factor in American strategy and in the Europe-first decision. The United States devoted nearly

40 per cent of its total effort in World War II to the Pacific but much of that effort was eaten up in shipping and the amount of force it could bring to bear was much less in Asia than in Europe. As a result the American strategy in the Pacific was to avoid Japanese strong-points and initiate operations that would conserve men and material.

Insofar as the United States never came to grips with the main forces of the Japanese Army, America pursued a peripheral strategy in the Pacific. There were good military reasons for doing so, chief of which was that there was no base near Japan to serve as a staging area, as England did in Europe. The island-hopping campaign the Americans pursued worked, in the sense that it brought the Army and Navy ever closer to the home islands of Japan and gave the Navy important bases in the Pacific for the post-war period, but there was a political price. In Europe, the process of closing in on the Germans carried with it the dividends of putting American troops in Antwerp, Paris, and Rome. In Asia, the process of closing in on the Japanese only gave the United States control of relatively unimportant islands.

Mainland Asia presented special problems as a scene for military operations, problems that were well nigh insurmountable. Size, population, and the nature of the Asian economy were at the head of the list. An American army corps in France was a powerful force there; a unit of equal size in China was simply swallowed up by distance and population. In Europe, a half-million soldiers could surround the Ruhr and effectively strangle Germany; in China, with its underdeveloped economy, there was no single area that was crucial. Potentially strategic bombing could pay high dividends in Europe; in Asia, with its targets scattered and with no one target of overwhelming importance save within Japan itself, the return on investment from bombing was low.

American military policy in the Pacific was geared only in a negative way to the nation's foreign policy aims. The military effort was dedicated to the destruction of Japan.

This was a goal of the first magnitude, to be sure, since Japan's program went beyond the end of European colonialism in Asia and included the closing-off of Asia and the Pacific to European and American exploitation. If Japan won, the natural resources, investment opportunities, and markets of Asia would be denied to the Americans as well as to the Europeans, with important effects on the American economy. Just stopping the Japanese was not enough, however, for it became increasingly clear as the war went on that it would be difficult, perhaps impossible, to restore the old order in Asia. The native populations would resist. Nor did Roosevelt want to return to business as usual, for he was a sincere opponent of old-style colonialism and wanted the British out of India, the Dutch out of the East Indies, the Americans out of the Philippines, and the French out of Indochina. The United States pledged itself to give independence to the Philippines upon the conclusion of hostilities.

For the Americans, the key question was the form that independence would take, and here, as always, power would reside with the man with a gun on the spot. Except in Japan, the Philippines, and the East Indies, that man would not be an American. This fact opened the possibility that governments of the left would replace the old colonial rulers, and they might shut the Americans out of their economy just as thoroughly as the Japanese would have done. The fundamental dilemma for American political activites in the war in Asia was how simultaneously to drive out the Japanese, to prevent the resurgence of European colonialism, and to foster the growth of democratic, capitalist local governments, all without actually making the effort necessary to put the man with the gun on the spot. In China, and to a lesser extent elsewhere, it turned out to be an insoluble dilemma.

In Asia, American priorities combined with military necessities to shape events. The first priority, as in Europe, was the defeat of the enemy. Next came the elevation of China under Chiang Kai-shek to great-power status, which required in the first instance establishing Chiang's control in China, a control that was increasingly contested by the communists under Mao Tse-tung. Chiang was corrupt, inefficient, and dictatorial – the senior U.S. Army officer in China referred to him contemptuously as 'Peanut' – but he was willing to maintain the Open Door for America. No matter how badly the Americans wanted Chiang and his landlords and war lords to rule China, however, there was little they could do to support him without troops on the scene, and the military realities precluded sending large numbers of American troops to China.

In China, the political and the military possibilities clashed. In Southeast Asia the situation was reversed. Communications between the United States and India–Burma were long and tortuous, but they did exist. There were British bases and an allied command. American troops could have gone into the area. They did not do so in any significant number because the priority was low. On Asia's offshore islands the situation was radically different. At the end of the war America had overwhelming force on all the major island groups, from Australia through the East Indies north to the Philippines. Most important of all, America had complete control of Japan.

The strategy that put America on the key islands grew out of military necessity, personality conflict, and political motivation. After falling back from the Philippines in the early spring of 1942, the Americans began building a base of operations in Australia. They already had one in the Central Pacific on Hawaii. Top Army and Navy officials did not get on well with one another and each service had a different idea as to the proper manner of conducting the war; the disagreements were so sharp that, unlike the situation in Europe, Navy admirals refused to subordinate themselves to Army generals, and vice versa. The result was a division of the area into two theaters, the Southwest Pacific and the Central Pacific, with the Army under General Douglas MacArthur responsible for the Southwest and the Navy under Admiral Chester Nimitz in charge in the Central Pacific. MacArthur's base was Australia; his strategy was to move northwards through the East Indies, the Philippines, and Formosa to get at Japan. Nimitz, in Hawaii, wanted to advance westward through the Central Pacific. In the end, both approaches were used.

When MacArthur got to Australia after his flight from Bataan, he announced 'I shall return' to the Philippines. (The War Department liked the phrase but thought the statement should read, 'We shall return', since presumably MacArthur would need help. MacArthur refused to change it, and 'I shall return' it remained.) Senior officers in the Navy objected; they felt that making the effort to get back into the Philippines was not worth the men and material required. Better by far, the Navy reasoned, to bypass the Philippines and go straight to Formosa or some other island base, or even to concentrate exclusively on the Central Pacific. MacArthur's critics, and their number was large, believed that the only reason the United States returned to the Philippines (in 1944) was to enhance MacArthur's personal prestige.

MacArthur's egotism was great, but his desire to go back to the Philippines involved something more than personal satisfaction. He had spent much of his life in the Far East, considered himself an expert on Orientals, and believed that the future lay with Asia. Europe was old and decrepit, Asia young and vibrant. MacArthur thought it would be madness for the United States to ever get involved in a land war in Asia, but this military judgement only reinforced his parallel belief that it was imperative for the United States to control the offshore islands, particularly the Philippines and Japan. The General knew that if the United States bypassed the Philippines, leaving the Japanese garrison intact, it would be difficult for America to reassert herself when the Japanese surrendered. The people who would pick up the arms the Japanese laid down would be members of the Hukbalahap, a communist-led guerrilla organization that already controlled vast sections of the colony. If the Huks once gained power, it might be impossible to root them out, and the Huks were unfriendly toward native landlords, American investors, and the idea of America retaining military bases in the Philippines.

During the Japanese occupation, according to a State Department report, the 'Philippine Islands have been governed very largely under the same laws and by much the same men as under the Commonwealth'. MacArthur was well aware of this, and his aim was to keep the same men in power, collaborationists though they might be. By early 1945 his program was being implemented. Mac-Arthur picked Manuel Roxas to lead the country, a man whom the Americans themselves described as being 'in the peculiar position of an exonerated collaborationist . . .' MacArthur put Roxas on his staff as a brigadier general, sent him to the United States on a prestige tour, and in April 1946 helped Roxas become the first President of the new nation. Behind Roxas stood, according to the American Office of Strategic Services, 'some economically powerful groups'. MacArthur saw to it that the Filipino authorities received American arms to put down the Huk rebellion and undo the land reform the Huks had carried out in the area they once controlled. Thanks to MacArthur, America had her bases and American investors had their property in the Philippines.

In China, unlike the Philippines, the Americans did not have troops and could not control events. The United States wished to have the Kuomintang under Chiang rule over a great power, so that China could serve as a counter to Russian and Japanese expansion in the Far East and in order to bring China into the modern world community both as a market and a producer of materials. Americans realized that to accomplish this the Kuomintang would have to be reformed and its policies liberalized. They encouraged Chiang to root out the rampant corruption, introduce at least a modicum of efficiency, make an accommodation with Mao and the communists, introduce some meaningful land reform, and in general modernize along Western lines.

The tactical mistakes made in attempting to implement this program were manifold, the most spectacular being the personalities of the key American officials sent to China. More important was the strategic error. Everything rested on the twin assumptions that Chiang wanted reform and could put it through, assumptions that turned out to be totally unwarranted. But most Americans regarded the Chinese communists with horror and there seemed to be no alternative between Mao and Chiang. Events therefore ground on with what appeared to be a tragic inevitability. America sent huge loans to China, often in the form of direct cash, but with a foreboding of failure since they were really bribes to Chiang and his chief supporters, who threatened to quit the war against Japan if their palms were not crossed. The possibility that the Chinese might surrender, thus freeing the bulk of the Japanese armies for employment against the Americans, frightened Washington sufficiently to keep the money flowing. It also kept the Americans from sending aid to the Chinese communists, who were undoubtedly more efficient in carrying on the struggle against the Japanese than Chiang was. The tragedy was that the policy gave Chiang the notion that he could do as he wished as long as he remained simultaneously anti-communist and anti-Japanese, which meant the end to whatever fleeting impulses he may have had towards reform.

Throughout the war the situation within the Kuomintang's armies was desperate. Senior officers lived in luxury while the enlisted men suffered from body-wracking disease, seldom ate, were usually shoeless, and had insufficient equipment (one in three had a rifle, mostly without ammunition). American officials wanted improvement, for it was imperative that China's vast manpower resources be used against Japan, since if Chinese troops did not carry the burden of the war someone else would have to. No one in Washington wanted American soldiers fighting the Japanese on mainland Asia, while the alternative – a Russian entry into the war – carried with it political implications for control of post-war Asia that disturbed many State Department officials. Russia was in any case so tied up by the Germans that there was little hope of bringing her into the Pacific war. It was clear enough that sending money to Chiang would not retrieve the situation, so in early 1942 Washington sent General Joseph W. Stilwell to China to serve as Chiang's Chief of Staff. The brilliant, irascible Stilwell was told to modernize Chiang's armies.

Stilwell was a realist and soon reported that the task was hopeless. He characterized the Kuomintang as a form of 'gangsterism' and was certain the Chinese people would overthrow Chiang after the war. Stilwell fumed because of Chiang's undeclared truce with the Japanese – whenever the enemy advanced, Chiang's forces fell back without offering resistance – but still tried again and again to force some improvement. The American general believed that Chinese troops, given proper training, support, and leadership, would be among the best in the world (a judgement proven sound in Korea a few years later), so he proposed reform after reform. But Chiang hated Stilwell, refused to listen, and insisted that Roosevelt relieve the American general. The Americans had a counter-proposal – they urged Chiang to give Stilwell command of all Chinese troops.

The idea that one man could change the course of history was problematical at best, but Stilwell was willing to give it a try. He thought he could see to it that lend-lease goods got into the hands of Chinese troops, rather than being sold by the rulers on the black market, and felt he could make a working arrangement with Mao so that there would be some co-ordination in the struggle against Japan. The trouble was that he would have to do it against the wishes of Chiang, thus forcing a choice between himself and the

Kuomintang. Stilwell recognized that the future of China was involved; on 26 September 1943, he declared: 'Chiang Kai-shek believes he can go on milking the United States for money and munitions by using the old gag about quitting if he is not supported . . . . I believe he will only continue his policy and delay, while grabbing for loans and postwar aid, for the purpose of maintaining his present position, based on one-party government, a reactionary policy, or the suppression of democratic ideas with the active aid of his gestapo.' But if Stilwell did replace Chiang, where then would America's China policy be? The United States could not expect to run China indefinitely.

Stilwell had made it either him or me, and it was Stilwell who went. Roosevelt sent Patrick J. Hurley to China as his personal representative; Hurley reported that 'if you sustain Stilwell in this controversy you will lose Chiang Kai-shek and possibly you will lose China with him'. Over General Marshall's strong protests, Stilwell came home (in late 1944), where he was not allowed to describe the realities in China, and General Alfred Wedemeyer replaced him. Wedemeyer's feelings about Chiang paralleled those of Stilwell, but Wedemeyer was more circumspect. The United States continued to support Chiang and hope for the best.

Wedemeyer's appointment, meanwhile, signified the end of the illusion that the Chinese could do in Asia what the Russians were doing in Europe – supply the hordes of fighting men necessary to defeat the enemy. This in turn meant that the United States would have to turn to the Russians in Asia, too, a policy Marshall advocated, with the recognition that Stalin would naturally demand a price for the blood his people would shed. The alternative, substituting the atomic bomb for mass armies, was not yet available.

The problem of the Chinese communists also remained. Chiang was using the only respectable troops he had against Mao, who in turn deployed a force of up to two million men. Full-scale civil war threatened, a war that would be dangerous to the Americans on two counts: it would reduce the potential forces that could be thrown against Japan and it might lead to Chiang's overthrow and Mao's victory. The Americans therefore tried simultaneously to force Chiang to bring the communists into the government and to persuade Mao to co-operate with Chiang. Neither of the Chinese groups, however, would make any but the most impossible demands of the other, and nothing was accomplished. Wedemeyer suggested sending American arms to the communists, on the grounds that only they were fighting the Japanese, but Chiang got wind of the project and vetoed it.

During the last stages of the war Chiang also was able to obtain Russian promises, honored for the most part, not to support the Chinese communists and to urge them to unite with the Kuomintang. In return, Chiang leased Port Arthur to the Russians and made Dairen a free port, while recognizing Soviet control of Outer Mongolia. In Asia as in Europe, Stalin was the extreme conservative, basing his decisions solely on Russian national interests and ignoring or selling out the communist parties of the world. He regarded Mao as an adventurist whose wild schemes would anger the West and thus endanger Russian gains in the Far East.

American policy, like Stalin's, was caught in the quicksand of the attempt to save Chiang. Both ignored the realities. In May 1945, for example, President Truman sent Edwin A. Locke, Jr, a banker, to China as his personal representative for economic affairs. Locke believed that America ought to invest in China in order to create 'a large, permanent and growing market for U.S. goods . . .' Such a program required peace with the Chinese communists, plus reform, neither of which Chiang favored – and which in any case he was incapable of carrying out. But as long as the only alternative to Chiang was Mao, the Americans could do no other than to try to patch things up between them.

For two years this hopeless policy continued, even

though realism was not entirely absent from the upper reaches of the American government. After the war Truman sent Marshall to China to mediate; Secretary Stimson warned his former Chief of Staff, 'Remember that the Generalissimo [Chiang] has never honestly backed a thorough union with the Chinese Communists. He could not, for his administration is a mere surface veneer (more or less rotten) over a mass of the Chinese people beneath him.' Despite this realism, and despite the proclaimed neutrality of the Marshall Mission, America continued to give material support to Chiang. It was never enough, primarily because nothing short of a total American occupation of China would have been sufficient to prevent Mao's eventual victory. Such an occupation would have required a million soldiers or more, far more than America was willing to expend even for Europe, and there never was the slightest possibility that either the American people or government were willing to make the sacrifice required to prop up the gangsters in the Kuomintang.

Stalin's willingness to co-operate in Asia with the Americans extended beyond China. Roosevelt first met with the Russian leader in late 1943, in Teheran. The American President's hatred of de Gaulle dovetailed with his general opposition to European colonialism and led to a proposal for Indochina. Roosevelt suggested that the colony be placed under a Four-Power trusteeship after the war (China, the United States, Russia, and Britain). Stalin immediately endorsed the proposal, adding that Indo-chinese independence might follow in two or three decades. What such a trusteeship would mean for Indochina was vague, but given the composition of three of the Four Powers it was obvious that the French landowners would remain, while the Viet Minh, a local guerrilla force dominated by Ho Chi Minh and the communists, would be excluded from power. Only the British, fearful for their own Empire, objected to thus snatching away a colony from France.

The situation within Vietnam did not lend itself to an

easy solution, whether it was to be the restoration of France or the imposition of a trusteeship. The Japanese had allowed the French to maintain administrative control of Indochina until March 1945, when they gave limited encouragement to nationalist sentiment by replacing the French with a local puppet government under the Bao Dai. The Viet Minh then went into active resistance, drawing their support from the peasant tenantry (in Vietnam 3 per cent of the landlords owned 60 per cent of the land). Ho informed Washington that he wanted independence within five to ten years, land reform, a democracy based on universal suffrage, and national purchase of French holdings. He copied much of his Declaration of Independence from the American one. All this availed Ho nothing, for the American position had changed. Whatever Roosevelt's personal feelings towards de Gaulle, good relations with France were imperative if communism were to be thwarted in Europe, still the main theater, and relations with France would turn in large part on the American attitude towards colonialism.

The same was true for the British, who as long as Churchill ruled had set their faces against any changes in the *status quo ante bellum*. They insisted on bringing the French back. There was, in addition, the general American fear of communism in Asia, of which Ho was obviously a part and potentially a leader. The Americans therefore agreed, in July 1945, that the British would take the Japanese surrender south of the 16th parallel in Indochina, while Chiang's troops would do so to the north. The British held the fort until the French could scrape up some troops to come in, while Chiang's troops looted with abandon until the French returned. America had taken its hard line with Japan in 1941 in large part because of the Japanese occupation of Indochina, and it was at least consistent that at the end of the war she would move again to prevent the tip of Southeast Asia from falling into Ho's unfriendly hands, distasteful as French colonial rule might be.

Many American decisions in World War II – for

example, that allowing the French to reoccupy Indochina – were made quickly and without the benefit of deep analysis because they dealt with issues that were relatively low on the priority list. In some cases there were, later, the most serious repercussions, as in the agreement to divide Korea, with the Russians occupying the country north of the 38th parallel and the Americans the area south of that line. Both agreed that this was merely a matter of convenience, that the Japanese colony eventually would be reunited and given its independence, and both seem to have meant it at the time, although neither gave Korea a great deal of thought.

The most important decision of the war, however – to build and then use an atomic bomb – was thoroughly examined and discussed in the higher levels of the government. So many important personages participated, in fact, and their motives were so divergent, that it is impossible to say that there was one key factor making the result inevitable.

The Manhattan Project, the best-kept secret of the war, began in 1939, with the sole purpose of harnessing the energy of the atom to produce a bomb that could be carried by aircraft, and to do it before the Germans succeeded in building one. J. Robert Oppenheimer, one of the eminent scientists on the Project, later recalled, 'We always assumed if they were needed they would be used.' The tendency was to regard the bomb as simply another military weapon. As the work on the bomb drew near completion, Secretary Stimson asked Truman to appoint the Interim Committee to decide on how the bomb should be used. Truman put Stimson, George L. Harrison, the President of the New York Life Insurance Company, politician James Byrnes, scientists Vannevar Bush and James B. Conant, General Marshall, and others on the committee. It recommended that the bomb be used against the Japanese as soon as possible, against a military target, and without prior warning of the nature of the weapon.

The Interim Committee's recommendation was straightforward enough, but complications ensued. The Manhattan

Project scientists began to get balky. They realized better than anyone else that the bomb was not just another military weapon and they insisted that its use had to be regarded not as a simple military matter but as a foreign-policy decision of the first magnitude. Germany was already defeated, which to many of the scientists took all the urgency out of the Manhattan Project, and the proposed Russian entry into the war against Japan sealed the Japanese fate. Why risk world condemnation for using a bomb when its use was unnecessary? Some questioned the wisdom of dropping the bomb on the Japanese, a non-white people, since this would seem to the non-white majority of the world's people further evidence of America's racist policies (the British military commentator B. H. Liddell Hart later charged that the United States would never have used the bomb against the white people in Berlin).

Most of all, the scientists were concerned with America's image. Sixty-four of the men working on the Project signed a note saying, 'It may be very difficult to persuade the world that a nation which was capable of secretly preparing and suddenly releasing a new weapon, as indiscriminate as the rocket bomb and a thousand times more destructive, is to be trusted in its proclaimed desire of having such weapons abolished by international agreement.' They urged that the bomb be demonstrated on a barren island before Japanese observers. If the Japanese still refused to surrender, then the United States should turn the bomb over to the United Nations and let it assume the onus of making the decision to use it. 'This may sound fantastic,' they admitted, 'but in nuclear weapons we have something entirely new in order of magnitude of destructive power, and if we want to capitalize fully on the advantage their possession gives us, we must use new and imaginative methods.'

Despite the scientists, the military situation dominated the thinking about the bomb. Japan was clearly defeated, but not crushed. She had lost most of her Pacific Empire and

fleet, but she still retained much of China and the Asian
coast, her army was more or less intact, and her air force –
based on the frightening kamikazes – was a major threat.
Japan had an army estimated at up to 2,000,000 men in
Manchuria available for the defense of the home islands,
with some 5,350 kamikaze planes ready for use and some
7,000 under repair or in storage, with more than 5,000
young men training for the Kamikaze Corps. Most of the
planes were dispersed on small grass strips or in underground hangars and caves, where they were being conserved
for use against the American amphibious invaders. An
American invasion of the home islands would be a bloody
affair. Stimson wished to avoid it not only because he
feared the casualties, but also because he did not wish to
inaugurate a race war in the Pacific, where the white man
was so badly outnumbered.

A key factor was the Red Army. If Stalin would turn it
around, bring it to Asia, and declare war on Japan, the
Japanese Army in Manchuria would be tied down on the
continent and would therefore be unavailable for the
defense of the home islands. Under those circumstances,
Japan might well quit without a last-ditch fight. Contemplat-
ing the possibility of the Red Army taking care of the bulk
of the Japanese Army, on 18 June 1945 General Marshall
noted, 'The impact of Russian entry on the already hopeless Japanese may well be the decisive action levering them
into capitulation . . . .' The U.S. Navy thought the Japanese
could be starved into submission through a blockade, and
the Army Air Forces argued that even without the atomic
bomb the enemy could be forced through bombing to
surrender, but Truman and Marshall could not accept
either of these optimistic forecasts. If the United States
wanted an unconditional surrender, it could only get it by
destroying the Japanese Army. Since in the early summer of
1945 the atomic bomb had not yet been tested, it appeared
that the only way to destroy the Japanese Army was to fight
it, and in Marshall's view – and that of nearly everyone

else – it was preferable to have the Red Army do it than to shed barrels of American blood. As Truman later put it, 'The campaign against Japan was based on the assumption that we would not attempt to engage the masses of the Japanese Army . . . with our own ground forces.'

There was another alternative. However strong the Japanese Army was, whatever the cost the enemy could make the United States pay to overrun the home islands, Japan was a defeated nation and her leaders knew it. They could delay but not prevent the final defeat. Japan was fighting on only to avoid the humiliation of unconditional surrender. She wanted some explicit conditions to her capitulation, of which by far the most important was a guarantee that the Emperor would remain. As early as September 1944, the Japanese had approached the Swedish Minister in Tokyo to see what terms they could get, but the attempt came to nothing. In April 1945, a new cabinet came to power with a mandate to end the war as soon as possible. The Japanese approached the Soviets, asking for mediation; the Russians, who were by then anxious to enter the war against Japan when their troops were ready, in order to have a voice in the post-war settlements in Asia, stalled.

But thanks to their ability to read the enemy code, the Americans knew the Japanese were desperately trying to find a way out. An American intelligence report of 30 June put it bluntly: 'The Japanese believe that unconditional surrender would be the equivalent of national extinction, and there are as yet no indications that they are ready to accept such terms,' but they would surrender on conditions. The Americans had also agreed among themselves that the Emperor had to stay, since his elimination would have brought on social chaos in Japan. For reasons of domestic morale and politics, however, and because they definitely did want to humiliate the enemy who had launched the treacherous Pearl Harbor attack, the Americans decided not to inform the Japanese of their intentions about the Emperor.

At the February 1945 meetings with the Russians at Yalta, the Americans had done everything they could to get Stalin to promise to enter the Pacific War, including persuading Chiang to make concessions to the Russians on the Sino-Soviet border. Stalin agreed to come in within three months of the conclusion of hostilities in Europe – he would need that much time to shift troops from Germany to Manchuria. When in July the Big Three met again at Potsdam, the Americans remained as anxious as ever to have the Red Army help them out.

Then came the successful test of the first atomic bomb. It inaugurated a new era in the world's history and in the tools of American foreign policy. No longer, or so it seemed, would the United States have to rely on mass armies, either those of their allies or their own. The atomic bomb had numerous advantages – it was cheaper than mass armies; it was politically advantageous, since by using it the government could avoid conscription; it was quicker. For the next two decades, American foreign policy would pivot on the bomb.

The Americans began to use the bomb as an instrument of diplomacy immediately. As Churchill summed up the American attitude on 23 July, 'It was now no longer necessary for the Russians to come into the Japanese war; the new explosive alone was sufficient to settle the matter.' Later the same day, reporting on a conversation with James Byrnes, Churchill declared, 'It is quite clear that the United States do not at the present time desire Russian participation in the war against Japan.' They did not because they did not want the Russians to join the occupation of Japan or to make gains at Japan's expense in the Far East. On 23 July, Stimson recorded that even Marshall, who had pushed hardest for Russian entry, 'felt, as I felt sure he would, that now with our new weapon we would not need the assistance of the Russians to conquer Japan.'

At Potsdam, Truman casually informed Stalin that the United States had a 'new weapon' and was pleased when the Soviet leader did not press him for details. The Big Three then agreed to retain the Emperor after Japanese surrender, but refused to let the Japanese know this. Instead, they issued the Potsdam Declaration, calling again for unconditional surrender on pain of great destruction. The Japanese rejected the demand as it contained no guarantee on the Emperor, and Truman gave the order to drop the bomb as soon as one was ready.

What was the great hurry? This question has bothered nearly everyone who has examined the controversy raging around the decision to use the bomb. The importance of the question stems from three related factors: (1) the United States had no major operations planned before 1 November, so it had time to wait and see what the effect of the anticipated Russian declaration of war would be, or to see if the Japanese peace-feelers were serious; (2) the bomb was not used against a military target, so it did not change the military situation; (3) the Americans expected the Russians to enter the war on or about 8 August; they dropped the bomb on 6 August. When the Japanese did not surrender immediately, a second bomb fell on 9 August. The British physicist P. M. S. Blackett, and later others, charged that the sequence of events conclusively demonstrated that the use of the bomb was 'the first major operation of the cold diplomatic war with Russia'. Its purpose was to keep Russia out of the Far Eastern settlement and had nothing at all to do with saving American lives.

A parallel interpretation claims that the intention was to impress the Russians with the power of the bomb and to make it clear that the United States would not hesitate to use it. America had already deployed the bulk of her troops out of Western Europe, as had the British, so the Red Army in East Europe was by August of 1945 the most powerful force in all of Europe. To those concerned about a possible Russian advance across the Elbe, the bomb seemed a perfect deterrent.

These interpretations are not necessarily wrong; they are

just too limited. It is true that the death of Roosevelt allowed anti-Soviet sentiment to bubble up in Washington, especially in the State Department, but it is not at all clear that the anti-Soviet advisers were controlling events. In any case, if the motive was to keep the Russians out of the Far Eastern settlement, the Americans could have done that by negotiating a surrender in July and probably earlier, long before the Soviets were ready to declare war.

Nearly every individual who participated in the decision to use the bomb had his own motive. Some were concerned with the kamikazes, others wanted to punish the Japanese for Pearl Harbor, while there were those who thought the actual use of the bombs was the only way to justify to Congress and the people the expenditure of $2 billion on a secret project.

Life came cheap in the world of 1945. The Anglo-Americans at Dresden had slaughtered thousands and thousands of women and children in air raids that had no discernible military purpose. To kill a few more 'Japs' seemed natural enough, and the racial factor in the decision cannot be ignored.

The simplest explanation is perhaps the most convincing. The bomb was there. No one in the government seriously thought about not using it. To drop it as soon as it was ready seemed natural enough. As Truman later put it, 'The final decision of where and when to use the atomic bomb was up to me. Let there be no mistake about it. I regarded the bomb as a military weapon and never had any doubt that it should be used.' Still, he was aware of the indirect dividends. On 9 August the Russians declared war on Japan; Truman records that 'this move did not surprise us. Our dropping of the atomic bomb on Japan had forced Russia to reconsider her position in the Far East'.

Unfortunately, the first bomb on Hiroshima did not bring an immediate Japanese response. The Russians, meanwhile, rolled forward in Manchuria and Southern Sakhalin. The Japanese Manchurian army surrendered. In order to prod the Japanese, the United States dropped a second bomb, on Nagasaki, which insured that the Japanese government would surrender to the Americans. Even after the second bomb, however, the Japanese insisted on some guarantee about the Emperor. The Americans decided they would have to take what they could get, made the required promises, and got the surrender.

American troops occupied Japan, excluding the Russians, not to mention the Australians and British. Even though MacArthur, who headed the occupation, was supposed to be a Supreme Allied Commander responsible to all the governments which had been at war with Japan, in fact he ran affairs as he saw fit, checking his decisions only with the United States government. The conclusion of the war therefore found the United States either occupying, controlling, or exerting strong influence in four of the five major industrial areas of the world – Western Europe, Great Britain, Japan, and the United States itself. Only the Soviet Union was outside the American orbit.

It was an ironic conclusion. Of the Big Three powers, the United States had made the least sacrifices but gained the most. Her policy of avoiding direct confrontation with the armies of the Axis had saved hundreds of thousands of lives, while Roosevelt's insistence on maintaining the civilian economy at relatively high levels had strengthened the domestic economy. The United States was the only nation in the world with capital resources available to even begin to solve the problems of post-war reconstruction. She could use, or try to use, this capital to dictate the form the reconstruction took and to extend the areas of her own influence. America had, in addition, the atomic bomb. In 1945 it seemed the ultimate weapon, and American politicians, ignoring the scientists' warnings that others would soon make their own bomb, believed that they had a secret that would insure American military dominance for decades. The Russians desperately needed manpower to rebuild, but unless they were willing to abandon all pretense at military strength in Europe they would have to maintain an enormous army outside their borders. The bomb allowed the Americans to avoid such a waste of manpower.

There were problems. One existed on mainland Asia. Except in South Korea, America had no significant numbers of troops on the mainland. Whatever influence she wished to exert could be exerted only through proxies, and it was abundantly clear that the American proxies – France, Britain, the Dutch, and Chiang – were intensely unpopular with the great masses of Asians. The Japanese had shattered, for all time, the image of the white man in the Orient. No longer was he looked upon as a demi-God whose exploitation of Asians was inevitable. Asians had come to believe that they could control their own resources and lives. They wanted the white man out, out of Indochina, out of India, out of Malaya, out of the Dutch East Indies, out of the Philippines. American foreign policy would either have to adjust to this historic development or go crashing down with the rest of the white colonial rulers.

Even in Europe there were problems. The Soviets had made every sacrifice required to defeat the Nazis; they might be able to do the same in order to reconstruct. Certainly American loans could ease the burden, but if the loans had strings attached – strings that might include the nature of East European economic and social structure – the Soviets could, possibly, decide to create their own capital through forced savings and by stripping the areas in Germany and elsewhere they occupied. Stalin could then follow an independent, anti-American course in international affairs. What shape American relations with its wartime ally might take was still open, but increasingly hostility was the rule rather than the exception. To trace this development in American–Soviet relations, we must go back in time to February 1945, and Yalta.

4

The Beginnings of the Cold War

While the British and Americans held firmly . . . the whole position in
Africa and the Mediterranean . . . and the whole of Western Germany
containing 46 million Germans (compared to 18 million in the Russian
zone), the greater part of the demobilized and disbanded veterans of the
Wehrmacht and 70 per cent of Germany's pre-war heavy industry, they
undertook by negotiation and diplomatic pressure to reduce Russia's
position in Eastern Europe – which the Soviet Union had won because
the Red Army had defeated two thirds of the German Army.

WALTER LIPPMANN

THERE is no satisfactory date to mark the beginning of the
Cold War. Some historians have placed it at 1917, others as
late as 1947 or 1948, with most putting it somewhere in
between. Whatever date is chosen to mark the declaration
of war, it is certain that the issue that sparked it, gave it
life and shaped its early course, was East Europe. For
centuries East and West have struggled with each other for
control of the huge area running from the Baltic to the
Balkans, an area rich in human and industrial resources
and one that is strategically vital to both sides, either to
Russia as a buffer against the West or to Germany and
France as a gateway for invasion of Russia. In the first four
decades of the twentieth century, with a few exceptions,
East Europe had sided with the West. Local governments
were generally authoritarian, reactionary, and anti-Russian.
The ruling elites and the Church that supported them lived
in splendor, while the poverty-stricken masses provided the
cannon fodder first to hem in the Soviet Union and then, in
1941, to help attack it.

Neither the West nor the East has been willing to allow
East Europe to be strong, independent, or neutral. Russia

and the West each have wanted the area to be aligned with them and open for their own economic exploitation. The United States participated in this process in 1919, when President Wilson took the lead in breaking up the Austro-Hungarian Empire and establishing independent, Western-oriented governments designed, in part at least, to hold the Soviet Union in check. The attempt ultimately failed because of the inability of the capitalist states to stick together, a failure helped along by American refusal in the thirties to participate in European politics.

The climax came at Munich. For three years Stalin had sought to form an alliance with Britain and France, but London and Paris would do anything to avoid getting into bed with the Soviets, so they slept with the Nazis instead. Stalin, no more ready than the West to take on Hitler alone, then signed the Nazi–Soviet Pact, which provided for a division of East Europe between Germany and Russia. They soon began fighting over the spoils, however, and in 1941 Hitler took the rest of East Europe and drove deep into Soviet territory. The British and French, meanwhile, had tried to redeem their abandonment of East Europe by declaring war when Hitler invaded Poland, but the aid they gave to the defense of Poland was useless. In the conflict that followed, after France dropped out and America came in, the West made no significant contribution to the liberation of East Europe and when the end came the Red Army was in sole possession of the area to the east of a line drawn from Stettin on the Baltic to Trieste on the Adriatic.

Russia controlled East Europe. This crucial result of World War II destroyed the Grand Alliance and gave birth to the Cold War.

The West, with America leading the way, was unwilling to accept Russian domination of East Europe. Although the Anglo-Americans were ready to admit that Stalin had earned the right to have the major say in the politics of the region and that Russian security demanded friendly governments there, they were not prepared to abandon it altogether. The Americans especially wallowed in the illusion that it was possible to have East European governments that were both capitalistic and friendly to Russia. Nearly every important American leader acknowledged that East Europe could no longer maintain an anti-Soviet position, but at the same time they all wished to maintain the pre-war social structure. They wanted the landlords, the Church, and the factory owners to remain. They wanted East Europe open to American investment and tied to Western Europe through extensive trade (one of Truman's favorite proposals was the internationalization of the great river systems of Europe to facilitate this trade). They wanted, in short, East Europe to continue to serve as an economic colony of the West, contributing raw materials which the West would convert into finished products to be sold at high profits in the East. As Secretary of State James Byrnes put it, 'Our objective is a government [in Poland] both friendly to the Soviet Union and representative of all the democratic elements of the country.'

It was an impossible program. The division of East European society into elites and masses precluded democratic capitalism – only a form of Fascism was possible – and no capitalistic government in the region could be any other than anti-Soviet. It may be that Roosevelt realized this fundamental fact, but if so he was unwilling to explain it to the American people. When he reported on the Yalta conference in February 1945, he emphasized Stalin's agreement to hold free elections in East Europe. Roosevelt's report fed soaring American expectations about the shape of post-war East Europe – Poland, Bulgaria, Rumania, and the rest of the region would become, it was believed, democratic capitalist states closely tied to the West. There never was the slightest possibility that this would happen, but when it failed to occur, millions of Americans were outraged. They demanded liberation and roll-back and hurled insults at the Russians, while professional anti-communists searched for the betrayers of East Europe and found them in the highest circles of American government, including, in the minds of some, President Roosevelt himself. Even twenty-five years after the war, the West found it difficult to reconcile itself to the flow of Russian power into East Europe.

The struggle centered on Poland. There were two separate, but related, questions: Who would control the nation? and What would its boundaries be? The British had tried to answer the first by sponsoring, in London, a government-in-exile in which the Church, the Polish Army officer corps, and the landlords were dominant. The Americans had answered the second in early 1942 by refusing to discuss, as Stalin wished to do, the boundary question in East Europe. The United States insisted that such discussion had to be postponed until Hitler was crushed, partly because they did not want to enter into any secret agreements that could later be denounced, mainly because Stalin was insisting upon Russia's 1941 frontiers, which extended Soviet influence into East Europe as a result of the Nazi–Soviet Pact. The American mistake in refusing to agree to Stalin's 1942 demands was monumental, for not only did it feed the Russians' already great suspicion of the West, it also threw away the last, best hope of keeping the Soviets out of East Europe, since the 1941 frontiers were much more favorable to the West than those that Russia eventually imposed.

By the time of the Yalta meetings in early 1945 the Americans could no longer postpone the discussion of frontiers. The war was coming to an end and the Red Army had already overrun pre-war Poland. This strengthened Stalin's hand, as did the world-wide military situation. The United States was desperately trying to get Russian help in the war against Japan – it was at Yalta that Roosevelt agreed to put pressure on Chiang to recognize the autonomy of Outer Mongolia, the internationalization of Dairen, Russian control of Port Arthur, and so on, all in return for a Russian promise to support Chiang, not aid the

Chinese communists, and – most important – enter the Japanese war. But Stalin had no intention of aiding the Chinese communists anyway, just as he did little to aid the communists in Western Europe. He was not concerned with the future of international communism; he was concerned with Russian security, which was bound up with the fate of Poland and East Europe generally. If the United States wanted Russian co-operation in the war against Japan, it would have to acquiesce in the settlement in East Europe. All the Americans could do, however, was give verbal agreement to what was going to happen anyway, for the fundamental fact in East Europe was the presence of the Red Army.

Stalin was playing a strong hand. He already occupied the areas he most wanted, while in Italy and France the West had set the precedent he needed: 'Whoever occupies a territory also imposes on it his own social system.' The West had to have his help in the Pacific War. But the Americans had some trumps, too. Both as a result of previous agreements and because of the current military situation, they along with the British would be occupying the Ruhr Valley, by far the most valuable section of Germany and the only one that could begin to satisfy Stalin's demands for German reparations. Second, the Soviet Union had been devastated. Reconstruction would require capital, and in all the world only the United States had a sufficient supply. In order to obtain a loan from the United States, Stalin would have to take into account American sensibilities about East Europe.

A totaling-up of the balance sheet of pluses and minuses for the East and West in the struggle for Poland obscures rather than clarifies the situation, however, for the two sides were not playing a game, since there never was any doubt about the outcome. The main question was whether Stalin could impose his control without totally alienating the West. Britain had gone to war with Germany, at least officially, to preserve Polish independence; the United

States had millions of Polish-American voters; both Western powers had economic ambitions in the region; both were committed to an ideology that emphasized free elections, freedom of religion, and private property. No solution could have satisfied simultaneously the East and West, for what one wanted was incompatible with what the other needed. East Europe would have to fall into someone's orbit.

Given the general desire at Yalta to hold the Grand Alliance together, based on mutual need, the Big Three tried to find a face-saving formula. The Russians had created an alternative to the London-based Polish government-in-exile, the so-called Lublin Government, which was a Soviet puppet. In January 1945, Stalin had recognized the Lublin Poles as the sole government of Poland, a slap in the face to Churchill and a repudiation of long-standing British policy. At Yalta, Churchill and Roosevelt tried to retrieve the situation by insisting on a broadly based Polish government, one that would include major figures from the London government, and on free elections. They believed that they had achieved a miracle when Stalin agreed to 'free and unfettered elections as soon as possible on the basis of universal suffrage and secret ballot', and also to 'reorganize' the Polish government by bringing in Poles from London. Had these promises been kept in the sense that Churchill understood them, the old ruling classes in Poland probably would have been restored, thereby giving the West the best of all possible worlds. Stalin, however, had no intention of giving up Poland and he never accepted the Western interpretation of the Yalta agreements. It is possible that he did not fully realize that the West was serious, for he may have felt that all that was required was a face-saving formula, which he was willing enough to give. But if he thought the West would accept without protest his violations of the agreement, he was wrong.

Both sides wanted a puppet government in Poland, not so much because either wanted to exploit it economically (although that element was present) as for military reasons. Poland is a corridor that can lead either way. As Stalin put it at Yalta, 'For the Russian people, the question of Poland is not only a question of honor but also a question of security. Throughout history, Poland has been the corridor through which the enemy has passed into Russia. Twice in the last thirty years our enemies, the Germans, have passed through this corridor . . . . Poland is not only a question of honor but of life and death for the Soviet Union.' The West saw Poland in reverse, as the outpost of European civilization holding back the hordes of Asians ready to overrun the Continent. This great fear, a constant in European history, was heightened in 1945 because of the vacuum in Germany and because of the Red Army, by then incomparably the strongest power in all Europe. If the Red Army remained intact, if it occupied Poland and East Germany, if the United States demobilized, and if Poland fell into communist hands – all of which seemed probable in February 1945 – then there would be nothing to prevent the Russians from overrunning all Europe.

The West tried to stem the tide by limiting Poland's boundaries. It was too late to go back to Russia's 1941 frontier, for Stalin insisted on pushing far to the west and Poland would have to be compensated for what it lost to Russia at Germany's expense, but if the Anglo-Americans could hold the Soviets back they could hold down Polish gains in Germany. The West therefore proposed the 1919 Curzon Line, originally a British scheme, as the boundary between Russia and Poland. Stalin was furious, although more on emotional than practical grounds. The Curzon Line represented less than what he was demanding, but what really bothered him was the name itself, with its association with Russian exclusion from Versailles and the Western effort to strangle Bolshevism in the cradle. 'You would drive us into shame,' he declared. The White Russians and Ukranians would say that Stalin was a less reliable defender of Russian interests than Curzon and Clemenceau.

Stalin's outburst concealed more than it revealed. His concerns were less the Russo-Polish boundary than the Polish–German boundary and the nature of the Polish government. He therefore agreed to the Curzon Line, even making adjustments in it in favor of Poland, with the insistence that Poland be compensated by taking huge hunks of German territory. He intended to move Poland's western borders all the way to the Oder–Neisse line, taking not only East Prussia and all of Silesia but also Pomerania, back to and including Stettin. From six to nine million Germans would have to be evicted. The Anglo-Americans were alarmed, but there was little they could do about it. Considering German treatment of the Polish Slavs, it was difficult to argue that Stalin's proposal was anything less than fair, and in any case what mattered was not so much the frontiers of Poland as who would rule in Poland. By leaving the boundary question in abeyance and emphasizing Stalin's promise to hold free elections, Roosevelt came away from Yalta with a feeling of triumph. As the *New York Herald Tribune* later put it, 'Yalta left us with comforting illusions of a Western capitalist-democratic political economy reigning supreme up to the Curzon Line and the borders of Bessarabia.'

Stalin quickly began to shatter the American illusion. He refused to reorganize the Polish government in any significant way, suppressed freedom of speech, assembly, religion, and the press in Poland, and made no move to hold free elections. To a greater or lesser extent the Soviets did the same things in the rest of East Europe, making it perfectly clear that now that they had the region they had no intention of giving it up. They shut the West out completely. By any standard the Soviet actions were high-handed, their suppressions brutal.

The West was shocked and felt betrayed. Although it was obvious that Stalin was co-operating in the attempt to restore world-wide stability by refusing to aid the communists in Greece, Italy, France, China, and elsewhere, at a time when he could have created chaos by doing so, Americans came to believe that he was a would-be world conqueror. He was seen as another Hitler. The United States was determined to avoid another Munich anywhere, which came to mean opposing communism everywhere, including East Europe. Stalin either failed to realize this, or felt he had no choice. Time and again, at Yalta and later, Stalin emphasized Russia's security problem, her need to protect herself from Germany and the West by controlling the nations on her border, but increasingly Americans dismissed his statements as lies and denounced him as a paranoid whose aim was world conquest. Millions of American voters of East Europe origin, aided by the Catholic Church, businessmen who wanted access to the region's markets, anti-Soviets in the State Department, and military men who were sincerely worried about the new strategic balance in Europe, fed the flames. A kind of panic swept over the United States. It lasted for over a decade.

One of the first, and surely the most important, of those to feel the panic was President Truman. His inclination was to take a hard line with the Russians, an inclination that was fed by senior American officials stationed in Moscow. A week and a day after Truman assumed office, on 20 April 1945, he met with Ambassador Harriman to discuss America's relations with the Soviet Union. Harriman had just come from Moscow, where his chief intellectual adviser was George Kennan, one of the leading anti-Soviets in the Foreign Service. Kennan had advocated stopping lend-lease aid to Russia in 1944, on the grounds that America owed the Soviets nothing. He was opposed to the budding denazification policy the Americans intended to apply to Germany because he felt the Germans would soon be joining the United States in opposition to Russia. But Kennan stopped short of a call to arms. He believed the Russians would never be able to maintain their hegemony over East Europe, that United States–Russian post-war collaboration was unnecessary and what was needed was a clear recognition of each side's sphere of influence, that Stalin had no intention of marching further west, and most of all that 'it was idle for us to hope that we could have any influence on the course of events in the area to which Russian hegemony had already been effectively extended'. When Harry Hopkins, Roosevelt's close adviser, asked Kennan what the United States should do about the Russian domination of Poland, Kennan merely remarked that 'we should accept no share of the responsibility'. 'Then you think it's just sin,' Hopkins rejoined, 'and we should be agin it.'

'That's just about right,' Kennan replied.

Such a do-nothing policy could have been adopted; the indications were that this was the line Roosevelt intended to follow, although for different reasons from Kennan. Roosevelt felt that post-war collaboration was possible and that it could be achieved through the United Nations. To get Stalin's co-operation, Roosevelt was willing to overlook much, or like Kennan to adopt a realistic attitude towards developments in Poland. A few hours before he died, the President wired Churchill, who was urging him to take a strong stand on Poland. 'I would minimize the general Soviet problem as much as possible because these problems, in one form or another, seem to arise every day and most of them straighten out . . . .'

Harriman, however, rejected the do-nothing policy. He accepted Kennan's general analysis of the Soviets but felt Kennan did not go far enough. Harriman believed that Soviet ambitions were boundless but that with enough Anglo-American pressure they could be prevented from imposing complete control on East Europe. His attitudes, and his ability to persuade Truman, were crucial, for in April 1945 American–Soviet relations had reached a critical stage. Stalin had begun the process of imposing communist governments on East Europe. The San Francisco Conference to establish the United Nations was about to get underway – without American–Soviet co-operation the

U.N. would never amount to anything. The Anglo-American armies would soon be linking up with the Red Army in central Germany, and despite the signed agreements it was obvious that without honest co-operation between East and West the German problem could not be solved. Surely Stalin's attitude toward co-operation would be influenced by the American reaction to Polish developments, just as the American attitude would depend in part on what Stalin did in Poland. Stalin expected to be left alone, just as he had left the West alone while it suppressed the communist-oriented forces in Greece, Italy, and France.

The general situation on 20 April 1945, when the Harriman–Truman meeting began, was tense. Harriman began by explaining that one ingredient of Soviet policy was to extend Soviet control over East Europe. According to Truman, Harriman 'said that certain elements around Stalin misinterpreted our generosity and our desire to co-operate as an indication of softness, so that the Soviet government could do as it pleased without risking challenge from the United States'. But he emphasized that the Soviets would need American economic aid to reconstruct their country, so 'we could stand firm on important issues without running serious risks'. Truman stopped Harriman to inform him that he was 'not afraid of the Russians' and he 'intended to be firm', for 'the Russians needed us more than we needed them'. Truman's statement was a key to much that followed. American post-war policy was based, in part, on the belief that no matter what the United States did or said, the Russians could do nothing of significance about it because they had to have American money.*

* In November 1945, the House Special Committee on Post-War Economic Policy and Planning made clear what America wanted in East Europe. The Committee felt the United States should make a loan to Russia, since the Russian economy was in massive disarray due to the German 'scorched earth' policy and the war-time strain generally, but only after certain points had been clarified. These were: (1) the United States must be assured that aid would not go into arms; (2) the Russians

Harriman then declared that the West was faced with a 'barbarian invasion of Europe'. After continuing in this vein for a while, he lamely added that in international negotiations 'there is give-and-take, and both sides make concessions'.

Truman agreed. He would not, he said, 'expect one hundred per cent of what we proposed'. He did feel that 'we should be able to get eighty-five per cent'.

As a first practical step in the application of getting eighty-five per cent, Truman promised to tell Soviet Foreign Minister Molotov, who would soon be in Washington, that the Soviets had to hold free elections immediately in Poland. Truman added that he intended to put it to Molotov 'in words of one syllable'. At the conclusion of the meeting, Harriman confessed that he had rushed to Washington because he was afraid that Truman did not understand the true nature of the Soviet problem. 'I am greatly relieved,' Harriman said, 'to discover . . . we see eye to eye on the situation.'

Two days later Truman met with Molotov. For the most part it was a diplomatic function and the two men were cordial. Truman did point out that he wanted free elections in Poland 'because of the effect on American public opinion'. Molotov said he understood that point, but added that Truman should understand that Poland was 'even more important for the Soviet Union', since Poland was far from America but bordered on Russia. Truman brushed that aside and insisted that Molotov recognize that America was making Poland a test case, 'the symbol of the future development of our international relations.'

should make 'a full and frank disclosure' of their production statistics; (3) Russia must withdraw its occupation forces from East Europe; (4) Russia must disclose the terms of its trade treaties with East Europe; (5) relief should be administered on non-political grounds; (6) no loans would be made until American property rights in East Europe were assured. Other items called for opening Russia to Western travel and inspection.

The next afternoon, 23 April 1945, Truman held his first major foreign-policy conference. Secretary of State Stettinius, Stimson, Secretary of the Navy James Forrestal, Admirals Leahy and King, General Marshall, Harriman, and others attended. The subject was Poland. Truman set the tone by declaring that it was obvious 'that our agreements with the Soviet Union had so far been a one-way street and that this could not continue'. He then asked each man present to state his views. Stimson began by saying that unless the United States fully understood 'how seriously the Russians took this Polish question we might be heading into very dangerous waters . . .'. Forrestal took the opposite view; he said 'it was his profound conviction that if the Russians were to be rigid in their attitude we had better have a showdown with them now rather than later.' Harriman, too, thought the United States should be firm on Poland. Stimson interjected that he thought 'the Russians perhaps were being more realistic than we were in regard to their own security', and Leahy added that he never expected the Soviets to sponsor free elections in Poland. General Marshall said he favored a cautious policy with regard to Poland, for he wanted to avoid a break with the Soviets since it was imperative to get Russian help in the Pacific War.

Truman, who was to meet with Molotov at 5:30 P.M., still could go either way. His senior advisers were split. He could acquiesce in Soviet actions and let the Polish question ride, or he could continue to demand eighty-five per cent.

Truman decided upon the latter course. When Molotov arrived, the President shouted at him in the language of a Missouri mule-driver. The interpreter said 'he had never heard a top official get such a scolding'. At the end, Truman told Molotov that 'there was only one thing to do'. Stalin had to reorganize the Polish government by bringing in elements from the London Poles, and hold elections. Molotov finally remarked, 'I have never been talked to like that in my life.' Truman replied, 'Carry out your agreements and you won't get talked to like that.'

As D. F. Fleming has remarked, 'From the eminence of eleven days in power Harry Truman made his decision to lay down the law to an ally which had contributed more in blood and agony to the common cause than we had – and about Poland, an area through which the Soviet Union had been invaded three times since 1914 . . . . The basis for the Cold War was laid on 23 April in the scourging which Truman administered to Molotov, giving notice that in areas of the most crucial concern to Russia our wishes must be obeyed.'

The Russians were puzzled, as Stalin indicated on 24 April in a letter to the Anglo-American leaders. 'Poland borders on the Soviet Union which cannot be said about Great Britain or the U.S.A.' he began. Turning to complaints about Soviet actions in Poland, he remarked, 'I do not know whether a genuinely representative Government has been established in Greece, or whether the Belgium Government is a genuinely democratic one. The Soviet Union was not consulted when those Governments were being formed, nor did it claim the right to interfere in those matters, because it realizes how important Belgium and Greece are to the security of Great Britain.' He said he could not understand why in the West 'no attempt is made to consider the interests of the Soviet Union in terms of security as well'. Stalin found it inconceivable for the Americans to demand – as they in fact were doing – that Poland be returned to the semi-Fascists who had run the country before the war.

It was difficult for other outsiders, not just Stalin, to understand the American position. Throughout the war Americans had filled the international air-waves and newspapers with rhetoric about the need to eliminate spheres of influence and balance of power concepts, substituting for them a new era of peace and freedom backed by the collective security of the United Nations, an organization open to all democratic nations. American insistence on free elections in East Europe was based on high principle. Yet in practice the Americans maintained a hegemony over Central and South America through the instrument of military dictatorships. It was true that free elections in East Europe would result in anti-Soviet governments, but it was equally true that free elections in Latin America probably would bring to power anti-American governments.

This inner contradiction was recognized by some leading Americans. In May 1945, Stimson talked on the telephone with his Assistant Secretary of War, John J. McCloy, about how to square the American sphere of influence in the Western hemisphere with the United Nations. Stimson and McCloy agreed that allowing the Soviets to form a sphere of influence in East Europe would conjure up the risk of war and destroy the effectiveness of the U.N. They also agreed that American domination of Latin America had to be preserved. 'I think,' said Stimson, 'that it's not asking too much to have our little region over here which never has bothered anybody.' McCloy felt 'we ought to have our cake and eat it too: . . . we ought to be free to operate under this regional arrangement in South America, at the same time intervene promptly in Europe; we oughtn't to give away either asset.'

The United States, successfully, insisted that the U.N. Charter make provisions for regional security groupings, which in practice meant a continuation of American control of Latin America. Both Roosevelt and Truman also saw to it that Argentina, a dictatorship that was a haven for Nazis, got a seat in the U.N., despite Stalin's vigorous protests, and despite Argentina's refusal to participate in the war against Germany and Japan.

Truman's attitude towards the Polish issue was a compound of many elements, not the least of which was a desire to have his cake and eat it. In terms of domestic politics, there were millions of Americans of East European parentage, along with countless Catholic voters, who were enraged by Soviet actions, and Truman had to take their views into account. Churchill was bombarding the President with hard-line telegrams, and Truman had great respect for the Prime Minister. Harriman, the man on the spot in Moscow who presumably understood the Soviets best, had persuaded Truman that no matter how tough the United States got, the Russians would have to take it, for without American aid they could never reconstruct. Truman had recently been briefed on the Manhattan Project, where the atomic bomb was nearing completion, which added to his sense of power. Certainly ideology cannot be ignored. Men like Truman, Harriman, and Kennan were appalled by Russian brutality and communist denial of the basic Western freedoms.

Marxist historians have seen the origins of Truman's policy in the general American fear of another depression. They point out that it was widely assumed in America that a major depression would follow the war and the only prescription American leaders could suggest to ward off the disease was to expand foreign markets. East Europe was crucial, therefore, because of its economic importance. Stalin seems to have shared the assumption about an inevitable depression, and fear of depression did influence Truman's anti-Soviet stance. Equally important however was his concept, fed by Harriman and others, of the United States as the defender of Western civilization against the barbarian hordes. Americans saw themselves as picking up the cudgel laid down by Britain, France, and Germany to beat back the uncivilized Asians who threatened to over-run all of Europe. There were racist undertones to the policy, for insofar as the term Western civilization applied to the colored peoples of the world it meant white man's rule. Western Europe's day was over or ending, and the only white men left to take over in Southeast Asia and the Pacific as well as to hold the line in East Europe were the Americans.

Of all the ingredients in the policy mix, such as anti-communism, the equating of Stalin with Hitler, economic motives, and concerns over military security, the element that gave body to it all was an awesome sense of power. By every index available, save that of men in arms, the United States was the strongest nation in the world. Many Americans, including leading figures in the government, believed that they could use their power to order the world in the direction of democratic capitalism on the American model. There was also a will to use the power, for Americans in general shared the strange belief that everyone in the world wanted to be just like them ('We will lift Shanghai up and up, ever up, until it is just like Kansas City', a U.S. Senator once remarked). Most nations, probably all, believe in the moral goodness of their ideals, but few have had the conceit to imagine, much less constantly proclaim, that their particular ideals are universal. Americans did not hesitate to do so, and since they felt they had the power to carry out their wishes, a general policy of intervention resulted. The intervention, whether it involved sending troops or diplomatic notes, was against governments, not people, based as it was on the concept that the peoples of the world wanted to be just like Americans. Thus State Department official William C. Bullitt, speaking at the National War College in 1947, declared that 'Peace can come only when the Russian people throw off their Polit-bureau and take over the government for themselves.'

Clearly American policy during the Cold War was never so simplistic as to aim at unleashing the goodness of the masses of people by overthrowing their bad governments. For one thing, evil existed on all sides. Most of the right-wing governments in Latin America, for example, were standing affronts to American ideals, but as long as the alternative seemed to be limited to socialism or communism, America continued to support the dictators. Another limitation was the notion that many of the world's people did not know what was good for them. As the British had seen in Greece, to allow free selection of rulers might bring the communists to power; the thing to do was to prevent that tragedy by holding the line with the current government, no matter how dictatorial, until the people realized where their own best interests lay.

The most important limitation on American policy, however, was one that most Americans did not like to think about, seldom discussed, and frequently ignored. This was the simple fact that however great America's power was, it had its limits. Six per cent of the world's people, no matter how enormous their productive power, could not run the lives of the remaining 94 per cent. In practice, this led to restraints on what America tried to do – for example, America's diapproval of Stalin's action in East Europe was always verbal and no troops ever set forth on a crusade to liberate Poland. But caution in action led to frustration in feeling, a frustration felt not only by millions of ordinary Americans but by the President himself. Truman had unprecedented power at his fingertips and a program for the world that he believed was self-evidently good. Yet he could not block Soviet expansion.

American influence would never be as great as American power. Over the next two decades American leaders and the American people were forced to learn that bitter lesson. American power was vaster than anyone else's but in many cases it was not usable power and thus could not be translated into diplomatic victory. Vietnam would be the ultimate proof of America's inability to force others to do as she wished, but the process began much earlier, in 1945, with Truman's attempt to shape the course of events in East Europe.

Truman rejected the do-nothing advice of Stimson, Kennan, Leahy, and Marshall and adopted the get-tough policy of Harriman and Forrestal because he accepted an analysis of the Soviet Union that saw it as a barbaric nation bent on world conquest. There would be shifts in the policy, for in early 1945 America was not ready to go to a hot war with the Soviets. It was thought that the Red Army would be needed to defeat the Japanese, for one thing, and Truman wanted the Russians in the U.N., because he recognized that without them the world organization would never work. A life-long Democrat, and an extremely partisan one at that, he could not give up on Woodrow Wilson's dream of an effective international organization.

The United States government insisted on making an issue out of Poland while ignoring what the British were doing in Greece, but it did not feel that Poland was important enough to risk war. Truman never threatened to use force to impose his views because he still thought he could make Stalin behave by applying economic muscle. The world was weary of war, the American people were demanding demobilization, and the Red Army in Europe was too powerful for Truman to even consider war. He was, therefore, following a policy of trying to force Stalin to co-operate on American terms that was doomed to failure because the President would be satisfied with nothing less than eighty-five per cent. Given Truman's view of the Soviet Union, and given his desire to spread American ideals and influence around the globe as a fitting climax to the war, he felt he could demand no less. But Stalin would not give and the Grand Alliance broke up. Resources that might have been used to reconstruct a war-torn world went instead into new armaments.

In May 1945, Truman suddenly revealed the main outline of American use of economic preponderance to force compliance with its demands. On VE Day he signed an executive order that terminated lend-lease shipments to America's allies. Four days later Leo Crowley, the Foreign Economic Administrator, placed an embargo on all shipments to Russia and other European countries. Some ships headed for Russia were turned around and brought back to port for unloading. There had been no warning to either Russia or Britain, the two principal recipients, and both countries had been planning their reconstruction on the basis of a continuation of lend-lease. In a grand understatement Secretary Stettinius, then in San Francisco for the

U.N. organizational meeting, said the order was 'particularly untimely and did not help Soviet-American relations'. Stalin was irate, and Truman sent Harry Hopkins to Moscow to pacify him. It was Hopkins's job to explain to Stalin that the whole thing was a terrible mistake. Truman countermanded the lend-lease order and the flow of supplies resumed.

Stalin accepted the explanation, but as Stettinius's remark indicated the mistake was not one of policy but of timing. The United States had no intention of continuing to send supplies to either Russia or Britain once she no longer needed their help in the Pacific War. Even the manner in which lend-lease shipments were resumed showed as much, for only material that would be used against Japan was sent. No supplies that could be used for reconstruction were put on the cargo ships. What Stettinius found 'incredible' was that America had revealed the policy before the Soviets declared war on Japan, not the termination of lend-lease itself.

In the end the policy of applying economic pressure, pursued so actively, failed. In January 1945, Stalin had asked for a six billion dollar loan. The State Department refused to discuss the matter unless, as Harriman put it, Stalin became more receptive to American demands in Europe. Aid should only go to the Soviets, Harriman said, if they agreed to 'work cooperatively with us on international problems in accordance with our standards . . .'. Later in 1945 the Soviets asked for a one billion dollar loan. The United States government lost the request.* When it

* This remains the official explanation of the United States government. It was at this time that George Kennan, in a memorandum to Harriman and the Secretary of State, expressed the remarkable judgement that 'The Russians have no great need for foreign aid unless they insist on straining their economy by maintaining a military strength far beyond the demands of their own security'. He said he could see no justification for any aid to Russia. These views, he added, received Harriman's 'prudent and effective support and found acceptance, in the main, in Washington'.

was finally found, months later, the State Department offered to discuss the loan if the Soviets would pledge 'non-discrimination in international commerce', allowing American investment and goods into the Russian sphere of influence. Stalin rejected the offer. Instead the Soviets announced a new Five-Year Plan to rebuild heavy industry and to ensure 'the technical and economic independence of the Soviet Union'. The Russians would rebuild through forced savings at home, at the expense of their own citizens, and by taking whatever they could from the European areas they occupied.

In his discussions with Stalin on Poland, Hopkins could not move the Soviet dictator. The United States had to recognize the Russian puppet government or break relations, so in June it accepted the inevitable and established relations with the Polish government. America continued to try to force Poland to accept, as the State Department put it, 'a policy of equal opportunity for us in trade, investments and access to sources of information,' but there never was any chance that the policy would succeed. America had suffered what she considered to be a major defeat, which caused much resentment and was not forgotten.

Hopkins's other major task was to ensure Soviet entry into the Pacific War. On 28 May he jubilantly cabled Truman, 'The Soviet Army will be properly deployed on the Manchurian position by August 8th.' There was, naturally, a price. Stalin expected Truman to see to it that Chiang would keep the promises Roosevelt had made at Yalta; in return he would support Chiang's leadership in China. Truman had no objections. Hopkins also said Stalin expected to share in the occupation of Japan and he wanted an agreement with the Anglo-Americans as to zones of occupation, a demand to which Truman did not reply. It could, however, be worked out at Potsdam, where the Big Three had arranged to meet in July.

At Potsdam, Truman said, his 'immediate purpose was to get the Russians into the war against Japan as soon as possible', for he realized that 'Russia's entry into the war would mean the saving of hundreds of thousands of American casualties'. American lives could be saved, however, only by substituting for them Russian lives, which Stalin was not going to sacrifice for nothing. Truman recognized this, which indicated that he was willing to make concessions in return for the Soviet aid, an indication reinforced by his second object at Potsdam, 'to come out with a working relationship' with the Russians 'to prevent another world catastrophe'. As soon as the meeting began, however, irreconcilable differences emerged. Truman proposed as an agenda item an agreement on reorganizing the governments of Rumania and Bulgaria, with a view to early free elections, and the inclusion of Italy in the U.N. Stalin proposed for discussion the question of German reparations, trusteeships for Russia (among other things, he wanted a share of the Italian colonies in Africa), an end to the Franco regime in Spain, and a settlement of Poland's western frontier on the Oder–Neisse line, with a liquidation of the London government-in-exile. Arguments went on and on, with some minor agreements reached, but nothing important could be settled. Everyone did as they pleased in the areas they controlled and disapproved of what the other side was doing.

A typical exchange came on 22 July. Molotov raised the question of trusteeships. He had read in the foreign press that Italy had lost its colonies and he wanted to know who had received them and where the matter had been decided. Churchill replied by saying that the British Army had conquered all Italian colonies. Truman raised an eyebrow and queried, 'All?' Churchill said he had in mind Libya, Cyrenaica, and Tripoli, which the British took without help. Molotov interjected that Berlin had been conquered by the Red Army, with the implication that if the British retained sole possession of the Italian colonies, the Russians ought to have sole possession of Berlin.

Snipping and jabbing were the hall-mark of Potsdam.

The Russians had given the Poles control of eastern Germany. Truman and Churchill protested that this meant the forced evacuation or death of millions of Germans, as well as a unilateral decision by Russia to bring another occupying power into Germany. Stalin shrugged them off, saying all the Germans had already left the territory and the frontier question had been agreed to at Yalta, neither of which was true. The Soviets wanted to participate with Turkey in the control of the Black Sea straits. Truman proposed an international guarantee that the straits be open to all nations at all times, as a substitute for fortification or Russian participation in the control of the straits. Molotov asked if the Suez Canal was operated under such a principle. Churchill said the question of Suez had not been raised. Molotov retorted, 'I'm raising it.' Churchill explained that the British had operated Suez for some seventy years without complaints. Molotov replied that there had been many complaints: 'You should ask Egypt.'

The major issue at Potsdam, aside from the question of Soviet participation in the Pacific War, was Germany. At Yalta, the Big Three had agreed to divide Germany into four zones (one to the French), with each area governed by the local military commander. Together, the generals formed the Allied Control Council (A.C.C.) which would lay down rules for reuniting Germany. The A.C.C. would be governed by a rule of unanimity, a rule that proved disastrous for reunification, since the Anglo-Americans wanted one outcome, the French and Russians another. England and the United States aimed to create a politically whole Germany that would have self-sufficient industry; the other two occupying powers wanted to keep Germany divided and weak. No reconciliation of such divergent views was possible and at Potsdam none was really attempted. The Americans did agree that German industry should not exceed a certain level, but within less than a year they violated the agreement.

Potsdam did try to deal with the problem of German

reparations. At Yalta, Roosevelt had accepted Stalin's demand that $20 billion be the starting point for negotiations, with half that amount to go to the Soviet Union, but the foreign ministers had been unable to reach any precise agreement and left the question to be settled at Potsdam. Since the United States had already indicated that it would not continue lend-lease after the war, nor extend a loan to the Soviet Union, for Stalin the question of German reparations was crucial. Geography was against him, however, since the prime industrial area of Germany, the Ruhr, was in the British zone. His advantage was that the Ruhr could not feed itself and he controlled the major agricultural regions of Germany. In the end, a deal was made: the West essentially recognized the Oder–Neisse line as Germany's eastern border, while Stalin accepted twenty-five per cent of German capital equipment from the Western zones as his share of reparations. Fifteen per cent of this figure was to be in exchange for food from eastern Germany. Stalin also got *carte blanche* on reparations from the Russian zone, which he quickly stripped of whatever could be moved.

Perhaps more important than the agreements and arguments at Potsdam was the attitude Truman took back to the White House with him. At Potsdam, he later recorded, he learned that the only thing the Russians understood was force. He decided he would no longer 'take chances in a joint setup with the Russians', since they were impossible to get along with. The most immediate result of this decision was Truman's determination 'that I would not allow the Russians any part in the control of Japan .... As I reflected on the situation during my trip home, I made up my mind that General MacArthur would be given complete command and control after victory in Japan'. In the Pacific, at least, Truman was going to ask for, and get, more than the eight-five per cent he had said he wanted. The successful test of the atomic bomb while he was at Potsdam encouraged him to take this stance, to refuse to trust the

Russians (which was the equivalent of accepting a prolonged period of tension), but probably equally important was his image of Stalin.

At Potsdam, Truman had persistently attempted to get an agreement on the internationalization of the principal waterways of Europe. Stalin had just as persistently waved the question aside and asked for control of the Black Sea straits. To Truman, this 'showed how his mind worked and what he was after'. The President rejected the obvious interpretation – that Stalin only wanted the same rights in the Black Sea straits that England enjoyed at Suez or the Americans at Panama, or that the communist leader resisted internationalization of waterways because he wanted to block American economic penetration into East Europe. Instead, Truman decided that Stalin's actions demonstrated that 'the Russians were planning world conquest'.

Truman had made an incredible mental leap. Hitler was hardly in his grave; already Truman had substituted Stalin for Hitler as the madman who had to be stopped. The tone of the Cold War was established.

Potsdam was also important because it revealed the chief weapon of the Cold War. When Truman learned that the atomic bomb was a reality, he might have offered to his Russian allies a share in its future development or at least have told Stalin of its existence and something of its nature, thereby establishing an atmosphere of trust. Instead Truman casually informed Stalin that the United States had a new weapon and let it go at that. He also decided that as soon as the bombs were ready they should be used against Japan; part of the reason for haste was to force a Japanese surrender before Russia got into the war, or at least before the Red Army was in a position to get onto the Japanese home islands, for Truman was determined that the occupation of Japan would be exclusively American. More significant for the future was the notion in high American governmental circles that American possession of the atomic bomb would, in Stimson's words, result in 'less barbarous relations with the Russians', or as Byrnes put it in June 1945, the bomb 'would make Russia more manageable in Europe'.

The bomb, coupled with the financial position the United States enjoyed, gave Truman and his chief advisers an awesome feeling of power. They could not see how the Russians could avoid toeing a line, especially since in their view the line they were drawing was so eminently reasonable and was based on agreements Stalin had already signed. From Potsdam on, the bomb was the constant factor in the American approach to the Soviet Union. The new policy was aptly described by Stimson as wearing 'this weapon rather ostentatiously on our hip', which he himself later came to fear merely fed 'their suspicions and their distrust of our purposes and motives . . .'.

The bomb was a godsend. It seemed to give the Americans the best of all possible worlds. They could impose their will on any recalcitrant nation merely by threatening to use it. Stopping aggression would be simplicity itself – just drop the bomb. America could retain a powerful position in Europe without having to maintain a mass army there. One of the great fears in American military circles was that, having smashed Germany, the West now had to confront the Red Army and the only nation capable of doing so was the United States. But in the United States domestic political realities precluded the maintenance of a large standing army in the post-war period. The 'Bring Back Daddy' clubs and similar organizations, plus a widespread mutiny by enlisted men in both Europe and the Pacific shortly after the war, a mutiny designed to force their speedy return to the United States and civilian life, demonstrated that ordinary citizens would not serve in mass armies in peace-time. America's great corporations and the Republican Party, soon to take control of Congress, meanwhile had made it clear that taxes had to be cut and the budget balanced. The administration would have neither the men nor the money to engage actively in cold war.

Then came the bomb, which at a stroke solved all the problems. America could fight a cold war without demanding any sacrifices of her citizens, rich, poor, or middle class. The Red Army was neutralized, even overcome. America's leaders hoped that through a judicious use of financial credit and the veiled threat of the bomb the United States could shape the post-war world. In the fall of 1945 Truman met with de Gaulle, who was worried about the desire of General Lucius Clay, head of the American occupation zone in Germany, to restore unity to Germany and to raise its levels of production. De Gaulle was also concerned about the Red Army in central Europe. Truman off-handedly remarked that there was nothing to fear. If any nation did become aggressive, Truman explained, the United States would use the atomic bomb to stop it. The strategy would later be called massive retaliation. The trouble with it was that even as early as 1945 it bore little relation to reality.

The atomic bombs of the 1945–9 period were not powerful enough to deter the Russians, nor did America have enough of them to institute a real massive retaliation program. These truths were only gradually realized, especially by the politicians, but they colored the military situation from the beginning. Even had the U.S. Air Force been able to deliver all the bombs available in 1947 or 1948, they were not sufficient to destroy Russia totally. Tactically, they were not as helpful as was thought initially, since if the Red Army crossed the Elbe River and drove for France, the tactical targets would be West European cities and strategic points, which was hardly a military policy that commended itself to the West Europeans. U.S. Army plans in 1948, at a time when it appeared the Red Army might use force to drive the Anglo-Americans out of Berlin and possibly out of Europe altogether, called for a retreat to Spain, to be completed in less than a week.

The most that could have been done with the bombs, had the Russians met the West's worst fears and marched across the Elbe, would have been to punish the Soviets by dropping a few bombs on principal Russian population centers, which would have killed hundreds of thousands but which would not have hamstrung the Russian war machine. Stalin would have matched American destruction of Moscow with Soviet occupation of Western Europe. The Red Army was just as effective a deterrent as the atomic bomb.

There was a psychological as well as a military problem involved in massive retaliation. Whatever the limitations on the bomb, the world regarded it as the ultimate weapon, an attitude the American press and politicians encouraged, which in the end backfired on the Americans since it meant the bomb could only be used in the most extreme situation imaginable. To say that the United States would use the bomb to punish aggression was easy enough, but it proved extraordinarily difficult to find an aggression serious enough to justify using the bomb. When the communists took over Czechoslovakia, for example, no responsible American official thought the outrage serious enough to start dropping bombs on Moscow, but because the United States had put its faith in the bomb there were no other tools available to punish the aggressor. The United States, therefore, could do nothing. This had been clear, in fact, as early as 1945.

American possession of the bomb had no noticeable effect on Stalin's policy in East Europe. He and Molotov continued to do as they pleased, to refuse to hold elections or to allow Western observers to travel freely in East Europe. The region was not opened up to American economic penetration. At Foreign Ministers' meetings the Russians continued to insist that the West had to recognize the puppet governments in East Europe before peace treaties could be written. Byrnes's hope that the bomb would 'make Russia more manageable' proved abortive, and by the summer of 1946 both sides had accepted the fact of a divided Europe.

Russian mistrust of the West, added to their determination to maintain a tight grip on their satellites, had grown so great that Molotov refused to consider seriously Secretary of State Byrnes's proposal that the Big Four powers sign a treaty unifying Germany and guaranteeing German demilitarization, an offer sincerely made and one that represented the best hope of solving the German problem. Instead, the Soviets stopped removing machinery from East Germany and began instead to utilize the skilled German manpower to produce finished goods in their zone, goods they then shipped onto the Soviet Union. On 3 May 1946, meanwhile, General Clay unilaterally informed the Russians that they could expect no more reparations from the Western zones. Later that year, at Stuttgart, Secretary Byrnes gave a highly publicized speech in which he announced that Germany must develop exports in order to become self-sustaining. Byrnes refused to recognize the Oder–Neisse boundary, said the Germans should be given primary responsibility for running their own affairs and allowed to increase their industrial productivity (policies Clay had already been putting into practice), and emphasized that American presence in central Europe would not be withdrawn.

Solutions acceptable to both East and West were hard to come by in 1946. This applied especially to the atomic bomb, a weapon that had separated past from future as sharply as had man's discovery of fire. Whatever the limitations on the size and number of nuclear weapons in the first half-decade of the atomic age, it was obvious that the growth potential was almost unlimited. Control of the bomb was crucial to the future welfare of the world. How to get the weapon under control was not so clear. On the one hand, the United States had a monopoly, something no nation would ever be likely to give up lightly. On the other hand, all the atomic scientists agreed that it was only a question of time before the Soviets developed the bomb. If the Russians got atomic weapons on their own, and if they continued to be treated as just another military item to be used by sovereign nations as they saw fit, the world would live in continual terror.

What made a solution especially difficult was the post-war atmosphere in which America and Russia made their proposals for atomic control. There were almost daily crises in Germany between the occupying powers. Tension dominated the Middle East, reaching its peak in Iran and Turkey. According to the terms of a 1942 occupation treaty, the Russians were required to withdraw their forces from Iran six months after the end of the war. They refused to do so because Stalin wanted oil concessions from the Iranian government, concessions that would not equal those gained by Anglo-American companies but which would at least give the Soviets some of the Iranian oil. To put pressure on the government, the Russians started tanks towards the border and supported a revolt in northern Iran. As the crisis moved forward, Byrnes sent a strong note (6 March 1946) to Moscow demanding immediate withdrawal. Three weeks later Iran and the U.S.S.R. announced that the Soviet occupation troops would be pulled out and that a joint Iranian–Soviet oil company would be formed subject to ratification by the Persian Parliament. On 6 May the Russians withdrew; early in 1947 the Parliament rejected the oil company treaty.

The reaction to this major Soviet diplomatic defeat illustrated how far apart the former allies had drifted. To the Russians it seemed only fair that they be allowed to participate in the exploitation of Iranian oil, all the more so since the terms they wanted were less favorable than those enjoyed by the Anglo-American oil companies. To be forced out only showed that the West was up to its old tricks of encircling the Soviet Union and doing everything it could to keep it weak. To the Americans, the crisis proved once again that the Soviets were bent on world conquest.

Churchill interpreted the events for the benefit of the American public on 5 March 1946, in a speech at Fulton, Missouri. President Truman was on the platform with him. Churchill declared that 'from Stettin in the Baltic to Trieste in the Adriatic, an iron curtain has descended across the

Continent'. He wanted to lift that curtain, to liberate East Europe, and to hold the Russians back elsewhere, as in Iran and Turkey. He suggested that a fraternal association of the English-speaking peoples, operating outside the U.N., should do it. Their tool would be the bomb, which 'God has willed' to the United States alone.

Churchill's speech hardly helped American efforts, then going on, to find an acceptable solution to international control of the bomb. Stalin reacted with the full fury of a wounded animal at bay. He compared Churchill and his 'friends' in America to Hitler, charging that like Hitler they held a racial theory which proposed world rule for the English-speaking peoples. Stalin said Churchill's speech was 'a call to war with the Soviet Union' and reminded the West that twice in the recent past Germany had attacked Russia through East European countries that had 'governments inimical to the Soviet Union'. Within three weeks following Churchill's iron curtain speech the Soviets rejected membership in the World Bank and the International Monetary Fund, announced the start of a new Five-Year Plan designed to make Russia self-sufficient in the event of another war, built up the pressure on Iran, and mounted an intense ideological effort to eliminate Western influences within Russia.

But Stalin was no more ready for war than Truman, as events in Turkey showed. The issue there was control of the Dardanelles. In August 1946, Stalin demanded of the Turks equal partnership in running the Straits. This was an ancient Russian dream, of course, and it seemed to the Russians only just that they should have control of one of their major life-lines. But Under Secretary of State Dean Acheson interpreted the demand as a Soviet attempt to dominate Turkey, threaten Greece, and intimidate the remainder of the Middle East. He advised a showdown. Truman agreed: 'We might as well find out whether the Russians were bent on world conquest now as in five or ten years.' The United States told the Turks to stand firm. To back them up, the most modern American aircraft carrier sailed into the area. The Soviets backed down.

In this atmosphere of threat and counter-threat, bluff and counter-bluff, achieving workable international control of atomic weapons was almost hopeless. Still, the Americans tried. On 16 March 1946, the United States released its plan, the Acheson–Lilienthal proposal. It called for international control reached through a series of stages. The proposal was an honest attempt to avoid the horrors of a world in which Russia and the United States rattled nuclear-tipped sabers at each other. It did not, however, satisfy the Soviets, for during the transitional stages the Acheson–Lilienthal proposal reserved to the United States full control of its own bombs. 'Should there be a breakdown in the plan at any time during the transition,' the proposal read, 'we shall be in a favorable position with regard to atomic weapons.' The Soviets, meanwhile, would not be allowed to develop their own bomb.

Given the tension in Soviet-American relations, it was unthinkable that the United States could go further in sharing the bomb; it was equally unthinkable that the Russians could accept. The Soviet counter-proposal called for an end to the production and use of atomic weapons and insisted on the destruction within three months of all existing stocks of atomic bombs. Only then would they discuss international control.

No way could be found out of the impasse. In April 1946, Truman appointed Bernard Baruch, financier and adviser to Presidents, as the American delegate to the U.N. Atomic Energy Commission. Baruch thought the Acheson–Lilienthal proposal had gone much too far because it contained no reference to Russia's veto power. Baruch wanted majority rule at all stages; since the United States controlled a majority in the U.N., this meant not only that the Soviets could not veto the use of the bomb against themselves if violations were discovered, they could not even prevent – except by force – inspection teams roaming at will through their country. It could hardly have been expected that they would accept Baruch's proposal. Indeed, the U.S. War Department told Baruch that there was no chance the Russians would agree, for it certainly did not serve Soviet interests to accept a system under which the United States would have a continuing monopoly of atomic power, enforced by a U.N. agency controlled by the United States, and Stalin would never open his nation to free inspection by a U.N. commission dominated by the United States.

Baruch, however, insisted upon the elimination of the veto. He was backed by Army Chief of Staff Eisenhower, who advised him that only through effective international control of atomic energy could there be any hope of preventing atomic war, but who also insisted that national security required that methods of such control be tested and proven before the United States gave up its monopoly. 'If we enter too hurriedly into an international agreement to abolish all atomic weapons,' Eisenhower pointed out, 'we may find ourselves in the position of having no restraining means in the world capable of effective action if a great power violates the agreement.' He warned that the Russians might deliberately avoid the use of atomic weapons and undertake aggression with other, but equally decisive, weapons.

This was the central dilemma for the United States in its efforts to get some international control of atomic energy before it was too late, more important by far than the veto or inspection. The question Eisenhower raised was straight-forward enough: if the United States gave up the atomic bomb, how could it stop the Red Army? The only alternative to American possession of the bomb was to build up a mass army, or get the Russians to demobilize, and in 1946 there was absolutely no possibility of doing either one. Both sides made various concessions, but neither would back down on the crucial point. America insisted on retaining the bomb until it was satisfied with the effectiveness of international control, and the Russians would not give up the veto. In the end, Congress established the U.S. Atomic Energy Commission and prohibited any exchange of information on the use of the bomb with any nation, including the British, whose scientists had helped develop the weapon in the first place.

The only real hope of eliminating the bomb, which in the political atmosphere of 1946 was never very great, was gone. America would never give up its monopoly as long as the Red Army was intact and American leaders regarded Stalin and his associates as the Huns at the gate, and the Russians would never demobilize as long as the Americans had the bomb. In a relatively short period of time the Russians would have their own bomb; eventually the United States would be maintaining a large standing army. An arms race unprecedented in the world's history would be underway. This forced a qualitative change in American foreign policy and in international relations generally. Every crisis struck terror into the hearts of people everywhere. There was no security, no defense. Much of American foreign policy after Baruch's proposal was a search for a viable method of using the bomb to achieve overseas goals. The bomb had already failed America once, in East Europe, where the Soviets refused to behave. How effectively it could be used elsewhere remained to be seen. Russian probes towards Iran and Turkey had been met and stopped. By the end of 1946 spheres of influence in Europe were clearly drawn, but elsewhere who belonged to whom was up in the air. Perhaps, as with Iran and Turkey, there would have to be a confrontation at each point around the world until the line was drawn and accepted everywhere. The Cold War would meanwhile continue to be fought under the shadow of atomic weapons.

[5]

The Truman Doctrine and the Marshall Plan

The language of military power is the only language which disciples of power politics understand. The United States must use that language in order that Soviet leaders will realize that our government is determined to uphold the interests of its citizens and the rights of small nations . . . . The Soviet Union's vulnerability is limited . . . but it is vulnerable to atomic weapons, biological warfare, and long-range power . . . . The United States should entertain no proposal for disarmament or limitation of armament as long as the possibility of Soviet aggression exists.

CLARK CLIFFORD, *Special Counsel, in a memorandum to President Truman, September 1946*

THERE are limits to the extent that even the most powerful nation can project its influence beyond its borders. In a democracy, one of the most important limitations is the mood on the domestic scene, which involves both a general perception of a need to exert influence and a willingness to make the sacrifices required to generate usable power. In the United States, at the beginning of 1947, neither was present. If there was no retreat to isolation as in 1919, there was a popular feeling that America could handle her foreign problems through her commitment to the United Nations and through possession of the atomic bomb. In late 1946 the Republicans had won control of Congress by emphasizing a modified version of Harding's return to normalcy – demobilization, business as usual, a cut-back in the role and spending of the government, and lower taxes. These domestic facts severely restricted the Truman administration's ability to carry on the Cold War.

So did the absence of a precise strategic theory for conducting the Cold War, or indeed even a hot one. American strategists were in a state of confusion, understandably enough since they had so many new factors to take into consideration. No one knew how to use atomic bombs effectively, either as diplomatic or military weapons. There was much talk of push-button warfare and of the need for instant preparedness because of the speed with which the next war would be fought, but these were really predictions about the future. The immediate threats were the Red Army, which was limited to Eurasia as a scene of operations, and various national liberation forces, mostly communist and centered in Asia. The resulting confusion in building a viable strategy was well illustrated by Marshall's, Eisenhower's, and Truman's advocacy of universal military training (U.M.T.), which envisioned a mass reserve army, somewhat on the Prussian model, that could march soon after mobilization day. The strategy has solid historic roots – Americans had always relied on mobilization, not forces in being, for their defense – but it had little relation to the post-war situation.

The type of mass reserve that U.M.T. would have created could have been used to support foreign policy objectives or to stop a thrust by the Red Army into Western Europe only if it could have been quickly transported overseas. This in turn would have required a large standing navy and merchant fleet, plus an air force to protect the ships, plus extensive bases to receive the troops on arrival. In 1946 only the Navy existed on the scale required. U.M.T. was designed to save money by avoiding a standing army, but it would have cost more money than the public was willing to pay to implement it.

Some strategists, notably General Alfred Gruenther in the Pentagon, were beginning to argue that U.M.T. was all wrong in concept. It was well-suited to meet America's role in the world wars – mobilize a mass army and send it overseas to tip the balance in favor of the allies – but had little if anything to do with current requirements. America could not match the Red Army on the ground, Gruenther argued, and in any case the deterrent to the Red Army was the atomic bomb. What the Army needed was a relatively small but highly trained force of regulars who could be used to counter Soviet moves on the periphery of Europe. The critics of U.M.T. were groping for a strategy of deterrence to support a policy of containment, but they too were unsuccessful in selling their doctrine and therefore could not obtain the needed funds.

By the beginning of 1947 the United States had almost completed the most rapid demobilization in the history of the world. The Army had been cut from eight to one million men; the Navy from three and one-half million to less than a million; the Air Force from over 200 to less than 50 effective combat groups. As General Marshall later recalled, 'I remember, when I was Secretary of State I was being pressed constantly, particularly when in Moscow [March 1947], by radio message after radio message to give the Russians hell . . . . When I got back, I was getting the same appeal in relation to the Far East and China. At that time, my facilities for giving them hell – and I am a soldier and know something about the ability to give hell – was $1\frac{1}{3}$ divisions over the entire United States. That is quite a proposition when you deal with somebody with over 260 and you have $1\frac{1}{3}$.'

Foreign policy and military policy were moving in opposite directions. Truman and his advisers wanted to meet the communist challenge wherever it appeared, but save for the atomic bomb they had nothing with which to meet it. Stimson and Forrestal, among others, urged Truman to stop the demobilization process by dramatically warning the nation about the scope of the Soviet threat. On 16 October 1945, Forrestal stated at a Cabinet meeting 'that this was a situation of such gravity that in his view the President ought to acquaint the people with the details of our dealings with the Russians and with the attitude which the Russians have manifested throughout', and in January 1946 he advised Truman to call in 'the heads of the important news services and the leading newspapers . . . and state to them the seriousness of the present situation and the need for making the country aware of its implications abroad'. Throughout 1946 the Secretary of the Navy pressed Truman, but the results were meager, for Truman wanted a balanced budget and was enough of a politician to realize that the public would not support higher taxes for a larger, more efficient military establishment.

Simultaneously with the decrease in military force there was an increasing fear in Washington of the scope and nature of the threat. America's leaders saw communist involvement in every attack on the *status quo* anywhere and convinced themselves that the Kremlin was at the center of a master-plot to conquer the world. They regarded all communists as conscious agents of Russian policy, men who acted only in accordance with Stalin's will.

In a speech at the National War College in mid-1947, William C. Bullitt, formerly of the State Department, nicely summed up the attitudes then dominant in Washington. 'The Soviet Union's assault upon the West is at about the stage of Hitler's maneuvering into Czechoslovakia,' he asserted, which immediately linked Stalin with Hitler. 'The final aim of Russia is world conquest,' which outlined the scope of the problem. The Soviet method, however, differed from Hitler's and was more dangerous. Because of the American atomic monopoly the Russians would not inaugurate large-scale war, but rather would seek to avoid armed conflict while advancing their aims through internal subversion. In either case, their agents would be proxies. In China, Indochina, and Greece, where indigenous forces were trying to overthrow governments, Bullitt saw only 'active tools of world-wide communism'. By ignoring the complex jumble of historic, economic, racial, social, and other factors that led to the conflicts, and by ignoring the fact that Stalin was giving no active support to the Greek rebels, Chinese communists, or Vietnamese, Bullitt and the many others in the administration who thought like him made the problem easy to analyze.

American politicians, especially Truman, were justly famous for their tough-minded realism about domestic affairs. They were impatient with simple arguments and analysis, cynical in the deals they made, and fully aware of the complexities involved in any given domestic situation. That these same realists could make simplistic judgements about internal affairs in foreign countries was a phenomenon of American life. It was based, in part, on a world-view that other peoples yearned to be like Americans. This assumption was at the root of America's foreign policy. It denied historical and cultural diversity and led to the belief that when other nations or people did not act like the United States it was because something had gone wrong, usually with the leadership. Americans found it impossible to believe that any people could actually want to be communist. Bullitt had talked of the Russian people throwing off their Polit-bureau and taking over the government for themselves. Until that was done, Bullitt maintained, the Kremlin-directed enemy would be everywhere. France and Italy had strong communist parties and communist representation in their cabinets. In South America the communists were 'hard at work and had done a particularly effective job of infiltrating into the governments'. Even the United States was not safe from the disease; it was at this time that Truman ordered a loyalty check on every federal employee.

Since the challenge was world-wide, it had to be met everywhere, at once. As one step, Bullitt advocated a 'European Federation of Democratic States' in order to 'face up to Russia'. He was thinking primarily in terms of a military organization, which made sense only if coupled with American leadership, since the United States alone had the capital resources and productive capacity to supply the implements of war to European troops. Meeting the Russian threat by arming Europeans was in practice a continuation of the wartime policy of lend-lease, merely substituting Stalin for Hitler as the enemy. Another part of the response was to provide economic and technical aid to threatened nations. There was general agreement in the government that communism thrived on chaos and poverty; the way to meet it was to promote stability and prosperity. George Kennan was the most vocal advocate of economic aid as the proper containment policy; he was bitterly disappointed as America concentrated increasingly on military assistance.

At the end of 1946 most discussion of the optimum American response to the Soviet challenge revolved around three possibilities: build up America's own military resources; send military aid to threatened nations; give economic and technical assistance to needy peoples. They were not mutually exclusive, and most government officials wanted some kind of combination of all three, with the emphasis on one. All rested on the same assumptions Bullitt had expressed about the nature of the threat. And all would cost money.

The Republican Congress controlled the money and it saw no pressing reason to spend it on any of those courses. Neither did a majority of the American people. In January 1947, there was a feeling that post-war tensions with the Russians were easing, based primarily on the completion of peace treaties signed by the Big Three with the Eastern European countries that had fought alongside Hitler. These treaties constituted a practical recognition by the United States of the Soviet sphere of influence in East Europe, for they were all signed with communist satellite governments. Robert Taft, the leading Republican in the Senate and head of the economy-in-government drive, expressed the current mood when he objected to any administration attempt to divide the world into communist and anti-communist zones, for 'I do not want war with Russia'. The Democrats accused Taft – and other Republicans who resisted signing up for a crusade against communism – of isolationism, but despite the bad connotations of the word there was no denying that a majority of the American people did not want to embark on a crusade.

To obtain the economic and military resources to carry out an active foreign policy, Truman had to convince the bulk of the people of the reality and magnitude of the Soviet threat. To do that, he needed a dramatic issue. While he waited for one to come along, he began his preparations to move into some of the current trouble spots. Greece stood near the top of the list. Great Britain had been supporting the government there, but a severe storm in January 1947 had raised havoc with the British economy and under-scored the impossibility of Britain continuing to play a leading world role. As early as September 1946, the American government had quietly prepared programs for military aid for Greece, where the rebels, drawing supplies from Bulgaria and Yugoslavia, seemed on the verge of over-throwing the royalist government. In January 1947, the State Department sent an economic mission to Greece to see what could be done, and in February the Department began intensified planning to provide military aid. The United States was prepared to move into Greece whenever the British pulled out.

But Greece was on the periphery. Germany was the real key to a policy of containing the Russians. Germany's industrial and manpower resources and her geographical position made her essential to the defense of Western Europe. This fact had been clear to policy makers since Potsdam and had been the driving force behind Clay's policies of encouraging self-government in Germany and raising the level of industrial production. It was not so easy, however, to sell the policy of rearming Germany to the public, especially as evidence of Nazi atrocities con-tinued to be discovered and publicized.

There were also the allies to consider. Britain and France were working on a treaty – eventually signed in early 1947 – that pledged co-operation in the containment of a revived Germany. The Americans, seeing the danger in other, more easterly, quarters, considered an anti-Germany treaty backward-looking foolishness, and they were able to get the British to merge Anglo-American zones in Germany for economic purposes, but only because Britain needed to economize on occupation costs. Clay gave administrative duties to the Germans and the level of industrial output continued to rise. For the French, and some Americans, all this was happening rather too fast.

The issue began to come to a head in November 1946. George Meader, a government lawyer who had worked closely with Truman during the war, reported to the Senate War Investigating Committee on the conditions he found on an inspection trip in the U.S. zone in Germany. Meader charged that there was widespread misconduct on the part of Army personnel, including an alarmingly high venereal disease rate and flagrant miscegenation. The demands for luxurious accommodations by Army officers had created a desperate housing situation and high-ranking officers were deeply involved in black-market operations. More serious than the personal corruption was Clay's policy. Meader declared that denazification was a glaring failure because neither Clay nor anyone else pushed it. Clay had also allowed the Germans to raise their industrial production beyond the limits envisioned in the Potsdam agreements on Germany and had done nothing to break up the cartel system. Clay, in short, had made the Germans into allies, at a time when most Americans still regarded them as enemies who needed to be punished and re-educated.

The Truman administration, according to the *New York Times* of 2 December 1946, subjected the Senate committee to 'tremendous pressure . . . to suppress the report and drop the inquiry'. The newspaper also reported that Clay threatened to resign if the investigation was pressed. The Secretary of War, Robert Patterson, meanwhile sent the editor of the *Saturday Evening Post*, Forest Davis, to Germany to make a report on what was happening there. Davis had the full co-operation of the Army and was a guest at Clay's quarters. After three weeks he sent a ten-page report to Senator Taft, emphasizing that 'our record in the military government of Germany is magnificent' and urging Taft to oppose any investigation. Davis's main function was to convince the Republicans not to make political capital out of Germany by convincing them that the budding alliance with the Germans was absolutely necessary. He praised Clay for avoiding 'vindictiveness in his attitude or policies' toward the former Nazis and quoted with approval a comment Clay had made at dinner one evening, 'In the event of another war, the Germans probably would be the only continental peoples upon whom we could rely.'

Looking to the immediate future, Davis was greatly impressed by Clay's thoughts on the importance of the Western sectors of Berlin. Davis pointed out that 'Berlin affords us an unique observation post into Soviet Europe' and advocated an active intelligence network there. He wanted the Voice of America programs, which sent propaganda into East Europe, increased, for Berlin was not only a listening post but also an 'enormously useful outpost of our civilization'. This defined rather neatly the role the Americans had assigned to Berlin, a role it would play with increasing success over the next two decades. On the broader question of Germany as a whole, Davis agreed with Clay's advocacy of a bi-zonal solution. Clay wanted to abandon all efforts at reunification, still the official policy of both the United States and the Soviet governments, and instead accept as a fact the division of Germany into two parts. As a start, Clay wanted to merge the British, French, and U.S. zones, with immediate economic and political benefits and potentially great military advantages. This would also eliminate any danger of the Russians getting into the Ruhr.

On 29 January Taft received Davis's report. After some hesitation, he agreed to call off the investigation. This meant, in practice, a bi-partisan foreign policy with regard to Germany, with the broader implication of a Republican commitment to a policy of containment. All that remained was to make this clear to the Russians.

In January 1947, Secretary of State Byrnes resigned; his successor was General Marshall. This added to an already heavy military complexion to American foreign policy. General Walter B. Smith, Eisenhower's former Chief of Staff, was ambassador to Russia, while Clay in Germany and MacArthur in Japan ran the occupation of those countries independently of the State Department – indeed, they seemed to be responsible to no one. Marshall's first task was to prepare for a meeting of the Council of Foreign Ministers in Moscow, which would begin on 10 March, and he was spending most of his time on the German problem, the main issue on the agenda of the Moscow Conference.

The Moscow Conference was doomed before it started. Positions on Germany had hardened. Neither the Americans nor the Soviets had any intention of working toward a peace treaty with Germany and reunification, except on their own terms, which they knew in advance were unacceptable to the other side. All anyone could do at Moscow was put out propaganda.

While Marshall prepared for Moscow, events in Greece rushed forward. Truman would soon have his opportunity to swing the Republicans around on the need to spend more money for an active foreign policy. In January, Truman sent the Greek government an offer to provide advisers and funds for a program of economic stabilization. The Greek government had already complained in the United Nations that the insurgents were receiving outside assistance, and a United Nations mission had gone to Greece to investigate. Truman had sent his own agent to make a report. The British economy, meanwhile, had come to a near standstill as a result of the great storm, and it was increasingly doubtful that Britain could maintain its 40,000 troops in Greece. On 3 February the American ambassador in Athens reported a rumor that the British would be pulling out soon; a week later the ambassador recommended that the United States pick up the reins from the British. On 18 February

Truman's personal representative in Greece cabled that everything pointed to an impending move by the communists to seize the country, and two days later the American Embassy in London reported that the British Treasury was opposed to giving any further aid to Greece. The stage was set.

On 21 February 1947, the British Ambassador to the United States informed the State Department that London could no longer provide aid to Greece or Turkey. Britain would pull out by the end of March. To Secretary of State Marshall, this 'was tantamount to British abdication from the Middle East with obvious implications as to their successor'.

America was prepared to take up the burden, to begin a policy that would continue through the Cold War of directly replacing other imperialist powers. As Eugene V. Rostow, Under Secretary of State for Political Affairs, explained two decades later, 'In many ways the whole postwar history has been a process of American movement to take over positions of security which Britain, France, the Netherlands and Belgium had previously held.'

The first requirement was for the administration to work up a firm recommendation to make to the Congress. Within five days the State Department had consulted with the War Department, held meetings of its own, and was ready to move. Under Secretary Dean Acheson took the lead, as Marshall was busy preparing for the Moscow Conference. On 26 February Truman, Marshall, and Acheson met to discuss the result of the studies of the experts. Acheson made the presentation. He emphasized that if Greece were lost, Turkey would be untenable. Russia would move in and take control of the Dardanelles, with the 'clearest implications' for the Middle East. Morale would sink in Italy, Germany, and France. Acheson was describing what would later be called the domino theory, which held that if one nation fell, others would inevitably follow. In this case, Acheson maintained that a victory for the insurgents in Greece would mean the loss of Europe to communism. One rotten apple, he said, would infect the whole barrel. Put in those terms, the administration had no choice save to act vigorously and quickly. Truman felt, he later told his Cabinet, that 'he was faced with a decision more serious than had ever confronted any President', which took in quite a lot of ground and was in any case over-dramatic in its implications, for it implied that he was tossing in bed at night trying to decide what to do. Actually, he had long since made the decision and the real task was to sell the program to Congress.

At the meeting between Truman and the two senior State Department officials, Acheson recommended a program of military and financial aid to Greece and Turkey, with the emphasis on military support. The next day, 27 February, Truman called in the congressional leaders of both parties. Taft, regarded as the leader of the isolationist forces and a possible challenger to Truman for the Presidency in 1948, was not invited. Instead Truman concentrated on Senator Arthur Vandenberg, a Republican 'isolationist' turned 'internationalist' who, as chairman of the Senate Foreign Relations Committee, was one of the architects of the bipartisan foreign policy. Truman described the Greek situation in dark terms, then said he wanted to ask Congress for $250 million for Greece and $150 million for Turkey. Most, if not all, of what he said was news to the Congressmen, but the way in which he outlined the issues, coupled with Vandenberg's support for containment, won them over.

During the following weeks the State, Navy, and War Departments worked out the details of the aid program while Vandenberg and the other congressional leaders built support in Congress for the new policy. Not until 7 March did Truman go before his Cabinet to explain developments; there, perhaps unexpectedly, he found some opposition. Although Forrestal wanted a full mobilization for the struggle with the Russians ('I said that it would take all of the talent and brains in the country, just as it had taken all of them in the war, and that these abilities and talents should be harnessed in a single team'), others were not so convinced. The Secretary of Labor objected to pulling British chestnuts out of the fire. Someone wondered if it was good policy to support the corrupt, inefficient, right-wing Greek government. Most of all, however, the Cabinet was concerned about the way the public would receive such a sharp break with America's historic foreign policy, especially as it promised to be so expensive. As Truman laconically put it in his *Memoirs*, 'There was considerable discussion on the best method to apprise the American people of the issues involved.'

The day before, 6 March, Truman had begun to prepare the ground. In a speech at Baylor University in Texas he explained that freedom was more important than peace and that freedom of worship and speech were dependent on freedom of enterprise. This was standard American political rhetoric, of course, believed by Americans to be self-evident. Truman believed he could use that sentiment. His strategy, in short, would be to explain aid to Greece not in terms of supporting a rightist monarchy but rather as part of a world-wide program for freedom. This open-ended approach had been implicit from the first, as indeed it had to be, given the assumptions on which Truman was acting.

The State Department, meanwhile, was preparing a message for Truman to deliver to the full Congress. He was unhappy with the early drafts, for 'I wanted no hedging in this speech. This was America's answer to the surge of expansion of Communist tyranny. It had to be clear and free of hesitation or double talk.' Truman told Acheson to have the speech toughened, simplified, and expanded to cover more than just Greece and Turkey. He then made further revisions in the new draft.

George Kennan saw one of the revised drafts. Kennan had risen in prestige and power in the State Department since the end of the war and Marshall had just named him head of a new Policy Planning Staff. His rise was due in large part to a long telegram (over 7,000 words), which 20 years later he himself confessed 'reads exactly like one of those primers put out by alarmed congressional committees or by the Daughters of the American Revolution, designed to arouse the citizenry to the dangers of the Communist conspiracy'. In 1946 the telegram was well received. Truman read it, while Forrestal had it reproduced and made it required reading for thousands of senior officers. Kennan had sent the telegram on 22 February 1946, and it provided the intellectual justification for the policy of containment. Kennan was widely understood in Washington to be the father of that policy.

Despite all this, Kennan was horrified when he read the speech Truman was to deliver to the Congress. First, he saw no need for any military aid to Turkey, where no military threat existed. So too in Greece – Kennan was all for helping the Greek government, but thought it should be done through political and economic aid. In his view, the Soviet threat was primarily political. Kennan was also upset at the way in which Truman had seized the opportunity to declare a world-wide, open-ended doctrine, when what was called for was a simple declaration of aid to a single nation. Truman was preparing to use terms, Kennan later remarked, 'more grandiose and more sweeping than anything that I, at least, had ever envisaged'. Kennan protested, to no avail. He was informed that it was too late to change the speech.

The point Kennan had missed was the need to rally the public in support of a policy that broke sharply with America's past. Kennan was not a politician – in fact had hardly been in the United States for most of his adult life – while Truman was *the* expert on domestic politics. Like Truman, Kennan wanted to stop the communists, but he wanted to do so in a realistic way, at little cost, and with minimal commitments. Truman realized that he could never get the economy-minded Republicans – and the public that stood behind them – to shell out tax dollars to support a rather shabby king in Greece. Truman had to describe the Greek situation in universal terms, good versus evil, to get support for containment.

On 10 March, the day the Moscow Conference opened, Truman completed the preparation of the ground for his speech by calling in, once again, the congressional leaders. This meeting was larger than the earlier one, and this time Senator Taft was among those present. He evidently listened quietly as Acheson and Truman talked for two hours. Vandenberg 'expressed his complete agreement' with the new policy. Bipartisanship had won; everything was ready. At one P.M. on 12 March 1947, Truman stepped to the rostrum in the hall of the House of Representatives to address the joint session of the Congress. The speech was also carried on nationwide radio. He asked for immediate aid for Greece and Turkey, then explained the reasoning. 'I believe that it must be the policy of the United States to support free peoples who are resisting attempted subjugation by armed minorities or by outside pressures.'

The statement was all-encompassing. In a single sentence, Truman had defined American policy for the next twenty years. Whenever and wherever an anti-communist government was threatened, by indigenous insurgents, foreign invasion, or even diplomatic pressure (as with Turkey), the United States would supply political, economic, and most of all military aid. The Truman Doctrine came close to shutting the door against any revolution, since the terms 'free peoples' and 'anti-communist' were assumed to be synonymous. All the Greek government, or any dictatorship, had to do to get American aid was to claim that its opponents were communist. And the aid would be unilateral, as Truman never mentioned the United Nations, whose commission to investigate what was actually happening in Greece had not completed its study or made a report.

It has often been noted that Americans are slow to go to war but vicious once they are involved. This being so, Americans want their wars to be grand crusades on a world-wide scale, a struggle between light and darkness with the fate of the world hanging on the outcome. The Truman Doctrine met that desire. So did the bulk of his speech. At one of the meetings between the President and the congressional leaders, Vandenberg had warned Truman that if he wanted the public to support containment, he would have to 'scare hell out of the American people'. Truman did. He painted in dark hues the 'totalitarian regimes' which threatened to snuff out freedom everywhere. The time had come, he said, when 'nearly every nation must choose between alternative ways of life'. The President escalated the long, historic struggle between the left and the right in Greece for political power, and the equally historic Russian urge for control of the Dardanelles, into a universal conflict between freedom and slavery. It was a very broad jump indeed.

It was also brilliant. Ever since the promulgation of the Truman Doctrine, left-wing commentators and historians have emphasized the hostile reaction to it, and to be sure intellectuals and some Congressmen were unhappy. Kennan had already made his objections known. Walter Lippmann, the dean of the newspaper columnists, attacked Truman for bypassing the United Nations and because of the open-ended nature of his pledge of assistance. He was also disturbed at the no-strings-attached offer of assistance to the corrupt, reactionary, and 'obviously unrepresentative' Greek government, a sentiment some Congressmen shared. A few other Congressmen resented deeply the crisis treatment to which they had been subjected – Truman talked as if there had been another Pearl Harbor. A British diplomat was surprised and shocked by the 'enormous hullaballoo' that accompanied Truman's request and by the fact 'that the policy of aid to Greece was made to seem hardly less than a declaration of war on the Soviet Union'.

e these outbursts, and there were many others, the
lain fact was that Truman had struck a responsive chord
with the majority of his countrymen. Congress wrangled
over the aid bill, but given the good reception of Truman's
speech across the nation there was never any serious
question about passage. On 15 May 1947, Congress appropriated $400 million for Greece and Turkey. By later
standards the sum was small, but nevertheless America had
taken an immense stride. For the first time in its history, the
United States had chosen to intervene in a period of general
peace in the affairs of peoples outside North and South
America. The initial amount of aid was drastically limited,
but the symbolic act could not have been more significant.
The commitment had been made. It would take years to
persuade Congress and the public to provide all the
enormous funds needed for the new policy, but having
accepted the premises of the Truman Doctrine there was no
turning back.

The next step was to extend the Doctrine from the
periphery to the Continent of Europe itself. It was, in a way,
ironic that America had assumed the British protectorate
in precisely that area of Europe that Churchill had wanted
to concentrate on in World War II, an area the Americans
had insisted led nowhere and in which they refused to
fight. In the spring of 1947, having in effect finally extended
lend-lease to the periphery, some American leaders were
anxious to turn their attention back to what they continued
to consider the main theater, western Europe.

There was a certain amount of tension over this point,
for some officials wanted to make the Doctrine world-wide
immediately. Even before Truman spoke to Congress,
Vandenberg had defined the Greek crisis as a part of 'the
world-wide ideological clash between Eastern Communism
and Western Democracy', and Acheson had initiated a
State Department survey to investigate the possibilities of
broadening aid to other nations, especially in Asia. Forrestal
had sent a memorandum to Truman which warned that

the present danger was as great as that during World War II; the Secretary urged the President to quit the defensive and 'attack successfully' with an all-out economic effort to revitalize Germany and Japan before the 'Russian poison' conquered Europe, Asia, and Latin America.

General Marshall, however, disagreed. One of Marshall's major tasks during the war had been to set priorities, to decide what was more important and then concentrate scarce resources there. He had chosen Europe then, and he did so now. Marshall realized that no matter how eloquent Truman had been in persuading the Republican Congress about the communist threat, there was no chance of getting enough money from the legislature to support a world-wide program. He reminded one critic, who wanted to extend the Doctrine to China, that China was forty-five times as large and had eighty-five times as many people as Greece. Later, perhaps, money would be available for containment in Asia; until then the State Department would have to set priorities and keep its eyes on the main theater.

The situation in Europe was acute. When Marshall returned from the Moscow Conference, at which no progress on German reunification had been made, he reported that 'the patient [Europe] is sinking while the doctors deliberate'. The three Western powers had favored a federal government in Germany under a democratic constitution with free elections, while the Russians had insisted upon a strong central government under a provisional constitution prepared in an assembly composed of representatives of anti-Fascist organizations. The Soviets charged that the Western plan would bring a neo-Nazi government to power. The West replied that the Russian approach was unacceptable because it would guarantee communist participation, with fearful implications. 'Agreement was impossible' at Moscow, Marshall reported in a radio talk to the nation on 28 April, because the Soviet proposals 'would have established in Germany a centralized government adapted to the seizure of absolute control'.* As General Clay later put it, 'The principal result [of the Moscow Conference] was to convince the three foreign ministers representing the Western Powers of the intransigence of the Soviet position.' This in turn 'led them to work more closely together in the future', which meant it speeded the process of unifying the Western zones and bringing western Germany into the budding alliance against the Soviets.

While in Europe, Marshall had been shaken by the seriousness and urgency of the plight of Western Europe, where economic recovery from the ravages of war had been slow. Total economic disintegration appeared to be imminent; the great storm in Britain had only emphasized the danger. The Secretary of State's discussions with the Russians, according to Kennan, 'had compelled him to recognize, however reluctantly, that the idea of approaching the solution to Europe's problems in collaboration with the Russians was a pipe dream.' Stalin, Marshall concluded, wanted the European economy to come crashing down. In fact there is little evidence that Marshall went to Moscow hoping to find a method of collaborating with the Russians on European recovery and much evidence to indicate that the major American purpose was to convince France, Britain, and the West Germans that the time had come to take independent action.

The Truman Doctrine had cleared the way for a massive American aid program. The assumption that economic chaos was just as much a communist tool as guerrillas in Greece gave the program an authentically anti-Soviet ring.

* At Moscow, Molotov had – as always – pressed for Russian participation in the management of the Ruhr. The West, as usual, refused. The request had come as no surprise. Three months earlier, for example, the then Secretary of State, James Byrnes, had engaged in an informal conversation with Molotov late at night. After the third highball, Byrnes turned to Molotov and said, 'Mr Minister, I would like to know what you would really like in Europe.' Molotov replied that he was willing to give up practically anything else to get a quadripartite arrangement in the Ruhr.

Marshall ordered Kennan and the Policy Planning Staff to draw up a program for aid to Europe. Round-the-clock meetings began. The general aim was to revive the economy of Western Europe, which was imperative for both economic and military reasons. As Acheson explained, American exports were running at sixteen billion dollars a year, imports at less than eight billion. Most of the exports went to Europe. If the Europeans were to pay for them, they had to have dollars, which they could only get by procuring goods America could import. Otherwise, America's export market would dry up, with grave repercussions on the American domestic scene. Militarily, only with a healthy economy could Europe support the troops necessary to resist the Red Army.

The key was Germany. To get European production rolling again, Germany's coal mines and steel mills had to be worked at maximum capacity. Kennan emphasized this point. 'In my opinion,' he declared during the second day of his group's deliberations, 'it is imperatively urgent today that the improvement of economic conditions and the revival of productive capacity in the west of Germany be made the primary object of our policy . . . and be given top priority.' It would have been absurd to expect the Russians to co-operate in the revival of Germany without themselves controling the Ruhr, and indeed Kennan had no such expectations. The problem was that if the United States went ahead on its German program, the division of Europe would be complete, with the further consequence of a bipolar world and an end to even verbal attempts to co-operate with the Russians in achieving peace and stability. Everything pointed to a bipolar world anyway, to be sure, but if the United States took the lead in proposing programs that would bring western Germany into a revived Western Europe, responsibility for the split would rest with the United States.

There could be no progress in Europe without including Germany, and there could be no improvement in Germany without antagonizing the Russians. What to do about the Soviets thus became a prime consideration. Kennan insisted that the United States should 'play it straight' by inviting the Russians to participate in any Europe-wide recovery program. 'We would not ourselves draw a line of division through Europe.' He recognized the dangers. 'What if,' he himself asked, 'the Russians spiked it' by accepting the invitation and then 'trying to link it to Russian participation in the administration of the Ruhr?'. Since this was precisely what the Russians could be expected to do if they agreed to a multi-national program dominated by the Americans, the fear was real. Kennan's answer was straightforward: 'In that case I think we can only say "no" to the whole business as pleasantly and firmly as we know how....'

Even in making an offer to the Russians, Kennan wanted strict controls. He insisted that the Russians would have to open their economic records for American scrutiny and he wanted the East European economy integrated into that of Western Europe. Presumably this last point meant a return to pre-war conditions, when East Europe served as an economic colony of the West, exporting raw materials and importing finished goods. It also meant opening East European markets to American business interests, with long-range possibilities that might drastically weaken Soviet control of the region. Most students of the Marshall Plan have concluded that Kennan's limitations on Russian participation were so severe that, despite Marshall's famous sentence stating that the policy was 'directed not against any country or doctrine but against hunger, poverty, desperation and chaos', in fact Kennan and the State Department did not want Soviet participation and did all they could to prevent it within the context of making it appear that a genuine offer was being made.

Kennan applied the same formula in a more general way to the Soviet satellites. Insofar as they were free to accept the American offer and integrate their economies into those of Western Europe and the United States, Kennan was willing to offer aid to them. He insisted, however, that it be done in such a way that they would 'either exclude themselves by unwillingness to accept the proposed conditions or agree to abandon the exclusive orientation of their economies'.

Control was crucial. America was not going to give money to any European state, East or West, without some assurances. During the war, the use of lend-lease goods by the largest recipient, Britain, had been controled through the Combined Chiefs of Staff, where American domination made certain that the British fought where the Americans wanted them to. Even the goods that went to Russia were controled to the extent that the United States sent only material that could be used to wage war. The need with the Marshall Plan was to find a similar control, in order to make sure the recipients integrated their economies, provided opportunities for American investors, and opened their markets.

The need for control led to the rejection of the United Nations as the agency to revive the patient. Kennan's group thoroughly discussed this point. The United Nations had established the Economic Commission for Europe (E.C.E.) then in session at Geneva. 'There were many' in the Policy Planning Staff, Kennan later admitted, 'who feared . . . that if, in stimulating the preparation of a recovery program of Europe, we bypassed this commission, into whose area of responsibility the economic recovery of Europe plainly fell, we would be damaging the usefulness not only of the commission but of the United Nations itself in the entire field of world trade and economics.' This was, however, precisely what the Americans ultimately decided to do. It would have been risky to give money to a United Nations' agency to distribute, and in any case it was doubtful that Congress would have provided the funds for a massive United Nations' program.

A final aim of Kennan's group was 'to correct what seemed to us to be the two main misimpressions that had been created in connection with the Truman Doctrine'. These were the idea that America's foreign policy was a defensive reaction to communist pressure and that the Doctrine was a blank check to give aid to any area of the world threatened by the communists. Truman was more nearly correct, however, in saying that the Doctrine and the Marshall Plan 'are two halves of the same walnut'. The emphasis in Greece and Turkey was military, while initially in West Europe it was economic, but both were designed to contain the Soviets.

On 5 June 1947, speaking at Harvard University, Marshall announced the plan. His speech was pitched on a plan of dignity and reasonableness and indeed it was quite possible that Marshall himself, unlike his planners, still hoped for Soviet co-operation. His general proposals, like the man himself, were high-minded. He recognized the Continent-wide nature of the problem. Marshall recalled the disruption of Europe's economy because of the war and the destructive rule of the Nazis. Europe could not feed itself, so it was using up scarce foreign credits to buy food. If the United States did not provide help, 'economic, social and political deterioration of a very grave character' would result, with serious consequences for the American economy. The assistance should not be piecemeal, but 'should provide a cure rather than a mere palliative'. He asked the European nations to gather themselves together, draw up a plan, and submit it to the United States.

The reaction in Western Europe was immediate and enthusiastic. Even traditional fears of Germany quieted. Although Marshall had declared, 'The restoration of Europe involves the restoration of Germany. Without a revival of German production there can be no revival of Europe's economy,' the French were anxious to implement a program, for the Marshall Plan tied Germany to Western Europe generally and offered vast sums to everyone. French Foreign Minister Georges Bidault began meetings in Paris. He neglected to invite the Russians to participate, but pressure from the powerful French Communist Party made him change his mind. On 26 June, Molotov arrived in Paris with eighty-nine economic experts and clerks, which indicated that the Russians were seriously considering the proposal, as indeed they had to. As the American Ambassador to Moscow, General Smith, said, 'they were confronted with two unpalatable alternatives.' They were afraid of a Western bloc and realized that 'to refrain from participation in the Paris Conference would be tantamount to forcing the formation of such a bloc'. On the other hand, if they joined up, 'they would create the possibility of a certain amount of economic penetration by the western democracies among the satellite states.'

Molotov spent three days at the conference, most of it on the telephone talking to Stalin in Moscow. He finally proposed that each nation establish its own recovery program. The French and British refused. They insisted on following the American line of making the program Europe-wide. Molotov angrily walked out. He condemned 'the creation of a new organization standing over and above the countries of Europe and interfering in their internal affairs down to determining the line of development to be followed by the main branches of industry in these countries'. He warned that Europe would find itself captive to American corporations (a charge that became the subject of a best-selling book in France in the late sixties), that a revived Germany would dominate West Europe, and that the Plan would divide 'Europe into two groups of states.' Molotov returned to Moscow, where within a week the Soviets announced the 'Molotov Plan' for their satellites. The Poles and Czechs, who had wanted to participate in Paris, informed the West that they could not attend because it 'might be construed as an action against the Soviet Union.'

All that remained was for the Western Europeans to work out the details of a plan and for the American Congress to accept it. At the end of August, the sixteen Western European nations represented at Paris presented a plan calling for $28 billion over a four-year period. An American mission flew to Paris immediately, confered with the European leaders, and got the figure reduced to $22 billion. After thorough examination in the United States, the American administration accepted the program and Truman presented it to Congress on 19 December, although he further reduced the proposed amount to $17 billion.

Despite the reductions, the Plan faced a hostile Congress. 1948 was a Presidential election year. The Republicans did not want to give Truman a major diplomatic triumph or throw American dollars away. They called the Plan a gigantic 'international W.P.A.', a 'bold Socialist blueprint', and a plain waste of American money. Vandenberg ardently championed the bill. In presenting it to the Senate, he called it 'a calculated risk' to 'help stop World War III before it starts'. The area covered by the Plan, he declared, contained '270,000,000 people of the stock which has largely made America . . . . This vast friendly segment of the earth must not collapse. The iron curtain must not come to the rims of the Atlantic either by aggression or by default'. Administration witnesses before Congressional committees considering the Plan underscored Vandenberg's emphasis on containment. They pointed out that a rejuvenated Europe could produce strategic goods which the United States could buy and stockpile, preserve Western control over Middle Eastern oil supplies, and free Europeans from economic problems so they could help the United States militarily.

Indeed, as Walter LaFeber has pointed out, the Plan offered all things to all people. Those who feared a slump in exports and a resulting depression within the United States could envision a continued vigorous export trade; those who thought communist expansion would result from economic chaos saw salvation in an integrated, healthy European economy; those who thought the real threat was the Red Army fairly drooled at the thought of reviving Germany and then rebuilding the Wehrmacht. For the humanitarian, the Plan offered long-term aid to war-torn Europe.

Still, the Plan met intense opposition. Taft proclaimed that American money should not be poured into a 'European T.V.A.'. Like many of his Republican colleagues, he was deeply disturbed at European steps – however halting – towards socialism, and feared that the Europeans would use Marshall Plan money to nationalize basic industries, including American-owned plants. The National Association of Manufacturers laid down the principle that 'during the period of economic aid the participating countries should not undertake any further nationalization projects, or initiate projects which have the effect of destroying or impairing private competitive enterprise', and that 'aid should be extended to private competitive enterprises in the foreign countries instead of to governments or their agencies', all of which was consistent with the administration belief that the time had come for the world to adopt the American system. Even with these provisions, however, Congress would not budge. Committee meetings ground on, with no results.

All in all, 1947 had been a frustrating year for the new foreign policy. In Greece, guerrilla warfare raged on, despite increased American military assistance. The Chinese communists continued to push Chiang back. Russia retained her grip on East Europe; indeed, strengthened it, for immediately after Molotov left the Paris Conference he announced the formation of the Communist Information Bureau (Cominform), which the West assumed to be a substitute for the old Communist International, abolished during World War II. In Hungary, the Soviets purged left-wing anti-communist political leaders, rigged the elections on 31 August 1947, and destroyed all anti-communist opposition. Truman had been forced by the Republicans and the public generally to call off the peace-time drafting of young men into the armed services, demobilization continued, and U.M.T. failed, all of which left the administration with inadequate tools to pursue the policy of containment.

Truman was even unable to achieve unification of the

armed forces, a proposal designed to make them more efficient and cheaper. In July 1947, the Congress finally passed the National Security Act, which provided for a single Department of Defense to replace the three independently run services, gave statutory status to the Joint Chiefs of Staff, established a National Security Council to advise the President, and created a Central Intelligence Agency to gather information and to correlate and evaluate intelligence activities around the world. Truman appointed the leading anti-communist in his Cabinet, Forrestal, as the first Secretary of Defense, but the Act as a whole fell far short of what he, Marshall, and Army Chief of Staff Eisenhower had wanted. They had envisioned the creation of a single armed force, small but efficient, that could move quickly to trouble spots or be expanded rapidly through U.M.T. Instead they got a loosely federated system with an independent Air Force.

The Air Force doctrine was to punish misbehavior through strategic bombing, including the atomic bomb, which made the new service popular with Congress, since massive retaliation seemed a cheap way of providing for the national defense. Taft and some other senators indicated that they were nearly ready to abolish the Army and Navy and concentrate funds on the Air Force. This doctrine, however, did not fit in at all with containment; mass bombardment from the air was clearly not an effective answer to the problems raised in Greece or Hungary or even China. It did appear to be a good way to protect the United States from any mass assault, which indicated that its proponents were retreating to isolation and had not fully accepted the doctrine of containment, with its implication of an active military policy around the world.

The alternative to an American armed force that could stand up to the communists was one manned by Europeans, but this too had so far failed. The Greek government and army showed scarcely any improvement. In Western Europe, the proposing of the Marshall Plan had helped to draw a line across the Continent, but the unwillingness of Congress to appropriate the money had left the area much too weak to support any sizeable armed forces. The last, faint hope of redeeming Eastern Europe through the economic policies of the Marshall Plan had gone aglimmering when Molotov walked out of the Paris Conference. Indeed, the Molotov Plan and the Cominform had made the situation worse.

The Marshall Plan had now become the keystone to containment, and on 2 January 1948 Truman tried to get some action from Congress by dropping the $17 billion request and asking instead for $6.8 billion to cover the first fifteen months of the Plan's operation. He got no immediate response.

Then came Czechoslovakia.

In the post-war years, Czechoslovakia had been a good case study of the way in which American foreign and military policy moved in different directions. The nation had been jointly occupied by the American and Red Armies in 1945, but from the first Eisenhower, then head of the American occupation forces, had wanted to pull out. He had broad commitments in Germany, with not enough troops, and was being pressed by the War Department to redeploy even more men to the Pacific. After the Japanese surrender, the pressure for demobilization made the man-power situation worse. Eisenhower wanted a complete withdrawal from the American zone in Czechoslovakia by 15 November 1945, a proposal that Acheson (then Acting Secretary of State) wanted reconsidered. Acheson argued that the presence of American troops in Czechoslovakia 'has been welcomed by the populace' and warned that a United States withdrawal 'might create the impression, however erroneously, that the United States had disinterested itself in the affairs of this part of Europe'. He wanted two divisions (about 40,000 men) left in Czechoslovakia until the Soviets had withdrawn from their zone.

Secretary of War Stimson, in reply, told Acheson that

demobilization made it impossible to leave the troops in Czechoslovakia. He urged the State Department to do all it could to get the Soviets to pull out, but declared that in any case the American troops would have to be brought home. In the end, there was a mutual withdrawal on 1 December, but the Soviets kept a number of divisions on Czechoslovakia's borders. Czechoslovakia was, in addition, caught between Poland and eastern Germany on the north and Hungary on the south, which made Soviet influence there pervasive.

In May 1946, Czechoslovakia held her first post-war elections. The communists won 38 per cent of the vote and Klement Gottwald, who had spent World War II in the Soviet Union, became the Prime Minister. Neither the President, Eduard Benes, nor the Foreign Minister, Jan Masaryk, were communist, and both were greatly admired in the West. They attempted to maintain a balance between East and West, but the polarization of Europe – particularly after the Paris Conference – made the success of their policy increasingly doubtful. The end came in February 1948, when Gottwald refused to co-operate with Benes on a plan to reorganize the police and the Cabinet broke up. Gottwald issued an ultimatum for a new government under his power and a Soviet mission flew to Prague to demand Benes' surrender. On 25 February 1948, Benes capitulated and the communists assumed complete control. Two weeks later Masaryk was assassinated.

The coup did two things absolutely necessary for the adoption of the containment policy. First, as Truman noted, it 'sent a shock throughout the civilized world'. Americans had regarded Czechoslovakia as a model democracy, an example of what was possible in East Europe. Nearly everyone remembered, and discussed, Hitler and Munich. It seemed the same play was about to be performed, with new actors. Second, the coup dramatically illustrated the limitations of current American policy, for not only could the United States do nothing to help save

Czechoslovakia, it was doing nothing to prevent similar occurrences in the remainder of Europe.

Events now began to rush forward. On 5 March Clay sent a telegram from Germany. Although 'I have felt and held that war was unlikely for at least ten years', the General began, 'within the last few weeks, I have felt a subtle change in the Soviet attitude which . . . gives me a feeling that it may come with dramatic suddenness.' The Soviet officials in Germany had adopted a new attitude, 'faintly contemptuous, slightly arrogant, and certainly assured'. On 11 March, Marshall described the situation as 'very, very serious'. Three days later, the Senate endorsed the Marshall Plan by a vote of 69 to 17.

In Washington, London, and Paris there was a real warscare. Kennan interpreted the Russian move in Czechoslovakia (and the tough atmosphere in Berlin) as defensive reactions to the Marshall Plan and to the Western preparations to set up a separate German government in West Germany. If the Americans were going to consolidate Western Europe into a single military–economic unity, the Soviets were determined to do the same on their side of the curtain. This was especially important as it had now become clear to Stalin that Tito in Yugoslavia would not blindly take orders from the Kremlin. The defensive interpretation of Soviet actions, however, found little favor. In Europe, France, Britain, and the Benelux countries held a series of meetings in Brussels and on 16 March 1948 signed the Brussels Union, pledging mutual defense arrangements. In the United States, the C.I.A. solemnly assured Truman that the Red Army would not march within the next two months. At the end of March, when the Army and Navy wished to extend the cautious estimate another two weeks into the future, the Air Force would not concur. Averell Harriman warned: 'There are aggressive forces in the world coming from the Soviet Union which are just as destructive in their effect on the world and our own way of life as Hitler was, and I think are a greater menace than Hitler was.'

On 17 March Truman, noting 'the grave events in Europe . . . moving so swiftly', cancelled an engagement in New York and instead went before Congress. The President declared that the Soviet Union was the 'one nation' that was blocking all efforts toward peace. America must, he said, meet 'this growing menace . . . to the very survival of freedom'. He welcomed the Brussels Treaty and promised to extend American aid to the signatories 'to help them to protect themselves'.

Truman asked for an immediate favorable vote in the House on the Marshall Plan, but that was only a beginning. He also wanted U.M.T. and the resumption of Selective Service. Even after the Czech coup, however, Congress was not willing to respond wholeheartedly to a call to arms. The House gave Truman the Marshall Plan on 31 March (although it appropriated $4 billion, not the $6.8 billion Truman had requested), but it refused to pass U.M.T. or resume the draft.

Congressional action, however, had indicated only that the politicians did not want to use American boys to contain the Russians, not that they had rejected containment. The policy was acceptable; the implementation was still in debate. One of the administration's promises about the Marshall Plan, however, had been that it would strengthen Europe's economy to the point where the Europeans could man their own barricades. With invaluable assistance from Soviet actions, the administration had gotten agreement on a policy. The Truman Doctrine and the Marshall Plan had set forth some of the details of containment in Europe. The rest could now be worked out. Events in Berlin would help speed the process.

In July 1947, when George Kennan's influence within the government was at its peak, he published an article in the journal *Foreign Affairs* entitled 'The Sources of Soviet Conduct' and signed only 'By X'. Its author was soon widely known; its reception nothing short of spectacular. It quickly became the quasi-official statement of American foreign policy.

Kennan argued that the Soviets were motivated by two beliefs: (1) 'the innate antagonism between capitalism and socialism', and (2) the infallibility of the Kremlin. Their goal was world conquest, but because of the Soviet theory of the inevitability of the eventual fall of capitalism they were in no hurry and had no timetable. The Kremlin's 'political action is a fluid stream which moves constantly, wherever it is permitted to move, toward a given goal. Its main concern is to make sure that it has filled every nook and cranny available to it in the basin of world power'. The article in its entirety seemed a wholly satisfactory explanation of Soviet behavior and was accepted as such for at least a decade.

Kennan was an intellectual and he filled the X article with qualifications, although he would later complain that he had not qualified sufficiently and that therefore his article had been misread. He did not believe the Russians posed any serious military threat nor that they wanted war. The challenge Kennan saw was a political and economic one, which should be met on those grounds by 'long term, patient but firm and vigilant containment'.

The sentence in Mr X's article that was most frequently quoted, however, and the one that became the touchstone of American policy, declared that what was needed was 'the adroit and vigilant application of counter-force at a series of constantly shifting geographical and political points, corresponding to the shifts and maneuvers of Soviet policy'. This implied (and most readers thought this was what Kennan meant) that crisis would follow crisis around the world, as the Soviet-masterminded conspiracy used its agents to accelerate the flow of communist power into 'every nook and cranny'. It also implied that the threat was military, which made it the responsibility of the United States to meet and throw it back wherever it appeared. Containment meant building up the military strength of America and her allies, to be matched by a willingness to stand up to the Russians wherever they applied pressure.

Walter Lippmann immediately protested that the cost of Kennan's program would be fantastic, far beyond the ability of the American people to pay. Lippmann agreed with Kennan's analysis of the sources of Soviet conduct but thought the American response ought to be more limited and realistic. Kennan wrote Lippmann to assure him that he had not meant to say that the Russians wanted to invade anyone or that the task of American policy was to prevent them from doing so – quite the contrary. But almost every reader, not just Lippmann, thought that military resistance was precisely what Kennan meant,* and the policy-makers set themselves to watching for the next in that 'series of constantly shifting geographical and political points' against which the communists would move.

It came in Berlin. It had been expected, for the Ameri-

---

* Carefully read, the article was clear enough. For example, just as Marx stood Hegel on his head, so did Kennan turn Marx around. Kennan believed there was a strong possibility 'that Soviet power, like the capitalist world of its conception, bears within it the seeds of its own decay, and that the sprouting of these seeds is well advanced'. All America had to do was wait and the Soviets would 'mellow' or even collapse. Since this is precisely what the Soviets predicted would happen to the United States, the Cold War was all a terrible mistake. Both sides should have sat back to wait for the other to collapse.

cans, knowing in advance what the Russian reaction would be, had pushed ahead with the plans to unify the west German zones. They had used the failure of the 1947 meetings of the Council of Foreign Ministers to convince the French that there was no hope of co-operation with the Russians; what the French had in fact come to realize was that neither of the super-powers dared let the other camp control all of Germany, for a revived and unified Germany on either side would mean that that side could dominate the world. If Germany were unified, no matter what the guarantees, each antagonist feared that the other would sooner or later control it. In the circumstances, the only thing to do was to divide it. An economic merging of the three Western zones in Germany was then needed to speed European-wide recovery, along with some steps to restore West German sovereignty to improve German morale. In March 1948, as a part of these developments, Clay introduced a currency reform into the Anglo-American zones. The Russians, fearing a revival of German industry outside their control, and the merging of West Germany into an anti-Soviet block, responded with a partial blockade of Western movement into West Berlin. Clay then closed the borders of the American zone to Soviet traffic and announced that he intended to introduce the new currency into West Berlin. As the tension mounted, the Western powers met in London to consider the future of Germany. In June, they indicated that they intended to go ahead with the formation of a West German government.

Events moved swiftly in the spring of 1948. After the signing of the Brussels Treaty, the American Joint Chiefs declared that the American frontier lay on the Elbe and proposed a military alliance with the Brussels powers. They urged the establishment of a central military command for the new organization with an American supreme commander. At the time there were about twelve ill-equipped and poorly trained divisions in all Western Europe; military plans called for a withdrawal to the Pyrenees if the Red

Army marched. The Joint Chiefs wanted between eighty and eight-five divisions, which was almost as many as the the United States had mobilized for World War II and could obviously be had only through extensive rearmament of Western Europe. Unspoken but implicitly understood by everyone involved in the discussions was the fact that the only way to get the required number of men in arms was to use German troops. Because of British, Benelux, and especially French fears, however, this could not be broached at once. The first step was to form a Western Union without Germany but simultaneously with the current efforts toward West German independence.

Even in the United States acceptance of the program would not be easy. There were three major objections: the cost; the abandonment of America's historic position of no entangling alliances; and doubts about the wisdom of rearming the Germans. Truman would need all the help he could get. Following an April meeting of the National Security Council (N.S.C.), Forrestal noted the techniques that would be used: Under Secretary of State Robert A. Lovett 'outlined tentative proposals for as nearly concurrent action as possible by the Senate and the President . . . [in the form of] a statement that we were willing to consider steps looking to the construction of a regional agreement, if it proves to be in the interests of the security of the United States. The tactics would be to have this action initiated by the Republicans and to have the ball picked up immediately by the President.' When a member of the Council tried to move the discussion out of the narrow tactical field by asking aloud if such a 'regional agreement' might not be provocative to the Soviet Union, Lovett shrugged him off and said the purpose was 'to indicate to anyone [*sic*] that there would be a price to any decision to overrun – that it would not be simply a walk-in'.

Senator Vandenberg responded handsomely, In early June he introduced a resolution in the Senate that encouraged 'the progressive development of regional and other

collective arrangements' for defense and promised to promote the 'association of the United States' with such
organizations. That Vandenberg was unaware of the administration's plans became obvious when he stressed the value
of a simple political commitment in encouraging Europe
and explicitly repudiated the idea that the United States
should help in building up a sizeable force-in-being. The
administration gave verbal approval to his limitations and
on June 11 the Vandenberg Resolution breezed through
the Senate by a vote of 64 to 4.

At the beginning of the summer of 1948, the Soviets were
thus faced with a whole series of what they considered
threatening developments. The Marshall Plan was beginning to draw the Western European nations closer together.
France, Britain, and the Benelux had signed a military pact
which the United States had officially welcomed and had
indicated it intended to join. Americans were already
beginning to talk of bringing others into the proposed
organization, among them Canada, Portugal, Denmark,
Iceland, Norway, and Italy. Since these countries could
contribute little or nothing to ground defense, the Soviets
judged – rightly – that the Americans wanted them included
in order to use their territory for air and sea bases. The
United States was even dickering with Fascist Spain for
bases. Equally ominous was the Western determination to
give independence to West Germany. In the long run, this
could only mean that the West intended to merge West
Germany into the proposed anti-Soviet military organization.

Adding to Stalin's difficulties, his strongest satellite,
Yugoslavia, refused to play the role Russia had assigned to
it and struck out on an independent course. Stalin tried to
topple Tito, failed, and in despair expelled Yugoslavia
from the Cominform. The example Tito had set, however,
could not be so easily dismissed.

Soviet foreign policy, based on an occupied and divided
Germany, a weakened Western Europe, and tight control
of East Europe, faced total collapse. Whether Stalin had

expansive plans is unclear and at least doubtful, but what had happened made him shake, for the security of the Soviet Union itself now seemed threatened. As Kennan put it, in a grand understatement, 'There can be no doubt that, coming as it did on top of the European recovery program and the final elaboration and acceptance of the Atlantic alliance, the move toward establishment of a separate government in Western Germany aroused keen alarm among the Soviet leaders.' The victor in the war was being hemmed in by the West, with the vanquished playing a key role in the new coalition. Worst of all was the Western listening-post and outpost in the heart of the Soviet security belt, the Western sector in Berlin.

On 23 June 1948, Clay introduced the new currency into Western Berlin. Stalin responded immediately. He argued that since the West had abandoned the idea of German reunification, there was no longer any point to maintaining Berlin as the future capital of all Germany. The Western powers, through the logic of their own acts, ought to retire to their own zones. The Russians clamped down a total blockade on all ground and water traffic to Berlin. The British joined the Americans in a counter-blockade on the movement of goods from the east into western Germany.

In the West, there was sentiment to abandon Berlin. For many, it seemed foolish to risk World War III for the sake of a prestige objective, and there was force to Stalin's argument that if the West was going to create a West German nation it had no business staying in East Germany. Clay and Truman quickly scotched such talk. As Clay told the War Department, 'We have lost Czechoslovakia. Norway is threatened. We retreat from Berlin. When Berlin falls, western Germany will be next.' Then Europe would go communist. The frontiers of freedom, it seemed, were not on the Elbe, but beyond it. Like Stalin, the Americans felt they could not give an inch. Marshall declared, 'We had the alternative of following a firm policy in Berlin or accepting the consequences of failure of the rest of our European

policy,' a statement that described equally well Stalin's feelings. Truman provided the last word in a succinct, simple declaration: 'We are going to stay period.'

Clay wanted to shoot his way through the Russian blockade. He thought the United States might just as well find out immediately whether the Russians wanted war or not. Given the ten to one disparity of ground strength in Europe, Army Chief of Staff Omar Bradley was able to convince Truman that there must be a better way. It was found with air transport, which soon began flying round-the-clock missions into Berlin, supplying up to 13,000 tons of goods per day.

The war scare continued. On 15 July the N.S.C. decided to send two groups of B-29s to Britain; B-29s were known around the world as the bombers that carried atomic weapons. In his diary, Forrestal noted the rationale: (1) it would show the American public 'how seriously the government . . . views the current sequence of events'; (2) it would give the Air Force experience and 'would accustom the British' to the presence of the U.S. Air Force; and (3) 'We have the opportunity *now* of sending these planes, and once sent they would become somewhat of an accepted fixture,' whereas if America waited, the British might change their minds about the wisdom of having American bombers on their soil.

Whether the planes had atomic bombs on board or not is unknown. It is clear that the Air Force did not control the use of the weapons even if their bombers carried them. On 21 July, Forrestal formally requested that Truman turn over custody of the bomb to the Air Force so that the generals could decide when and where to use it. At the time the civilian Atomic Energy Commission (A.E.C.) controled the bomb. A.E.C. head David Lilienthal objected to Forrestal's request on the grounds that the atomic bomb was not simply another weapon. Truman agreed, saying 'the responsibility for the use of the bomb was his and that was the responsibility he proposed to keep'.

So the military did not get everything out of the crisis that it wanted, but it had made giant strides. The principle of American forward bases in Europe had been established; it was obvious that if they were to be effective they would have to be scattered and there would have to be more of them. The need for a closer military connection with Western Europe had been emphasized. The draft was reintroduced and the Army began to build up. To Kennan's great discomfort, the economic orientation of the Marshall Plan had been nearly forgotten, as containment took on a narrow military look.

Truman, triumphant after his re-election (foreign policy had not been an issue between the major parties in the 1948 campaign), pledged in his Inaugural Address aid to the European nations willing to defend themselves, while the new Secretary of State, Dean Acheson, pushed forward a treaty with the Europeans. On 4 April 1949 the North Atlantic Treaty was signed in Washington; Britain, France, Belgium, the Netherlands, Italy, Portugal, Denmark, Iceland, Norway, Canada, and the United States pledged themselves to mutual assistance in case of aggression against any of the signatories.

The N.A.T.O. Treaty signified the beginning of a new era. In the nineteenth century America had broken the bonds of a colonial, extractive economy and became a great industrial power thanks in large part to private European loans. In the first forty-five years of the twentieth century, the United States had gradually achieved a position of equality with Europe. The Marshall Plan, followed by N.A.T.O., began in earnest the era of American military, political, and economic dominance over Europe.

To the south, in Latin America, the United States had always been dominant. There Truman did not need to change the fundamental relationship, but he did move to rationalize it and make it more profitable. In his 1949 Inaugural Address, Truman announced the celebrated Point Four, in which he promised American technical aid

'to supply the vitalizing force to stir the peoples of the world into triumphant action, not only against their human oppressors, but also against their ancient enemies – hunger, misery and despair'. Truman's tendency to speak in sweeping generalities hid the fact that Point Four was aimed primarily at Latin America and had as its major goal the stimulation of private investment in the region.

The form that Point Four investment would take was clearly stated by the agency entrusted with its administration: 'Location, development and economical processing of mineral and fuel resources is a major aspect of the program of technical co-operation for economic development of underdeveloped countries.' With admirable candor, the agency declared that 'many underdeveloped mineral resources in the areas ... are of considerable importance to the more highly developed nations of the world, including the United States'. Point Four would ensure that the economy of Latin America remained colonial and extractive. There would be soaring profits for American corporations, good salaries for the local managers, and no change at all in the life style of the masses of Latin America. Cecil Rhodes once said he was interested 'in land, not niggers'. So, apparently, was Point Four.

In the spring of 1949 Truman enjoyed success after success. N.A.T.O. and Point Four were followed by a victory in Berlin; on 12 May the Russians lifted the blockade. They had decided – as Clay had felt they would – that the counter-blockade was hurting them more than they were injuring the West, and they realized there was no longer any hope of stopping the movement toward a West German government.* The Soviets still retained flickering hopes of getting something out of the Ruhr. During sporadic discussion between the Soviets and the Americans over Berlin 'the Russians mentioned the Ruhr repeatedly' and as the immediate price for lifting the blockade they got the West to agree to another Foreign Ministers' Con-

* The Bonn Republic came into being on 23 May 1949.

ference on Germany (it began in Paris on 23 May and was abortive).

It had been a good spring for Truman, but trouble lay ahead. The removal of the war scare, combined with the fear that N.A.T.O. was going to cost a good deal of money, began to put an end to bi-partisanship in foreign policy. The old issues, buried since Truman's dramatic speech on Greece, re-emerged. Should the United States be a world policeman? Should it commit itself in advance to the defense of any anti-communist government? How extensive a world role should America play? How much should it pay to play the role? And, at bottom, what was the nature and extent of the Soviet threat and how should it be met? Thoughtful Republicans, led by Senator Taft, began to question the wisdom of provoking the Soviets thousands of miles from America's shores. In the committee meetings to consider ratification of the N.A.T.O. Treaty, Congressmen began to ask embarrassing questions about the purpose of N.A.T.O.

Senator Henry Cabot Lodge wanted to know if N.A.T.O. was the beginning of a series of regional organizations designed to hem in the Russians. Acheson reassured him by stressing that no one in the administration contemplated following N.A.T.O. with 'a Mediterranean pact, and then a Pacific pact, and so forth'. Other Senators wondered why the United States did not rely upon the United Nations, where America controlled a majority of the votes. One reason was the Russian veto; another that the Europeans required some sort of special guarantee. Harriman warned that if N.A.T.O. was not carried through, 'there would be a reorientation' in Europe, a 're-strengthening of those that believe in appeasement and neutrality'. Acheson explained that 'unity in Europe requires the continuing association and support of the United States. Without it free Europe would split apart.' Or, as Senator Tom Connally declared, 'the Atlantic Pact is but the logical extension of the principle of the Monroe Doctrine'.

N.A.T.O., in other words, would speed the movement toward Western European unity while simultaneously allowing the United States to assume a new posture *vis-à-vis* Europe. What that posture would be was adequately, if somewhat crudely, summed up in the frequent references to the extension of the Monroe Doctrine. Europe would become, for the American businessman, soldier, and foreign policy maker, another Latin America.

All this obviously had great appeal, but serious questions remained. Could not as much be accomplished through the Marshall Plan? Why permanently split Europe, thereby abandoning all hope of ever re-opening the East European market? What was the substance of the military guarantees that Americans were making or supporting?

The last question was crucial. The West already had adequate power with the atomic bomb. N.A.T.O. as it stood added nothing to this power. The ground figures remained the same, with the Russians enjoying a ten to one advantage. Did the Secretary of State plan to send 'substantial' numbers of American troops to Europe? Acheson responded, 'The answer to that question, Senator, is a clear and absolute "No".' Did he plan to put Germans back in uniform? 'We are very clear,' Acheson replied, 'that the disarmament and demilitarization of Germany must be complete and absolute.'

This deepened the mystery rather than clarifying it. What would N.A.T.O. do? The problem, as French Premier Henri Queuille put it in a much-quoted statement, was easily described: 'We know that once Western Europe was occupied, America would again come to our aid and eventually we would again be liberated. But the process would be terrible. The next time you probably would be liberating a corpse . . . . The real frontier of Western Europe which must be defended must be moved well beyond the actual frontiers [i.e., into Germany], because once the geographic frontiers of these countries are crossed it will be too late for America to save very much.' The solution was not so easily seen. In the absence of an imminent attack, neither the Europeans nor the Americans were remotely prepared to undertake the rearmament effort on the required scale to match the Red Army. The Europeans, like the Americans, were unwilling to jeopardize their economic revival or take the internal political risk of building new standing armies.

Each side was trying to carry water on both shoulders. In order to persuade their peoples of the necessity of accepting a provocative alliance, the governments had to insist that the alliance could defend them from invasion. But the governments also had simultaneously to insist that no intolerable sacrifices would be required. As Robert Osgood noted, 'these two assurances could only be fulfilled, if at all, by the participation of West Germany in the alliance, but for political reasons this measure was no more acceptable to the European countries than a massive rearmament effort.'

German rearmament was also politically unacceptable in the United States – the crusade against Hitler had ended only four years previously – and the administration continued to insist that it had no intention of encouraging a German build-up. Nor, the Senators were assured, would N.A.T.O. lead to an arms race or require the Americans to provide military material to the Europeans. Taft was still opposed to the Treaty, but was persuaded to vote for it after the Senate specifically repudiated any obligation either to build up the armed forces of the eleven allies or to extend to them continued aid for the twenty-year period covered by the Treaty. The Senate then ratified the N.A.T.O. Pact by a vote of 84 to 13.

On 23 July 1949, Truman signed the North Atlantic Treaty. It marked the high point of bi-partisanship and of containment in Europe. It also completed one phase of the revolution in American foreign policy. America had entered an entangling alliance. American security thereafter could be immediately and drastically affected by changes in the overseas balance of power over which the United States could not exercise much effective control. It meant that the

United States was guaranteeing the maintenance of foreign social structures and governments for the next twenty years. It committed the United States to close peacetime military collaboration with the armed services of foreign nations. It signified the extent both of America's break with her past and of her determination to halt communist expansion.

The presence among the members of Italy (and later Greece and Turkey) made a mockery of the words North Atlantic in the title; Portugal's presence made the assertion that it was an alliance in defense of democracy a hollow claim. So was the concept that N.A.T.O. represented a pact between equals, for the United States had no intention of sharing the control of its atomic weapons with its N.A.T.O. partners, and the bomb was the only weapon that gave N.A.T.O.'s military pretensions any validity at all. Acheson's denials to the contrary notwithstanding, the Treaty paved the way for German rearmament. It also underscored the Europe-first orientation of Truman's foreign policy, an orientation for which he would soon have to pay a price.

First, however, it was the Senate's turn to pay. On the very day that Truman signed the N.A.T.O. Treaty, he presented the bill to Congress. All the assurances by administration witnesses before the Senate Foreign Relations Committee that the Treaty would not inaugurate an arms race or cost the United States anything were brushed aside. Truman sent to the Congress a Mutual Defense Assistance Bill asking for $1.5 billion for European military aid. The President described the object in modest terms: 'The military assistance which we propose for these countries will be limited to that which is necessary to help them create mobile defensive forces'; in other words, to equip and bring up to strength Europe's twelve or so divisions.

There was immediate opposition. Such a limited program would hardly give a 'tangible assurance' to the peoples of Western Europe that they would be protected from the Red Army. Suspicious Congressmen asked how long the program would last and how much it would cost. General Bradley gave a partial answer: 'Our whole contention is that it is going to take time . . . it may take five years, ten years, for these countries to build up their defenses to the point where they can stop an aggressor.' The Military Assistance Program of 1949 was, in short, only a small down-payment on a large, long-term investment. Senator Taft and other skeptics said this would never do, for the military assistance would be large enough only to provoke the Russians and precipitate an arms race without being adequate to halt the Red Army. Taft charged that the administration was committing the United States to a futile, obsolete, and bankrupt strategy of defending Europe by large-scale land warfare. He much preferred a unilateral American defense of Europe through building up the American Air Force and stepping up the production of atomic bombs.

This got to the heart of the matter, for despite all the intricate committee systems N.A.T.O. eventually created to handle the multi-national forces-in-being, and despite all the 'goals' for ground strength N.A.T.O. commanders continued to put forward, in point of fact the meaning of N.A.T.O. was that the United States promised to use the bomb to deter a Russian attack. Bradley and most Navy officers doubted that such a strategy was realistic. They argued that if the Soviets wanted West Europe badly enough, they would march and accept the fairly limited damage the atomic bombs of that time could render. They were outvoted, however, for the good reason that if they were right the only alternative was to build up Western ground strength to match the Red Army, a politically impossible task.

The United States' promise to use the bomb to deter Russian aggression made sense only if the Americans had bases in Europe from which to deliver the bombs and if the Americans retained their monopoly. The great need was bases for the American bombers, which was the first and most important accomplishment of N.A.T.O. As Osgood wrote, 'The United States backed up its guarantee to come to the defense of Europe by, in effect, extending the protective umbrella of the Strategic Air Command with the atomic bomb. In return, Europe provided the bases that the United States needed in order to strike effectively at the heart of Russia.' This, however, could have been accomplished through bilateral agreements and did not require a multi-national treaty; it also did not require military aid to the N.A.T.O. countries. Opposition to Truman's military-assistance program continued.

Then, on 22 September 1949, Truman announced that the Soviets had exploded an atomic bomb. 'This is now a different world,' Vandenberg painfully recorded. It was indeed. The urge to do something, anything, was irrepressible. Six days later Congress sent the N.A.T.O. appropriations to the President for his approval. Truman ordered the development of the hydrogen bomb accelerated. Nothing, however, could change the fact that America's promise to defend Europe with the bomb had been dissipated almost before it had been given. If the Russians could make the bomb, they surely could develop the means to deliver it, first to Western European targets and then to the United States itself. The Soviets now had two trumps, the bomb and the Red Army, to the West's one.

Within the next six weeks the Operations and Plans Division of the U.S. Army completed a draft program for German remilitarization and began a campaign to get N.A.T.O.'s acceptance. On strictly military grounds this was the only sensible response, given the assumption that the Russians did entertain thoughts of European conquest. Field Marshal Montgomery, General Clay, and the U.S. High Commissioner in Germany, John J. McCloy, joined the Army in calling for German rearmament, and the Joint Chiefs approved the draft plan. The State Department, however, resisted on political grounds, as did Truman. Since neither France nor Britain, not to mention the other

N.A.T.O. nations, showed any inclination of creating a mass army,* this left it up to the Americans.

Aside from the considerable political difficulties inherent in any rearmament program, America's military leaders were still groping for a feasible strategy for the Cold War. The Russian explosion of the atomic bomb made resolution of the debate imperative. As Samuel Huntington has stated, 'Before World War II, American strategy implicitly assumed that the geographical remoteness of the United States from other powers, the superiority of the American fleet in western hemisphere waters, and the struggles which ensue on the Eurasian continent before the balance of power there could be upset, all would give the United States sufficient time in a crisis to convert its manpower and industrial potential into operational military strength.' This assumption seemed no longer valid. While pre-war strategy stressed mobilization potential, post-war strategy had to stress forces-in-being, of which the United States had almost none.

The question, as Huntington stated it, was 'Could a democracy arm to deter or could it only arm to respond?'. An election year was coming up. The House was changing Truman's tax revision bill into a tax reduction bill. The Soviet threat was largely theoretical – the Red Army had not marched beyond the positions it held in May of 1945, not even into Czechoslovakia. How much support, if any beyond what they were already paying, would the American people give to a policy of deterrence designed to forestall a threat that could only with difficulty be seen to endanger

---

* Not even with American equipment. France was especially suspicious, in view of her World War II experience, when America had rearmed her divisions, then insisted that they be used as Eisenhower directed, which was to say as an instrument of American policy. Europeans could see little point to accepting American arms if it also meant accepting American orders, the central problem in the N.A.T.O. organization both then and later. A strategy that uses American equipment and European lives to counter the Red Army has little appeal to the Europeans, especially since only the Americans can decide when or where to use the troops.

American security? Billions of dollars would be needed. Even if the tax-payers agreed to pay the bill, could the economy afford it? These were serious questions, but so were the ones on the other side of the fence. Could America afford not to rearm? Would not the failure to do so automatically abandon West Europe to the communists? It seemed to many in the government that it would.

In Asia the problem had reached crisis proportions. Mao's troops were on the verge of driving Chiang off the mainland. American support for Chiang had been limited and halting, partly because of the Europe-first orientation of the Truman administration, mainly because of the budget ceilings within which the Congress forced the government to operate. That Chiang could have been 'saved', that one of the great historic events of the century could have been reversed by a few million or even billion more dollars of aid, is one of the will-of-the-wisps popular among the Asia-first wing of the Republican party. It is patent nonsense. The point was, however, that millions of Americans believed that more aid would have saved Chiang. A great nation had been 'lost' to communism because Congress was stingy.

This widespread attitude underscored one of the basic assumptions of American foreign policy during the Cold War. Americans high and low implicitly assumed that with good policies and enough will, the United States could control events anywhere. If things did go wrong, if Poland or China did fall to the enemy, it could only happen because of mistakes, not because there were areas of the world in which what America did or wanted made little difference. The assumption that in the end every situation was controllable and could be made to come out as the United States wished – what Senator William Fulbright later called 'the arrogance of power' – colored almost all foreign policy decisions in the fifties and sixties. It also prepared the way for the right-wing charge that the Truman administration was shot through with traitors, for there could be no other explanation for American failures.

The roots of the assumption were deep and complex. The American belief that the United States was different from and better than other countries was part of it. American success in 1917–18 and 1941–5 contributed to the conceit that the United States could order the world. So did the awesome feeling of power that came with a monopoly of the atomic bomb, American productivity, and the American position at the conclusion of World War II. There were racial connotations to the idea. Although most Americans were too sophisticated to talk about the 'white man's burden' and the 'little brown brothers', they still believed in white superiority. Many also held to the notion that the peoples of the Third World thought of Americans as being different from Europeans because the United States had come into being through a revolution. This idea ignored American economic exploitation of the Third World, ignored the fact that the American Revolution had not been a major social upheaval like the one that the Third World was currently undergoing, and ignored America's persistent hostility to anti-colonial revolutions in the post-World War II decade. American leaders were fond of asserting that the United States could lead the emerging nations because America had never been a colonial power, an absurdity of such proportions as to stagger the imagination, but one that was nevertheless believed and frequently trumpeted.

Given all the power America had at her disposal, given American good will, and given the eagerness of peoples everywhere to follow the American example, how could it be that East Europe and China fell to the communists? The junior Senator from Wisconsin, Joseph R. McCarthy, had one answer. On 9 February 1950, in a speech at Wheeling, West Virginia, he declared, 'I have in my hand 57 cases of individuals [in the State Department] who would appear to be either card-carrying members or certainly loyal to the Communist party, but who nevertheless are helping to shape our foreign policy.' A few days later the figure had gone up to 205 communists in the Department; at another time the figure was 81. The charge, however, was consistent – America had been betrayed.

McCarthy's charges came less than eight weeks after Chiang fled to Formosa, five days before the Soviet Union and Communist China signed a thirty-year mutual aid treaty, and three weeks before Klaus Fuchs was found guilty of giving atomic secrets to agents of the Soviet Union. The last was, perhaps, the most important cause of the spectacular popularity of McCarthy and of the forces he represented, for it seemed to be the only explanation of how the backward Russians matched America's achievements in atomic development so quickly. McCarthyism swept the country. The Republicans suddenly had an issue that could bring them, after twenty years ('twenty years of treason', according to McCarthy), back to power.

Much of McCarthyism was froth, screaming accusations without substance. At one point McCarthy said he would stand or fall on the case of a man who 'has a desk in the State Department' and who was boss of an 'espionage ring'. The man was Owen Lattimore; McCarthy charged him with being Russia's 'top secret agent' in the United States. Lattimore, a professor at the Johns Hopkins University and sometime adviser to the State Department on Far Eastern affairs, was guilty – according to McCarthy – because of a memorandum that he had submitted to the Department on 18 October 1949. The central theme of Lattimore's memorandum was that 'the aim of the United States policy should be to enable the countries of the Far East to do without Russia to the maximum extent. This is a much more modest aim than insistence on an organization of hostility to Russia; but it is an attainable aim, and the other is not.' That such views could be regarded as treason indicated how far McCarthyism could go. Lattimore was eventually cleared, but it took years and cost him a small fortune.

Others, less well known, also suffered. State legislatures across the land instituted loyalty oaths for all teachers;

investigations of subversive activity in Washington and in state capitals ruined the reputations of hundreds, if not thousands, of men. McCarthy never had a majority of the public behind him, but he nevertheless enjoyed broad support, and the threat he represented was real enough. The Federal government, to fight back, strengthened and extended its loyalty investigations. At times it seemed that everyone in America was checking on everyone else for possible communist leanings. McCarthy's personal flamboyance only disguised the fact that millions of Americans agreed with his basic premiss – America had failed in the Cold War not because of inherent limitations on her power, nor because of her refusal to rearm, but because of internal treason. Even those public figures who did speak out against McCarthy, and their numbers were few, objected to his methods, not his assumptions. The opponents also wanted to ferret out the guilty, but they insisted that the rights of the innocent should be protected.

There was an Alice in Wonderland quality to the entire uproar. Truman administration officials, up to and including Acheson, had to defend themselves from charges that began with their being soft on communism and moved up to treason. The Democrats were bewildered and angry. With some justice, they wondered what more they could have done to stand up to the Russians, especially in view of the funds available, funds drastically limited by the very Republicans who now demanded blood for the State Department's shortcomings. Chickens had come home to roost. From the time Truman had 'scared hell out of the American people' in March 1947 to the explosion of the Russian bomb and the loss of China, the Democratic officials in the State Department had been stressing the world-wide threat of communism along with the danger of internal subversion in foreign governments. McCarthy and his adherents followed the same path, only they went further along it.

The great McCarthy upheaval, with its enormous popular support, could not be explained in a few glib phrases, although there was some truth in most of the explanations McCarthy's opponents tossed off. There was in McCarthyism an appeal to the inland prejudice against the Eastern seaboard establishment and the things it stood for in the popular mind – the New Deal, among others. Antiintellectualism was always prominent in the movement. McCarthy drew strong support from those Asia-firsters who had been opposed to the trend of American foreign policy, with its European orientation, at least since the early days of World War II. Americans of East European origin were among the first to flock to McCarthy's standard; the Catholic Church in America came with them. Above all, McCarthy provided a simple answer to those who were frustrated as America seemed to suffer defeat after defeat in the Cold War.

One of the appeals of the McCarthy explanation of the world situation was that it would not cost much to set things right. All that was required was to eliminate the communists in the State Department. Few of McCarthy's supporters, and none of those like Senator Taft who tolerated him, were ready to go to war with Russia to liberate the satellites or to send millions of American troops to China to restore Chiang. They did want to root out those who had sold out America at Yalta, Potsdam, and in China; then, with honest patriots in the State Department, world events would develop in accordance with American wishes.

The administration could not accept such a limited program for the Cold War, but it too wanted the same results. It was difficult, however, to develop a comprehensive program in this atmosphere of fear, even hysteria. Nevertheless, something had to be done. China had been lost. Russia did have the bomb. The Europeans were not willing to assume the burden of rearmament. The McCarthy assault was there. The United States had practically no usable ground power. And the President, primarily for domestic political purposes, was still trying to cut the budget. His new Secretary of Defense, Louis Johnson, had set out to 'cut the fat' from the Defense Department. He began by canceling the Navy's supercarrier. Truman set a limit of $13 billion for defense in the up-coming budget, by no stretch of the imagination enough to support a get tough with the Russians' stance. American foreign policy had arrived at a crossroads.

On 30 January 1950, Truman had authorized the State and Defense Departments 'to make an over-all review and re-assessment of American foreign and defense policy in the light of the loss of China, the Soviet mastery of atomic energy and the prospect of the fusion bomb'. Through February, March, and early April, as events whirled around it, a State-Defense committee met. By 12 April it had a report ready, which Truman sent to the National Security Council. It came back as an N.S.C. paper, number 68; it was, as Walter LaFeber says, 'one of the key historical documents of the Cold War'. N.S.C. 68, Senator Henry Jackson declared, was 'the first comprehensive statement of a national strategy'.

N.S.C. 68 began by listing the four alternatives of American policy as: (1) continuation of the present course of action without strengthening American capabilities or reducing American commitments; (2) preventive war; (3) withdrawal to the western hemisphere, a Fortress America policy; and (4) the development of free-world military capabilities. In the light of the Russian bomb, the communist victory in China, and McCarthy, the first was not a viable alternative; the second was probably beyond American capacities and in any case would have meant the sacrifice of West Europe to the Red Army; the third had no appeal whatsoever to the leading figures in the administration. The fourth alternative was the only logical choice.

As one of the principal authors stated, N.S.C. 68 advocated 'an immediate and large-scale build-up in our military and general strength and that of our allies with the intention of righting the power balance and in the hope that through means other than all-out war we could induce a change in the nature of the Soviet system'. The statement became the basis for American foreign policy over the next twenty years. How the change was to be brought about was unclear, except that it would not be through war. N.S.C. 68 postulated that while the West waited for the Soviets to mellow, the United States should rearm and thereby prevent any Russian expansion. The program did not look to the liberation of China or of Eastern Europe, but it did call on the United States to assume unilaterally the defense of the non-communist world.

N.S.C. 68 represented the practical extension of the Truman Doctrine, which had been world-wide in its implications but limited to Europe in its application. The document provided the justification for America's assuming the role of world policeman. It did so on the basis of an analysis of the Soviet Union shared by the top officials in State, Defense, and the N.S.C., which held that the Soviets were dedicated not only to preserving their own power and ideology but to extending and consolidating power by absorbing new satellites and weakening any 'competing system of power'. Implicit in the analysis was the idea that whenever the West lost a position of strength, whether it be a military base or a colony undergoing a war of national liberation, the Kremlin or the Chinese communists, or both, were behind it. This came close to saying that all change was directed by the communists and should be resisted. The analysis also assumed that if America were willing to try, it could stop change. This was satisfying to the McCarthyites, but the willingness to abandon East Europe, China, and Russia to communism was not. The McCarthyites, however, had no very clear idea on how to liberate the enslaved peoples either.

If the assumptions of N.S.C. 68 were granted, it seemed to be a rational statement of international goals. A re-armed America would turn back the communists whenever and wherever they tried to thrust outward. The concept of unlimited American power guided policy makers through the fifties and sixties; it was called into serious question only with American failures in South Vietnam. The concept of an international communist conspiracy directing all social and political change in the world always had its critics, especially in the American intellectual and liberal communities, but even at the height of the Vietnamese struggle the Secretary of State could maintain that the historic, complex civil war raging there was the result of Communist China's machinations. And not even bloodshed along the Russo-Chinese frontier could convince some Americans that the monolithic communist bloc was a thing of the past. At the beginning of the seventies, millions of Americans still accepted the basic assumptions of N.S.C. 68.

N.S.C. 68 was realistic in assessing what it would cost America to become the world policeman. The Joint Chiefs' representative on the State-Defense committee that drew up the program had come to the meetings believing that the most money that could be gotten from Congress was around $17 billion a year. He quickly learned that the State representatives were thinking in much bigger terms, and he adjusted. In the end, although N.S.C. 68 did not include any specific figures, the State Department officials estimated that defense expenditures of $35 billion a year would be required to implement the program of rearming America and N.A.T.O. Eventually, more could be spent, for N.S.C. 68 declared that the United States was so rich it could use 20 per cent of its gross national product for arms without suffering national bankruptcy. In 1950, this would have been $50 billion.

That was a great deal of money, even for Americans. It was necessary, however, because the danger was so great. The document foresaw 'an indefinite period of tension and danger' and warned that by 1954 the Soviet Union would have the nuclear capability to destroy the United States. America had to undertake 'a bold and massive program' of rebuilding the West until it far surpassed the Soviet bloc;

only thus could it stand at the 'political and material center with other free nations in variable orbits around it'. The United States could no longer ask, 'How much security can we afford?' nor should it attempt to 'distinguish between national and global security'.

Truman recognized, as he later wrote, the N.S.C. 68 'meant a great military effort in time of peace. It meant doubling or tripling the budget, increasing taxes heavily, and imposing various kinds of economic controls. It meant a great change in our normal peacetime way of doing things.' He refused to allow publication of N.S.C. 68 and indicated that he would do nothing about revising the budget until after the Congressional elections. He realized that without a major crisis there was little chance of selling the program to the Congress or the public. He himself had only two and a half years to serve, while N.S.C. 68 contemplated a long-term program. If the Republicans entered the White House, the chances were that their main concern would be to lower the budget, in which case the nation would have to wait for the return of the Democrats to really get N.S.C. 68 rolling. Thus when Truman received N.S.C. 68 in its final form in early June 1950 he made no commitment. What he would have done with it had not other events intruded is problematical.

While Truman was studying the paper, he may have noted a sentence that declared it should be American policy to meet 'each fresh challenge promptly and unequivocally'. If so, he was about to have an opportunity to put it into practice. The crisis that would allow him to implement N.S.C. 68 was at hand.

TRUMAN had pried the money for containment in Europe from a reluctant Congress only with the help of the crisis created by the British withdrawal from Greece and the fall of Czechoslovakia. In June 1950, he desperately needed another crisis, one that would allow him to prove to the American people that he and the Democratic party were not soft on communism, to extend containment to Asia, to shore up Chiang's position on Formosa, to retain American bases in Japan, and most of all to rearm America and N.A.T.O. The whole package envisioned in N.S.C. 68, in short, could be wrapped up and tied with a ribbon by an Asian crisis.

The possibilities were there. In China, Mao's armies were being deployed for an assault on Formosa, where the remnants of Chiang's forces had retreated. The United States had stopped all aid to Chiang, thereby arousing the fury of the Republican Asia-firsters. Truman was under intense pressure to resume the shipment of supplies to the Nationalist Chinese. Former President Herbert Hoover joined with Senator Taft in demanding that the U.S. Pacific Fleet be used to prevent an invasion of Formosa. Others wanted to use the fleet to carry Chiang's forces back to the mainland for the reconquest of China.

A critical moment was at hand, for if the Chinese communists drove Chiang off Formosa they would complete their victory. Eventually, the United States would have to recognize the communist leaders as the legitimate rulers of China, which would mean giving Chiang's seat on the U.N. Security Council to Mao. America would no longer be able to regard Chiang as head of a government in exile or maintain the fiction that he would someday return to his rightful place. This in turn would require a new definition of the economic and political relations between China and America.

Since late 1949 Truman had consistently refused to pro-vide aid to Chiang, who had proved to be a poor invest-ment at best. The President insisted – rather late in the game – that the United States would not be drawn into the Chinese Civil War. This policy was consistent with the European orientation of his administration and, in terms of the money Congress had made available for foreign aid, realistic. Its only possible outcome, however, was an end to Chiang's pretensions and an American acceptance of the Chinese communists among the family of nations. The domestic political results for the Democrats of such a course of events were frightening to contemplate. If Truman wished to quiet the McCarthyites at all, he would have to rethink his China policy.

In Japan, too, changes were necessary. The United States was preparing to write a unilateral peace treaty with Japan, complete with agreements that would give the United States military bases in Japan on a long-term basis. It was quickly apparent that all would not go smoothly, however, as in early 1950 the Japanese Communist Party staged a series of violent demonstrations against American military personnel in Tokyo. Even moderate Japanese politicians were wary of granting base rights to the American forces. They wanted their independence returned, but without strings. The U.S. Air Force was confronted with the possibility of losing its closest airfields to eastern Russia.

In Korea, all was tension. Post-war Soviet-American efforts to unify the country, where American troops had occupied the area south of the 38th parallel, Russia the area to the north, had achieved nothing. In 1947 the United States had submitted the Korean question to the U.N. General Assembly for disposition. Russia, fearful of the implications, had refused to go along. The Soviets reasoned that if the question of Korea could be given to the General Assembly, where the United States controlled a majority, nothing would prevent the Americans from giving the problem of Germany to the Assembly too. The Soviets therefore refused to allow the U.N. Temporary Commission on Korea to enter North Korea. Elections were held in South Korea in May 1948; Syngman Rhee became President of the Republic of Korea. The Russians set up a government in North Korea. Both the United States and the Soviets withdrew their occupation troops; both continued to give military aid to their respective zones, although the Russians did so on a somewhat larger scale.

Rhee was a petty dictator and an embarrassment to the United States. In January 1950 Dr Philip C. Jessup, U.S. Ambassador-at-large, told the Korean National Assembly that the United States was dissatisfied with the severe restraints on civil liberties which it had imposed. In April, Acheson told Rhee flatly that he either had to hold previously scheduled but consistently delayed elections or lose American aid. Rhee gave in, although on the eve of the elections he arrested thirty of his leading opponents in anti-communist raids. Still his party collected only 48 seats, with 120 going to other parties, mostly on the left. The new Assembly immediately began to move for unification on North Korea's terms. Rhee was faced with the total loss of his position.

Like his close friend and stronger supporter, Chiang Kai-shek, Rhee's position was tenuous because he was losing American backing. On 2 May 1950, Senator Tom Connally, Chairman of the Senate Foreign Relations Committee, said he was afraid that South Korea would have to be abandoned. He thought the communists were going to overrun Korea when they got ready, just as they 'probably will over-run Formosa'. Connally said that he did not think Korea was 'very greatly important. It has been testified before us that Japan, Okinawa, and the Philippines make the chain of defense which is absolutely necessary.' His statement was widely reported in the United States and Japan, causing consternation in MacArthur's headquarters in Tokyo and Rhee's capital in Seoul. Connally's position was consistent with the entire policy of the Truman administration to date, but it ran counter to the thoughts just then being set down in N.S.C. 68 and, with the concurrent rise of McCarthyism, the abandonment of Rhee and Chiang was rapidly becoming a political liability of the first magnitude.

By June 1950, a series of desperate needs had come together. Truman had to have a crisis to sell the N.S.C. 68 program; Chiang could not hold on in Formosa nor Rhee in South Korea without an American commitment; the U.S. Air Force and Navy needed a justification to retain their bases in Japan; the Democrats had to prove to the McCarthyites that they could stand up to the communists in Asia as well as in Europe. The needs were met on 25 June 1950. North Korean troops crossed the 38th parallel in force and quickly sent the South Koreans running.

MacArthur's headquarters in Tokyo later claimed it was as 'astonished as if the sun had suddenly gone out', which was certainly not true. The Americans in Tokyo, like those in Washington, had a good general idea of what was coming and had their countermeasures prepared. Intelligence reports on North Korean intentions had been specific enough to allow the State Department, days before the attack, to prepare a resolution to submit to the Security Council condemning North Korea for aggression. At the time, the Russians were boycotting the United Nations for its refusal to seat Red China. State was prepared to take its resolution to the General Assembly if the Russians came back to the Security Council and exercised their veto. Truman, too, was ready with his countermeasures. Within hours of the attack he ordered MacArthur to dispatch supplies to the South Koreans, then ordered the U.S. Seventh Fleet to sail between China and Formosa to prevent an invasion. He also promised additional assistance to counter-revolutionary forces in the Philippines and Indochina.

These were sweeping policy decisions, hardly the kind that would be made without deliberation. Using the Seventh Fleet to protect Formosa constituted a complete reversal of policy with respect to the Chinese Civil War, with enormous long-term implications. Having MacArthur ship supplies to Rhee's troops carried with it the implication that the United States would defend South Korea, an implication borne out by the State Department resolution for the United Nations. Among other things, the decision carried with it the possibility of the introduction of American troops into the battle, for it was already doubtful that the South Koreans would be able to hold out unaided. At least since 1941 America had pursued a policy of avoiding involvement in ground wars on mainland Asia, but now it prepared to do so. In addition, if American troops were needed, this would require rearmament within the United States.

N.S.C. 68 had declared that the United States must be prepared to meet 'each fresh challenge promptly and unequivocally'. It would have been difficult to better Truman's record in the forty-eight hours following the North Korean invasion. For a man who had been surprised, he recovered with amazing speed.

The fact that the Korean conflict, initially, brought so many benefits to Truman, Chiang, and Rhee has led some historians and journalists to charge that Rhee started the war with covert support from America and Chiang. D.F. Fleming and I.F. Stone have pointed out that the North Koreans had everything to gain by waiting, while Rhee had everything to lose, since the new South Korean Assembly would be pushing for unification. They add that if the Russians sponsored the invasion they surely picked an odd time to do it, since their absence at the United Nations made it impossible for them to block action there.

While the circumstantial evidence is strong, these charges go too far. The North Korean offensive was too strong, too well co-ordinated, and too successful to be a counter-attack, as

Fleming and Sone suggest. It was true that Rhee had talked of reunifying Korea by force under his leadership; for that very reason, and as a part of the over-all policy, the Americans had refused to give him tanks or other offensive weapons. The North Koreans decided they could overrun the Peninsula before the Americans could reinforce the South Koreans – an assessment that was not far wrong – and they moved. They may even have expected the United States to stay out of the conflict altogether, for Acheson had preceded Senator Connally in publicly declaring that Korea was outside the American defense perimeter. The probability is that the Russians did not know the North Koreans were going to attack and in many ways the United States was better prepared to respond than the Russians were. What is true in the Fleming–Stone charges is that the United States knew the invasion was coming.

On 25 June, the day the attack began, the United States launched a massive diplomatic counter-attack. In the Security Council, they pushed through a resolution branding the North Koreans as aggressors, demanding a cessation of hostilities, and requesting a withdrawal behind the 38th parallel. The resolution was a brilliant stroke, for without any investigation at all it established war guilt and put the United Nations behind the official American version. Its sweeping nature tended to commit the United Nations in advance to any step the United States might wish to take in Korea and, with the help of latter resolutions, it gave the United States the benefit of United Nations' cover for military action in Korea.

Within twenty-four hours Truman began to indicate what the extent of that action would be. In a statement released at noon from the White House, he formally extended the Truman Doctrine to the Pacific by pledging the United States to military intervention against any further expansion of communist rule in Asia. He announced that he was extending military aid to the French, who were trying to put down a nationalist uprising in Indochina, and to the

Philippines, where the Huks continued to challenge the government. The decision to aid the French in Indochina, incidentally, was not a casual one – America had already been giving some aid, and Truman merely stepped it up. In the excitement of Korea, however, the American pledge to support the French in their struggle against Ho Chi Minh and his Vietminh was little noticed. Truman also ordered the Seventh Fleet to 'prevent any attack on Formosa', declaring that the determination of the island's future status 'must await the restoration of security in the Pacific, a peace settlement with Japan, or consideration by the United Nations'. America had thus become involved in the Chinese Civil War, the Philippines insurrection, and the conflict in Indochina.

At the same time the United States entered the Korean War. Truman announced that he had 'ordered United States air and sea forces to give the Korean Government troop cover and support'. His Air Force advisers had, apparently, convinced him that America's big bombers would be able to stop the aggression in Korea by destroying the communist supply lines. Truman may have believed that it was possible to defeat the North Koreans without any commitment of American ground troops, just as he evidently expected that the French could defeat Ho Chi Minh without having to use American soldiers.

Truman tried to limit the sweeping nature of his actions. The Seventh Fleet would not only resist a Chinese invasion of Formosa but would also be used to prevent Chiang from continuing his air and sea operations against the mainland. By implication, then, the United States would protect Chiang on Formosa but would not help him return to China proper. More important, Truman was careful to refrain from linking the Russians to the Korean attack. On the day of his White House announcement, Truman sent a note to Moscow assuring Stalin that American objectives were limited and expressing the hope that the Soviets would help in restoring the *status quo ante bellum*. This implied that all the United States wished to do was to contain, not destroy, North Korea. The implication was underscored by an American resolution in the Security Council introduced and passed on the same day, 27 June, which recommended to the members of the United Nations that they aid South Korea in restoring peace.

The underlying assumption of Truman's approach to the war was that communist aggression in Asia could be stopped at a fairly low cost in lives. American money and equipment would do the job in Indochina and the Philippines; the American navy would save Chiang, American bombers would force the North Koreans to pull back. Much of this was wishful thinking. It was based on the American Air Force's strategic doctrine and its misreading of the lessons of air power in World War II, on the racist attitude that Asians could not stand up to Western weapons and methods, and on the widespread notion that communist governments had no genuine support. Lacking popularity, the communists would be afraid to commit their troops to battle.

The question of who would fight and who would not was quickly answered. In the process Truman's assumptions about Asians and communists were badly battered, although he himself never abandoned them. The North Koreans drove the South Koreans in a headlong retreat. American bombing missions slowed the aggressors not at all. The South Koreans fell back so rapidly that two days after Truman sent in the Air Force he was faced with another major decision. He would either have to send in American troops to save the position, which meant accepting a much higher cost for the war than he had bargained for, or face the loss of all Korea. Holding a position on the Peninsula would be difficult, but getting back without a bridgehead would be almost impossible.

On 30 June Truman ordered United States troops stationed in Japan to proceed to Korea. He promised that more would soon be on their way from the United States. In an attempt to keep the war and its cost limited, he emphasized that the United States aimed only 'to restore peace and . . . the border'. At the United Nations, the Americans announced that their purpose was the simple one of restoring the 38th parallel as the dividing line. The policy, in other words, was containment, not roll-back.

It had been arrived at unilaterally, for Truman had not consulted his European or Asian allies before acting. The unilateral nature of American actions in response to the world crisis was always clear, despite heavy-handed propaganda attempts to define the action as 'collective security'. The United States rammed its resolutions through the United Nations without discussion or investigation. Under the terms of the 27 June resolution, the United States established a military command that took orders from Washington, not the United Nations. Although MacArthur delighted in calling himself the United Nations Commander, and although sixteen nations did make small contributions to the United Nations forces, MacArthur reported to and took his orders from the Joint Chiefs. 'Even the reports which were normally made by me to the United Nations were subject to censorship by our State and Defense Departments,' he later declared. 'I had no direct connection with the United Nations whatsoever.'

So the United States undertook to stop the communists, wherever and whenever they appeared. In Korea, after the dark days of late June and early July, the program began to work. American and South Korean troops held on in the Pusan bridgehead. By the beginning of August it was clear that MacArthur would not be forced out of Korea and that the North Koreans would receive no help from the Chinese or the Russians (one or two extra divisions in July would have pushed MacArthur into the sea). The American build-up around Pusan was reaching impressive proportions and it was obvious that when MacArthur's troops broke out of the perimeter they would be able to destroy the North Koreans.

In Washington, there was a surge of optimism. Perhaps

it was possible to do more than contain the communists. MacArthur wanted to reunify Korea, an idea that found great favor in the White House. It would mean roll-back, not containment, and thus represented a major policy change, but the opportunity was too tempting to pass up, especially since the Chinese and Russian failure to enter the war at the decisive moment indicated that they would not come in later. On 17 August Warren Austin, the American delegate to the United Nations, hinted at the new policy. Speaking in the Security Council, he remarked that 'the United Nations must see that the people of Korea attain complete individual and political freedom. . . . Shall only a part of the country be assured of this freedom? I think not.' Thus did the United Nations membership learn that its commitment to defend South Korea had been extended. On 1 September, Truman put the seal on the policy when he announced that the Koreans had a right to be 'free, independent, and united'. The Americans were replaying World War II, when they had liberated the capitals of Western Europe. Pyongyang, the Americans boasted, would be 'the first Iron Curtain capital' to be liberated. This seemed to mean that others would follow.

The risks were obvious. Truman moved to minimize them by building up American strength. Congress had voted all the funds he had requested for defense since June; on 9 September the President announced that the rapid increase in the Army would continue and that he would send 'substantial' numbers of new troops to Europe. Simultaneously, Acheson met with the British and French foreign ministers at the Waldorf-Astoria Hotel in New York City. On 12 September he dropped, as one official called it, 'the bomb at the Waldorf'. The United States proposed to create ten German divisions. French and British protests were loud and numerous, and various compromises on control were necessary, but Acheson insisted. To make German rearmament on such a scale palatable to the Europeans, the United States sent four divisions to Europe and three months later,

Truman appointed Eisenhower, who was popular in Europe, as the supreme commander of an integrated European force.

With the French and British taken care of, German rearmament under way, and Congress willing to vote funds for defense, the Truman–Acheson foreign policy was rolling. On 15 September MacArthur put the frosting on the cake by successfully outflanking the North Koreans with an amphibious landing at Inchon, far up the Korean peninsula. In a little more than a week, MacArthur's troops were in the capital, Seoul, and they had cut off the bulk of the North Korean forces around Pusan. On 27 September the Joint Chiefs ordered MacArthur to destroy the enemy army and authorized him to conduct military operations north of the 38th parallel. On 7 October American troops crossed the parallel. The same day the United Nations approved (47 to 5) an American resolution endorsing the action.

The optimism in Washington had led the administration to go beyond containment. All eyes now turned to China and Russia. How would they react to the loss of a satellite? Truman and Acheson had assumed they would not interfere, but even if they did, the J.C.S. told MacArthur to go ahead as long as 'in your judgement, action by forces now under your control offers a reasonable chance of success'. This broad authority, it is important to note, came after full discussion and consideration in the highest levels of the American government. Truman later implied, and millions believed, that MacArthur had gone ahead on his own, that it was the general in the field, not the government at home, that had changed the political objective of the war in the middle of the conflict. Such was never the case. Truman, with the full concurrence of the State and Defense Departments and the Joint Chiefs, made the decision to liberate North Korea and accept the risks involved.

The Chinese did not co-operate. They issued a series of warnings, culminating with a statement to India for transmission to the United States, that China would not 'sit back with folded hands and let the Americans come to the border'. When even this was discounted, the Chinese publicly stated on 10 October that if the Americans continued north, they would enter the conflict. The Russians were more cautious, but when on 9 October some American jet aircraft strafed a Soviet airfield only a few miles from Vladivostok, they sent a strong protest to Washington. Truman immediately decided to fly to the Pacific to see MacArthur and make sure he restrained the Air Force. Fighting Chinese forces in Korea was one thing, war with Russia another. The Americans were willing to try to liberate Pyongyang, but they were not ready to liberate Moscow.

The Truman–MacArthur meeting at Wake Island in October accomplished its main purpose, for the Air Force thereafter confined its activities to the Korean peninsula. More important was what it revealed. Commentators have concentrated almost exclusively on two aspects – MacArthur's desire to broaden the area in which his forces could operate, and the General's statement that the Chinese would not come into the war, or, if they did, there would be the greatest slaughter. On the second point everybody, not just MacArthur, was wrong.* On the first, the differences between Truman and MacArthur were more those of method than of goals. MacArthur was excessively dramatic in the way he put things and he had a milliennial quality about him, but like Truman his immediate aim was to liberate North Korea. At various times he indicated that he also wanted to help Chiang back onto the mainland, a long-range goal that Truman had not accepted as realistic, but for the immediate future the General and the President were together. They differed on means. MacArthur was not at all sure he could unify Korea without striking at the Chinese bases across the Yalu. Truman, more concerned

* At the MacArthur Hearings, Senator Brien McMahon complained that 'everybody that had to do with it turned out to be wrong', when he learned that all agencies of the government thought Chinese intervention improbable. Senator Saltonstall asked Acheson, 'They really fooled us when it comes right down to it, didn't they?' Acheson replied, 'Yes, sir.'

about Europe and the dangers there, especially since neither the German nor the American rearmament programs were yet well under way, insisted on keeping limits on the area of military operations.

Even this difference, however, was not made clear at Wake Island, for the Chinese had not been seen nor were they expected in Korea. MacArthur flew back to Tokyo to direct the last offensive. By 25 October his forces reached the Yalu at Chosan. That day, Chinese 'volunteers' struck South Korean and American troops around the Chosin Reservoir. After hard fighting, MacArthur's units fell back. The Chinese then retired. They had, by their actions, transmitted two messages: (1) they would never allow MacArthur's forces to proceed unmolested to the Yalu or to take valuable industrial sites in the northern quarter of the Korean peninsula, and (2) their main concern continued to be Formosa, and like Truman they wanted to limit the fighting in Korea. The second message was reinforced by Peking's acceptance of an invitation to come to the United Nations to discuss the Formosa situation and, hopefully, the Korean War.

Truman and Acheson, like their more bombastic commander in the field, were not ready to accept a negotiated peace. They discounted the Chinese intervention, continued to dream of liberating North Korea, and had no intention of abandoning the recent commitment to Chiang's defense. A negotiated settlement with the Chinese would bring the wrath of the Republicans on their heads, and Congressional elections were only a few days away. Most important, the rearmament program was just getting under way. If peace came, there would be no N.S.C. 68 and American foreign policy would be back where it was before the Korean War – much bluster and little muscle.

The Chinese delegates were scheduled to arrive at the United Nations on 15 November. A week earlier, an Air Force spokesman in Washington announced that 'an earlier ban against flights within three miles of Manchuria' had been lifted and United States planes in Korea 'are operating right up to the Chinese border along the Yalu River'. Simultaneously, 79 B-29s and 300 fighter planes attacked Sinuiju, on the Korean side of the Yalu. The pilots claimed that the 630 tons of bombs and 85,000 incendiaries they used destroyed 90 per cent of the city. The lull in the fighting was over.

MacArthur planned to launch another ground offensive on 15 November, which would have coincided with the announced date of arrival of the Chinese delegates at the United Nations. The delegates, however, were delayed. On 11 November MacArthur learned of the delay, and later that the Chinese delegation would arrive at the United Nations on 24 November. For unexplained reasons, MacArthur put off his offensive, finally beginning it on the morning of 24 November. The headlines that greeted the Chinese delegates when they arrived at the United Nations declared that MacArthur promised to have the boys 'home by Christmas', after they had all had a good look at the Yalu. The Americans were once again marching to the border, this time in greater force.

Europeans were incensed. So, in the end, was Truman, although for different reasons. The French government charged that MacArthur had 'launched his offensive at this time to wreck the negotiations . . .' and the British *New Statesman* declared that MacArthur had 'acted in defiance of all common sense, and in such a way as to provoke the most peace-loving nation'. It need hardly be added that the Chinese delegation at the United Nations soon packed its bags and returned to Peking, taking with it only what it had brought plus some additional bitterness.

The failure of the negotiations did not upset Truman, but the failure of the offensive did. MacArthur had advanced on two widely separated routes, with his middle wide-open. How he could have done so, given the earlier Chinese intervention, remains a mystery to military analysts. The Chinese poured into the gap and soon sent MacArthur's men fleeing for their lives. In two weeks the Chinese cleared much of North Korea, isolated MacArthur's units into three bridgeheads, and completely reversed the military situation.

The Americans, who had walked into the disaster together, split badly on the question of how to get out. MacArthur said he now faced 'an entirely new war' and indicated that the only solution was to strike at China, which meant – among other things – that MacArthur believed the Chinese had acted on their own, for he did not mention the Soviets. This assumption was not accepted in Washington. As Ambassador Austin put it at the United Nations, there was 'only one conclusion [that] can be drawn from the action of the Peiping regime; it has acted against the interests of the Chinese people and on behalf of Russian colonial policy in Asia'. If that were true, going to war against China meant going to war against Russia, and neither West Europe nor the United States were ready for that. The thing to do now, the administration decided, was to return to the pre-Inchon policy of restoring the *status quo ante bellum* in Korea while building N.A.T.O. strength in Europe. All talk of liberating Iron Curtain capitals disappeared. Never again would the United States attempt by force of arms to free a communist satellite.

The lesson had been learned, but not fully accepted as yet, and it was enormously frustrating. Just how frustrating became clear on 30 November, when at a press conference Truman called for a world-wide mobilization against communism and in response to a question declared that if military action against China was authorized by the United Nations, MacArthur might be empowered to use the atomic bomb at his discretion. Truman casually added that there had always been active consideration of the bomb's use, for after all it was one of America's military weapons.

Prime Minister Attlee, after a conference with Churchill and a debate in the Commons, flew right over to Washington. He brought with him a set of questions that, taken together, constituted an examination of the basic assumptions of the

Truman-Acheson policies. In a series of meetings in early December, Attlee hammered away at the Americans. There was much talk in Washington (and Tokyo) of pulling out of Korea altogether. Attlee feared that if this were done the humiliation of defeat would lead the Americans to all-out war with China. He suspected that such a development was exactly what MacArthur wanted. Truman, Acheson, Bradley, and the newly appointed Secretary of Defense, General Marshall, all assured Attlee that every effort would be made to stay in Korea and promised that as long as MacArthur held on there would be no atomic bombs dropped.

Somewhat reassured, Attlee urged the Americans to negotiate with the Chinese. Acheson patiently explained why that could not be done. The Chinese would 'ask for recognition of their government, for a seat in the United Nations Security Council, and for concessions on Formosa. They might even insist that any Japanese peace settlement had to have their assent.' It seemed perfectly obvious to Acheson that such demands, if met, would spell disaster for the free world; six months earlier, however, the policy of the American government had been, supposedly, one of regularizing relations with China, which Acheson had then realized included recognition, an end to Chiang Kai-shek, and a Chinese seat in the Security Council.

Attlee was not sufficiently impressed by Acheson's list of the evils that would flow from negotiations, so Truman entered the discussion to remind the Prime Minister that 'the problem we were facing was part of a pattern. After Korea, it would be Indochina, then Hong Kong, then Malaya.' The possible loss of British colonies did not convince Attlee either, but it was time for dinner and the first meeting broke up.

The next day Attlee began the discussion by remarking that as he understood it Acheson's policy was to continue to fight in Korea and to refuse to negotiate. This, he said, was sterile. It would result in either an all-out war with Chin

or, eventually, in negotiations. Why not enter negotiations now? The basic difference in outlook then began to emerge. Attlee said that China was not a Russian satellite, that it was ripe for 'Titoism', and that the West ought to aim to divide the Russians and the Chinese, not force them together. 'If we just treat the Chinese as Soviet satellites,' he said, 'we are playing the Russian game.'

The world-view from London was obviously different than that from Washington. With the discussion now revolving around basic issues, Acheson undertook to convince the Prime Minister of the necessity for current American policy. First Acheson explained that it was not possible 'for any administration to offer to the American people a foreign policy' which was isolationist in the Pacific and interventionist in Europe. This was what Truman and Acheson had learned since 1948 – they could not get tough with the communists in Europe without getting tough with the communists in Asia.

Next, the Secretary of State threatened. If America accepted the Chinese aggression in Korea and negotiated, he said, 'it could not fail to affect our entire thinking about aggression – and not only in Asia but also in Europe'. If America abandoned Chiang and Rhee, Attlee had to understand, she would also abandon N.A.T.O.

The performance failed to move Attlee. He tried to convince the Americans that they could not go on forever making unilateral decisions and fighting the communists wherever they appeared. He urged them to hold the United Nations together and to adopt a policy of making friends in Asia by pursuing positive goals rather than blustering their way with troops right up to the Chinese border. Attlee said that nothing could be more dangerous than for the Asians to split away from the West.

America could not go it alone, in Attlee's view, nor could she make friends in Asia by supporting reactionary governments like Rhee's and Chiang's and adopting a stance of permanent hostility towards the greatest of all the Asian

nations. The Americans would not agree. Their sense of power was so great, their conceit that the people of Asia yearned to follow the American lead and were only led astray by evil rulers was so overwhelming, that they did believe they could go it alone. Two decades of American foreign policy in Asia was summed up in Acheson's rejoinder to Attlee's remark that nothing could be more dangerous than for the Asians to split away from the West. 'Weakening the United States,' Acheson said, 'would be definitely more dangerous.'

Attlee was beginning to understand, although not accept, the American position. He told Truman he appreciated the political problems that Chiang raised, but he hoped Truman would remember that 'whatever we did would have to be done through the United Nations, and it could not be done there by the efforts and votes of just the United States and the United Kingdom, important as we are'.

Attlee still missed the key point. Truman and Acheson believed that the United States and the United Kingdom were important enough; indeed, they believed that the United States alone was important enough, especially since, as Truman put it the next day, the Chinese people would soon realize that their real friends were in Washington, not Moscow. 'You won't bring them to that realization,' Attlee responded without smiling, 'if you keep fighting them.' The next day he returned to London.

Attlee had accomplished something, for Truman stopped talking about the atomic bomb in his press conferences and the Americans agreed to stay in Korea if at all possible. But in the end Attlee's mission was a failure. He had forced the Americans to justify their policy but he had been unable to persuade them to abandon it or their assumptions.

With Attlee's departure, Truman and Acheson quickened the pace of their policy. They accomplished so much that by the end of January 1951 only the most extreme McCarthy-ite could complain that they were ignoring the communist threat. Truman put the nation on a Cold War footing. He got emergency powers from Congress to expedite war mobilization, made selective service a permanent feature of American life, submitted a $50 billion defense budget that followed the guidelines of N.S.C. 68, sent two more divisions (a total of six) to Europe, doubled the number of air groups to 95, obtained new bases in Morocco, Libya, and Saudi Arabia, increased the Army by 50 per cent to 3.5 million men, pushed forward the Japanese peace treaty, stepped up aid to the French in Indochina, initiated the process of adding Greece and Turkey to N.A.T.O., and began discussions with Franco which led to American aid to Fascist Spain in return for military bases there.

Truman's accomplishments were breath-taking. He had given the United States a thermonuclear bomb (March 1951), and rearmed Germany. He pushed through a peace treaty with Japan (signed in September 1951) that excluded the Russians and gave the Americans military bases, allowed for Japanese rearmament and unlimited industrialization, and encouraged a Japanese boom by dismissing British, Australian, Chinese, and other demands for reparations. Truman extended American bases around the world, hemming in both Russia and China. He had learned, in November of 1950, not to push beyond the Iron and Bamboo Curtains, but he had made sure that if any communist showed his head on the free side of the line, someone – usually an American – would be there to shoot him.

There had to be a price. It was best summed up by Walter Millis, himself a Cold Warrior and a great admirer of Forrestal. The Truman administration, Millis wrote, left behind it 'an enormously expanded military establishment, beyond anything we had ever contemplated in time of peace . . . . It evoked a huge and apparently permanent armament industry, now wholly dependent . . . on government contracts. The Department of Defense had become without question the biggest industrial management operation in the world, the great private operations, like General Motors, du Pont, the leading airplane manufacturers . . .

had assumed positions of monopoly power which, however unavoidable, at least seemed to raise new questions as to the legal and constitutional organization of the state.' The administration produced thermonuclear supergiant weapons, families of lesser atomic bombs, guided missiles, the B-52 jet bomber, new super carriers and tanks and other heavy weapons. It had increased the risk of war while making war immeasurably more dangerous.

One other thing bothered Millis. For all that the Truman administration accomplished, 'what it failed to do was to combine these men and weapons into a practicable structure of military policy competent to meet the new political and military problems that now stood grimly before us. We were to face them in a large measure of bewilderment as to where the true paths of military policy might lead.'

Millis might have added that the bewilderment extended to foreign policy, as there was no way to split sharply the activities of the soldiers and the diplomats. Truman gave America power and a policy but it seemed to many that with all the power he had generated, and the justification he had given for the policy, the policy itself was much too modest. Containment had never been very satisfying emotionally, built as it was on the constant reiteration of the communist threat and the propaganda line that divided the world into areas that were free and those that were slave. Millions of Americans wanted to accept their Christian obligation and free the slaves. Others wanted to destroy, not just contain, the communist threat, for if it were allowed to exist the Cold War would go on forever, at a constantly increased cost. There were those who felt that the only justification for a garrison state was the old one of putting it on a temporary basis, which was to say, to fight a war to destroy the threat.

This criticism of the Truman-Acheson policy, which centered around the towering figure of MacArthur, turned Attlee's criticism on its head. The Prime Minister had warned the Americans that they could not do it all alone, not forever anyway. He said they would either have to fight all-out or negotiate, and he urged them to negotiate. MacArthur wanted to fight all-out. American liberals and self-styled realists derided MacArthur and his followers for the simplicity of their views, but the liberals' views were built on the shaky foundation of a series of simple-minded assumptions about the nature of the world. In addition, there was no denying MacArthur's appeal or the frustration built into the containment program, an appeal and a frustration based on Truman's and Acheson's own descriptions of the world scene.

If America made permanent Cold War its policy, with a commitment to continuous military superiority to back an attitude of unrelenting hostility toward China and Russia, without ever doing anything to destroy the communist nations, it would be accepting permanent tension, permanent risk, and a permanent postponement of the social and economic promises of the New and Fair Deals. In a halting but devastating manner, the Republicans were in effect proclaiming that America could not have guns and butter (although their butter would have been lower taxes for the rich and middle class, not social programs). Truman and Acheson mistakenly thought America could have both.

The difference in outlook soon erupted into one of the great emotional events of American history. In January and February 1951 MacArthur resumed the offensive and drove the Chinese and North Koreans back. By March he was again at the 38th parallel. The administration, having been burned once, was ready to negotiate, especially since now that the Chinese were retreating they would not be likely to raise embarrassing issues at the peace table. MacArthur sabotaged the efforts to obtain a ceasefire by crossing the parallel and by demanding what amounted to an unconditional surrender from the Chinese. Truman was furious. He decided to remove the General at the first opportunity.

It came shortly. On 5 April Representative Joseph W. Martin, Jr, Republican, read to the House a letter from

MacArthur calling for a new foreign policy. The General wanted to reunify Korea, unleash Chiang for an attack on the mainland, and fight communism in Asia rather than in Europe. 'Here in Asia,' he said, 'is where the communist conspirators have elected to make their play for global conquest . . . . Here we fight Europe's war with arms while the diplomats there still fight it with words.'

General Bradley's response, in the Congressional hearings that followed Truman's dismissal of MacArthur, was that to extend the war to China would be to fight the wrong war at the wrong time in the wrong place against the wrong enemy. The two statements, Bradley's and MacArthur's, were much quoted and set the tone of the controversy. Aside from the problem of a soldier challenging civilian supremacy by trying to set foreign policy, the debate centered on Europe-first versus Asia-first. This, however, was not the root question, for the choice of a battleground was simply one of methods, not policies. MacArthur was not challenging only, or even primarily, the Europe-first priority, but rather the doctrine of containment. Initially, he had a large majority of the people with him. He returned to the United States to receive a welcome that would have made Caesar envious. Public opinion polls showed that three out of every four Americans disapproved of the way Truman was conducting the war.

The American people seemed to be rejecting containment, Truman had rejected victory; that left only Attlee's alternative of peace. Even Attlee, however, had wanted peace only in Asia, and as Truman pointed out to him time and again, Congress would not accept a policy of intervention in Europe and isolation in Asia. As it was, Truman was in trouble because he spent most of the money Congress voted for defense on N.A.T.O. at a time when most Americans assumed that the effort was going into Korea. If the Korean War came to a sudden end, so would N.S.C. 68 and the entire program that went with it.

Truman was playing a complicated and delicate game,

and he had reached a dead end of neither war nor peace. New approaches were needed. In May, one was suggested by Assistant Secretary of State Dean Rusk, a favorite with the China lobby, who explained that the United States recognized Chiang because he 'more authentically represents the views of the great body of the people of China'. Rusk promised American help for the Chinese people if they ever tried to throw off the communist 'tyranny'. Visions of a gigantic guerrilla war within China (and some day in East Europe and even Russia itself) danced through Rusk's head. America could air-drop supplies to the freedom-loving peoples. It would be lend-lease all over again.

Walter Lippmann was shocked. He said that if the Rusk policy were to be adopted 'then the Administration has worked itself into a fantastic predicament. It has made the issue with Red China not the repulse of its aggression in Korea but that of its survival. Regimes do not negotiate about their survival . . . . These issues can be settled only by total victory.' This was, indeed, the long-range hope, but it would not be brought about at the price of American lives and it was a policy for the future. American money and arms would suffice to contain communism and eventually the slaves themselves, with American material aid, would overthrow the tyrants. This tied everything together. Rusk's policy made the defensive nature of containment acceptable by saying eventual victory would come while it made eventual victory acceptable by saying that the slaves themselves, not American boys, would die for it.

Meanwhile, it was necessary to keep the small war going until the defensive preparations were complete. This was the meaning of the American rejection of a Soviet offer on 23 June for a pure and simple military armistice in the field. The Russians had omitted the three political conditions on which the Chinese and North Koreans had laid such stress: withdrawal of American troops from Korea, the return of Formosa to China, and the seating of the Peking government in the United Nations. Presumably Russia had the power to enforce what amounted to a surrender on China and North Korea. Certainly Stalin thought so and certainly this fitted in with the American beliefs about the nature of monolithic communism. No one ever found out, for, as I. S. Stone wrote, the American leaders regarded the possibility of peace talks 'as a kind of diabolic plot against rearmament'. Republican leader Thomas Dewey said, 'Every time the Soviets make a peace move, I get scared. . . . Every time Stalin smiles, beware.' Within a week, the Secretary of Defense, the Economic Stabilizer, the Chairman of the Joint Chiefs, the Chief of Naval Operations, the Defense Mobilizer, Averell Harriman, and General Eisenhower had all warned against any letdown in the mobilization effort. On 4 July Truman said that even if the Korean War should end, 'we face a long period of world tension and great international danger.' MacArthur joined the chorus.

The pressure from the United Nations and the N.A.T.O. allies to negotiate could not be totally ignored, however, and on 10 July 1951, peace talks – without a ceasefire – began. They broke down on 12 July. For the remainder of the year they were on again, off again. The front lines began to stabilize around the 38th parallel while American casualties dropped to an 'acceptable' weekly total. The war, and mobilization, continued.

Truman had won. Administration witnesses at the MacArthur hearings (held by the Senate to examine foreign policy and MacArthur's dismissal) argued convincingly that America could neither destroy Russia or China nor allow them to expand. Public opinion swung back to Truman's side. America remained committed to containment and permanent Cold War. MacArthur's alternative of victory, like Attlee's of peace in Asia, had been rejected. America girded for the long haul.

The Cold War would be fought Truman's way. There would be clashes on the periphery but none between the major powers. America would extend her positions of strength around the communist empire and where American soldiers went, American businessmen would follow. The military–industrial complex in the United States would become a major social and economic force, a handy tool to fight economic depression that avoided the dangerous political consequences of New and Fair Deal social programs while offering – seemingly – something for everyone. The United States would make no settlement, no compromise, with China or Russia, nor would she consult her allies on major decisions. America would build up the mightiest armed force the world had ever known and, if necessary, defend the barricades of freedom alone.

When Truman became President he led a nation anxious to return to traditional civil–military relations and the historic American foreign policy of non-involvement. When he left the White House his legacy was an American presence on every continent of the world, an enormously expanded armament industry, American corporations in Europe and Latin America on a scale surpassing Herbert Hoover's wildest dreams, and an end to all but verbal commitment to the one-third of the nation Franklin Roosevelt had characterized as ill-fed, ill-clothed, and ill-housed. Yet so successfully had Truman scared hell out of the American people, the only critics to receive any attention in the mass media were those who thought Truman had not gone far enough in standing up to the communists. For all his troubles, Truman had triumphed.

8

Eisenhower, Dulles, and the
Irreconcilable Conflict

'WE can never rest,' General Eisenhower declared during his 1952 campaign for the Presidency, 'until the enslaved nations of the world have in the fulness of freedom the right to choose their own path, for then, and then only, can we say that there is a possible way of living peacefully and permanently with communism in the world.' Like most campaign statements, Eisenhower's bowed to both sides of the political spectrum. For the bold he indicated a policy · of liberation, while the cautious could take comfort in his willingness to someday live peacefully with the communists. Since the Americans believed, however, that no one would freely choose communism, Eisenhower's statement had a major internal contradiction.

The emphasis, therefore, was on liberation. John Foster Dulles, the Republican expert on foreign policy, author of the Japanese peace treaty, and soon to be Secretary of State, was more explicit than Eisenhower. Containment, he charged, was a treadmill policy 'which, at best might perhaps keep us in the same place until we drop exhausted.' It cost far too much in taxes and loss of civil liberties and was 'not designed to win victory conclusively'. One plank in the Republican platform damned containment as 'negative, futile and immoral', for it abandoned 'countless human beings to a despotism and Godless terrorism'. It hinted that the Republicans, once in power, would roll back the atheistic tide, a hint that Dulles made into a promise when in a campaign speech he said that Eisenhower, as President, would use 'all means to secure the liberation of Eastern Europe'. Rollback would come not only in East Europe but also in Asia. The platform denounced the 'Asia last' policy of the Democrats and said, 'We have no intention to sacrifice the East to gain time for the West.'

The Eisenhower landslide of 1952 was a compound of many factors, the chief being the General's enormous personal popularity. Corruption in the Truman administration, and the McCarthy charges of communist infiltration into the government ('There are no Communists in the Republican Party,' a platform plank began), also helped. So did Eisenhower's promise to go to Korea and end the war there, not through victory but through negotiation. But one of the major appeals of the Eisenhower–Dulles team was its rejection of containment. The Republican pledge to do something about communist enslavement – it was never very clear exactly what – brought millions of former Democratic voters into the Republican fold, especially those of East European descent. Eisenhower reaped where McCarthy sowed. Far from rejecting internationalism and retreating to isolationism, the Republicans were proposing to go beyond containment. They would be more internationalist than Truman.

Republican promises to liberate the enslaved, like nineteenth-century abolitionist programs to free the Negro slaves, logically led to only one policy. Since the slaveholders would not voluntarily let the oppressed go, and since the slaves were too tightly controlled to stage their own revolution, those who wished to see them freed would have to fight. In the second half of the twentieth century, however, war was a much different proposition than it had been a hundred years earlier. Freeing the slaves would lead to the destruction of much of the world; most of the slaves themselves would die in the process.

There was another major constraint on action. The Republicans had accepted some of the New Deal, but essentially they were wedded to conservative fiscal views that stressed the importance of balancing the budget and cutting taxes. All of Eisenhower's leading cabinet figures, save Dulles, were businessmen who believed that an unbalanced federal budget was immoral. Government expenditures could be reduced significantly, however, only by cutting the Defense Department budget, which the Republicans proceeded to do. The cuts made liberation even more difficult.

In practice, then, Eisenhower and Dulles continued the policy of containment. There was no basic difference between their foreign policy and that of Truman and Acheson. Their campaign statements frequently haunted them, but they avoided embarrassment over their lack of action through their rhetoric. 'We can never rest,' Eisenhower had said, but rest they did, except in their speeches, which expressed perfectly the assumptions and desires of millions of Americans.

Better than anyone else, Dulles described the American view of communism. A devout Christian, highly successful corporate lawyer, something of a prig, and absolutely certain of his own and his nation's goodness, Dulles's unshakeable beliefs were based on general American ideas. They differed hardly at all from those of Truman, Acheson, Main Street in Iowa, or Madison Avenue in New York City. All the world wanted to be like America; the common people everywhere looked to America for leadership; communism was unmitigated evil imposed by a conspiracy on helpless people, whether it came from the outside as in East Europe or from the inside as in Asia; there could be no permanent reconciliation with communism for 'this is an irreconcilable conflict'. In January 1953, Dulles told the Senate Foreign Relations Committee that communism 'believes that human beings are nothing more than somewhat superior animals . . . and that the best kind of a world is that world which is organized as a well-managed farm is organized, where certain animals are taken out to pasture, and they are fed and brought back and milked, and they are given a barn as shelter over their heads.' This was somewhat more sophisticated than the way Eisenhower usually described the ideology that had millions of adherents, and far more sophisticated than the description employed by newspaper editors and television commentators, but it accurately summed up the American view of communism.

The Eisenhower administration, like its predecessor, based its policy on the lessons of history, or at least on one lesson, which was that appeasement was a disaster. The verbiage of the thirties helped shape the policies of the fifties. When the Chinese moved to capture tiny islands held by Chiang, for example, and America's N.A.T.O. allies indicated that they did not want to start World War III over such a trifling matter, Eisenhower talked incessantly about Munich and compared the Russian and Chinese leaders to Hitler. He could never understand why the Europeans could not see the threat as clearly as he did.

The Eisenhower–Dulles speeches helped hide the fact that they did nothing about their promise to liberate the enslaved, but perhaps more important to their popularity was their unwillingness to risk American lives, for here too they were expressing the deepest sentiments of their countrymen. On occasion the Republicans rattled the saber and always they filled the air with denunciations of the communists, but they also shut down the Korean War, cut corporate taxes, and reduced the size of the armed forces. Despite intense pressure and great temptation, they entered no wars. They were willing to supply material, on a limited scale, to others so that they could fight the enemy, but they would not commit American boys to the struggle. Like Truman they did their best to contain communism; unlike him they did not use American troops to do so. They were unwilling to make peace but they would not go to war. Their speeches provided emotional satisfaction but their actions failed to liberate a single slave. No one had a right to complain that the Republicans had been misleading, however, for the policy had been clearly spelled out in the campaign. The vague and militant talk about liberation was balanced by specific promises to end the war in Korea – without liberating North Korea, much less China – and balance the budget.

When General Marshall was Secretary of State he had complained that he had no muscle to back up his foreign policy. Truman agreed and did all he could to increase the armed forces. Dulles did not make such complaints. He worked with what was available – which was, to be sure, far more than Marshall had at hand in 1948 – for he shared the Republican commitment to fiscal soundness.

The extent of the commitment was best seen in the New Look, the term Eisenhower coined to describe his military policy. It combined domestic, military, and foreign considerations. The New Look rejected the premiss of N.S.C. 68 that the United States could spend up to 20 per cent of its G.N.P. on arms; it rejected deficit financing; it maintained that enough of N.S.C. 68 had been implemented to provide security for the United States and to support a policy of containment. It came into effect at a time of lessening tension. The Korean War had ended and Stalin's death (March 1953) made the world seem less dangerous. The New Look was based in large part on the success of the N.S.C. 68 program, for the first two years of the New Look were the high-water mark of relative American military strength in the Cold War. As Samuel Huntington has noted, 'The basic military fact of the New Look was the overwhelming American superiority in nuclear weapons and the means of delivering them.' Between 1953 and 1955 the United States could have effectively destroyed the Soviet Union with little likelihood of serious reprisal. The fact that America did not do so indicated the basic restraint of the Eisenhower administration, as opposed to its verbiage.

The New Look became fixed policy during a period of lessened tensions and American military superiority, but it did not depend on either for its continuation. In its eight years of power, the Eisenhower administration went through a series of war scares and it witnessed the development of Soviet long-range bombers, ballistic missiles, and nuclear weapons. Throughout, however, Eisenhower held to the New Look. His Defense Department expenditures remained in the $35 to $40 billion range.

In 1956, when the Soviets had nearly caught up to the American Armed Services, the Eisenhower administration subjected the New Look to careful scrutiny. Three alternatives were examined. Admiral Arthur W. Radford, Chairman of the Joint Chiefs, proposed to continue the existing level of military spending but to maintain a clear superiority in nuclear forces by major cutbacks in conventional strength. He wanted to begin by cutting the Army by nearly a half-million men. The Democrats in Congress went beyond Radford's proposal. They insisted on maintaining conventional strength at current levels while increasing Air Force appropriations by nearly $1 billion. Eisenhower chose a third course. Like Radford, he wanted to stabilize military expenditures; like the Senate Democrats he was opposed to reducing conventional forces. He disagreed with both on the fundamental question – should the United States maintain superiority? Eisenhower's answer was no. For him, and thus for the country, sufficiency was enough. He refused either to reduce the Army or to increase the Air Force. In fact, America retained superiority, but only because the Soviets did not increase their armament as rapidly as expected.

The key to the New Look was the American ability to build and deliver nuclear weapons. Put more bluntly, Eisenhower's military policy rested on America's capacity to destroy the Soviet Union. Soviet strides in military technology gave them the ability to retaliate, but not to defend Russia, which was the major reason Eisenhower could accept sufficiency. The United States did not have to be superior to the Soviet Union to demolish it.

To give up superiority was not easy, however, and it rankled with many Americans, especially in the military. Eisenhower had his greatest difficulties with the Army, for it suffered most from his refusal to increase the Defense

Department budget. Three Army Chiefs of Staff resigned in protest and one of them, Maxwell Taylor, later became the chief adviser on military affairs to Eisenhower's successors and saw his views triumph. The Army wanted enough flexibility to be able to meet the communist threat at any level. The trouble with Eisenhower's New Look, the Army Chiefs and some Democrats argued, was that it locked the United States into an all-or-nothing response. Wherever and whenever conflict broke out, the Chiefs wanted to be capable of moving in. To do so, they needed a huge standing army, with specialized divisions, elite groups, a wide variety of weapons, and an enormous transportation capacity.

Eisenhower insisted that the cost of being able to intervene anywhere, immediately, was unbearable. 'Let us not forget,' the President wrote a friend in August of 1956, 'that the Armed Services are to defend a "way of life", not merely land, property or lives.' He wanted to make the Chiefs accept the need for a 'balance between minimum requirements in the costly implements of war and the health of our economy . . .'. As he told the American Society of Newspaper Editors on 16 April 1953, 'Every gun that is made, every warship launched, every rocket fired signifies, in the final sense, a theft from those who hunger and are not fed, those who are cold and are not clothed.' The cost of one destroyer was equal to the cost of new homes for 8,000 people.

Still, the Army Chiefs had put their finger on the most obvious limitation of the New Look and massive retaliation. Eisenhower and Dulles tried to make up the deficit by signing up allies, as in World War II, who would do the ground fighting that had to be done. Eisenhower offered one reason when he pointed out that while 'it cost $3,515 to maintain an American soldier each year, for a Pakistani the price was $485, for a Greek, $424'. This was good economics, but poor politics, since the Pakistanis and the Greeks were not anxious to fight America's wars. They were more concerned with improving their own standards so that it would cost more to maintain their soldiers.

The New Look meant that Eisenhower had abandoned his former advocacy of universal military training, with its assumption that the next war would resemble World War II. More fundamentally, he had abandoned the idea of America fighting any more Korean wars. Eisenhower's policy emphasized both the importance of tactical nuclear weapons and the role of strategic airpower as a deterrent to aggression. He used technology to mediate between conflicting political goals. Big bombers carrying nuclear weapons were the means through which he reconciled lower military expenditures with a foreign policy of containment.

The New Look shaped foreign policy. Since it was almost his only weapon, Dulles had to flash a nuclear bomb whenever he wanted to threaten the use of force. To make the threat believable, the United States developed smaller atomic weapons that could be used tactically on the battlefield. Dulles then attempted to convince the world that the United States would not hesitate to use them. The fact that the N.A.T.O. forces were so small made the threat persuasive, for there was no other way to stop the Red Army in Europe. Both Dulles and Eisenhower made this explicit. If the United States were engaged in a major military confrontation, Dulles said, 'those weapons would come into use because, as I say, they are becoming more and more conventional and replacing what used to be called conventional weapons.' Eisenhower added, 'Where these things are used on strictly military targets . . . I see no reason why they shouldn't be used just exactly as you would use a bullet or anything else.'

Dulles called the policy massive retaliation. In a speech in January 1954, he quoted Lenin and Stalin to show that the Soviets planned to overextend the free world and then destroy it with one blow. Dulles held that the United States should counter the strategy by maintaining a great strategic reserve in the United States and that the free world should be 'willing and able to respond vigorously at places and with means of its own choosing'. The Eisenhower administration had made a decision 'to depend primarily upon a great capacity to retaliate, instantly, by means and at places of our own choosing'.

Dulles used massive retaliation as the chief instrument of containment. In 1956 he called his overall method brinksmanship, which he explained in an article in *Life* magazine. 'You have to take chances for peace, just as you must take chances in war. Some say that we were brought to the verge of war. Of course we were brought to the verge of war. The ability to get to the verge without getting into the war is the necessary art . . . . If you try to run away from it, if you are scared to go to the brink, you are lost. We've had to look it square in the face . . . . We walked to the brink and we looked it in the face. We took strong action.'

Dulles implicitly recognized the limitations on brinksmanship. He never tried to use it for liberation and he used it much more sparingly after the Soviets were able to threaten the United States itself with destruction. It was a tactic to support containment at an acceptable cost, within a limited time span under a specific set of military circumstances, not a strategy for protracted conflict.

In the *Life* article, Dulles cited three instances of going to the brink. All were in Asia. The first came in Korea. When Eisenhower took office, the truce talks were stalled on the question of prisoner of war repatriation. The Chinese wanted all their men held by the U.N. command returned, while the Americans insisted on voluntary repatriation, which meant that thousands of Chinese and North Koreans would remain in South Korea, for they did not want to return to communism. Truman and Acheson had first raised the issue. They could have had peace early in 1952 had they accepted the usual practice, firmly established in international law, of returning all prisoners, but they decided to offer a haven to those prisoners who wished to defect.

The talks, and the war, continued. The Chinese would not give.

After his election, but before his inauguration, Eisenhower made a trip to Korea. He returned on 14 December, convinced more than ever that involvement in a land war in Asia was a disaster for America. Determined to cut losses and get out, but locked into Truman's policy on prisoners – after Truman had made such an issue out of it, Eisenhower could hardly hand over the Chinese P.O.W.'s who did not want to return – Eisenhower warned that unless the war ended quickly, the United States might retaliate 'under circumstances of our own choosing'. On 2 February, in his first State of the Union message, the President said there was no longer 'any sense or logic' in restraining Chiang, so the U.S. Seventh Fleet would 'no longer be employed to shield Communist China'. Chiang then began bombing raids against the China coast. Armistice talks, which had broken down, recommenced in April, but again there was no progress. Dulles then warned Peking, through India, that if peace did not come the United States would bring in atomic weapons. Eleven days later the two sides agreed to place the question of prisoner repatriation in the hands of international, neutral authorities.

In its first test, massive retaliation had won a victory. Ominous portents for the future, however, soon appeared. Dulles's policy was based on a bipolar view of the world, which in his rhetoric was good *v.* evil or free *v.* slave but which in practice meant that Moscow and Washington ruled the world. He believed that the United States could make the major decisions for the free world while Russia would make them for the communists. He refused to accept, or perhaps even recognize, the diversity of the world, for he thought all important issues were related to the Cold War and was impatient with those who argued that the East–West struggle was irrelevant to many world problems. His negative expression of this belief in bipolarity was his denunciation of neutrality, which he characterized as immoral.

Syngman Rhee was no neutral, and he was willing to participate in the Cold War when it suited his purposes, but he refused to be a pawn in the State Department's hands. Peace in Korea meant the end of Rhee's hopes for ruling all of the peninsula. The end of the war may have signified victory for containment, but it also spelled defeat for Rhee. He refused, therefore, to accept any truce. To make one impossible, on 18 June 1953 he released 27,000 communist prisoners, who scattered over the countryside. On the 20th he threatened to pull his forces out of the U.N. command if a truce were signed.

China and America co-operated in putting pressure on Rhee. The Chinese launched a major offensive against South Korean troops, driving them to the south and demonstrating that Rhee could never fight on alone against them. The Americans sent high-level officials to Korea to plead with Rhee not to commit national suicide. Rhee remained recalcitrant, but eventually gave in when the American, British, and French Foreign Ministers all promised to fight side-by-side with Rhee if the communists should renew their aggression. On 27 July 1953, a military armistice was signed. Rhee had not been able to keep the United States committed to war in Asia against its will, but he had come close, and he had demonstrated how small nations could force the hands of great powers. He had also shown the limitations of massive retaliation. Dulles could hardly threaten to drop nuclear bombs on the Chinese because Rhee allowed Chinese prisoners of war to escape.

Some of the same general issues emerged in the second application of brinksmanship, which came in Vietnam. Vietnam also illustrated the continuity of policy between the Truman and Eisenhower administrations, based as they were on the same assumptions. In December 1952, the lame-duck Truman administration approved $60 million for support of the French effort against Ho Chi Minh's Vietminh. Truman, and later Eisenhower, labeled Ho a communist agent of Peking and Moscow, characterizing the war in Vietnam as another example of communist aggression.

When Eisenhower moved into the White House, the State Department presented him with a background paper on Vietnam that succinctly summed up the American position not only on Vietnam but on the entire Third World. In 1949 France had broken up Indochina and granted Laos, Cambodia, and Vietnam 'independence within the French Union'. All objective observers recognized this as a heavy-handed attempt to buy off the Vietminh without giving anything of substance in return. Even the U.S. State Department could not totally ignore the obvious sham, but it did its best to dismiss it.

In the background presentation to Eisenhower, the State Department said that 'certain symbols of the former colonial era remain'. These 'certain symbols' included total French control over 'foreign and military affairs, foreign trade and exchange, and internal security. France continues to maintain a near monopoly in the economic life' of Vietnam. The State Department told Eisenhower that French control of the reality of power in its former colonies was 'disliked by large elements of the native population', but said it was 'justified' because the French were bearing the major burden of 'defending the area'. But the only non-native troops in Vietnam were French and even State admitted that the bulk of the population 'disliked' French rule. American policy was to encourage an end to colonialism; yet in the face of all this State could still seriously assert that France retained 'certain symbols' of power and was 'defending the area'. Against whom, and for what?

Such nonsense could have meaning only to those who believed that the challenge to French rule came not from the Vietnamese but from the Chinese communists, acting in turn as proxies for the Kremlin, with the ultimate purpose of world conquest. If these beliefs were true, there was little point in fighting what Eisenhower called the tail of the snake, the Vietminh. Better to cut off the neck in Peking, or even the head in Moscow. Dulles tried that, warning the Chinese that if their troops entered Vietnam the United States would use nuclear weapons against China. The Chinese sent no troops, but they had never planned to anyway and Dulles's threat had absolutely no effect on the war in Vietnam.

While he served as Supreme Commander at N.A.T.O. Headquarters in Europe, and again in his first year in the White House, Eisenhower continually urged the French to state unequivocally that they would give complete independence to Vietnam upon the conclusion of hostilities. He made 'every kind of presentation' to the French to 'put the war on an international footing', i.e., to make it a clear Cold War struggle rather than a revolt against colonialism. If France promised independence, and Ho continued to fight, Eisenhower reasoned that the Vietminh could no longer pretend to be national liberators and would stand revealed as communist stooges. At that point, Britain and the United States could enter the conflict to halt aggression.

Eisenhower was badly confused about the nature of the war, but the French were not. Like Rhee, they were willing enough to talk about the communist menace in order to receive American aid, but they had no intention of giving up Vietnam. They knew perfectly well that their enemies were in the interior of Vietnam, not in Peking or Moscow, and they were determined to retain the reality of power. If the Americans wanted to fight communists, that was fine with the French; their concern was with continuing the exploitation of the Vietnamese.

Unfortunately the war did not go well for the French. By early 1954 the Vietminh controlled over half the countryside. The French put their best troops into an isolated garrison north of Hanoi, called Dien Bien Phu, and dared the Vietminh to come after them. They assumed that in open battle the Asians would crumble. The results, however, were the other way around, and by April it was the garrison at Dien Bien Phu that was in trouble. War weariness in

France was by then so great, and the French had attached so much prestige to Dien Bien Phu, that it was clear that the fall of the garrison would mean the end of French rule in Vietnam. Eisenhower and Dulles saw such an outcome as a victory for communist aggression and a failure of containment.

On 3 April 1954, Dulles and Radford met with eight Congressional leaders. The administration wanted support for a congressional resolution authorizing American entry into the war. The Congressmen, including Senator Lyndon B. Johnson of Texas, the Senate majority leader, were aghast. They remembered all too well the difficulties of the Korean War and they were disturbed because Dulles had found no allies to support intervention. Congressional opposition hardened when they discovered that one of the other three Joint Chiefs disagreed with Radford's idea of saving Dien Bien Phu through air strikes.

Eisenhower was as adamant as the Congressional leaders about allies. He was anxious to shore up the French but only if they promised complete independence and only if Britain joined the United States in intervening. Unless these conditions were met he would not move, but he was worried about what would happen if the French lost. On 7 April he introduced a new political use for an old word when he explained that all Southeast Asia was like a row of dominoes. If you knocked over the first one what would happen to the last one was 'the certainty that it would go over very quickly'.

To make sure the dominoes stood, Eisenhower went shopping for allies. He wanted 'the U.S., France, United Kingdom, Thailand, Australia, and New Zealand et al to begin conferring at once on means of successfully stopping the Communist advances in Southeast Asia'. He proposed to use the bulk of the French army already there, while 'additional ground forces should come from Asiatic and European troops'. America would supply the material, but not the lives. The policy had little appeal to Britain, Australia,

New Zealand, et al, but it was consistent with the approach of both Eisenhower's predecessors. The trouble was it had no chance of success. The proposed allies figured that if America would not fight in Korea, they would not fight in Vietnam. Even when Eisenhower wrote Churchill and compared the threat in Vietnam to the dangers of 'Hirohito, Mussolini and Hitler', the British would not budge.

The Vice President, Richard M. Nixon, then tried another tack. On 16 April he said that 'if to avoid further Communist expansion in Asia and Indochina, we must take the risk now by putting our boys in, I think the Executive has to take the politically unpopular decisions and do it'. Nixon was evidently confused about the premisses of the New Look, which made his suggestion impossible, since there were no troops available. In any case, the storm that followed his speech was so fierce that the possibility of using 'our boys' in Vietnam immediately disappeared from the suggestion pile. Eisenhower would never have supported it anyway, and his Army Chief of Staff, Matthew Ridgway, was firmly opposed to rushing into another ground war in Asia.

What to do? The question was crucial because a conference on Vietnam was scheduled to begin in Geneva on 26 April*. Like Truman in Korea, the Eisenhower admin-

---

* The conference had been called at the end of the Berlin Conference of Foreign Ministers in February 1954, the first meeting of the Foreign Ministers in nearly five years. The Berlin Conference came about because the West wanted to see how honest the Soviet successors to Stalin were in their professions of peaceful intent. Molotov at the Berlin Conference proposed that Germany be evacuated by foreign troops and the country neutralized, then unified. The West proposed German unity first, by free elections, rejecting any role for the East German Democratic Republic, after which a peace treaty could be drawn up. Dulles refused to discuss West German rearmament or Germany's role in N.A.T.O. Neither side would bend and the conference did not lead to any agreement. The French, however, insisted on another meeting; the great war weariness within France could be held in check only through the promise of a Foreign Ministers' meeting to discuss Vietnam. The Americans went along because it was necessary to prolong the life of the Laniel government in Paris; behind Laniel loomed the shadow of Mendès-France, the advocate of peace in Vietnam.

istration was flatly opposed to a negotiated peace at Geneva which would give Ho Chi Minh any part of Vietnam. The United States was paying 75 per cent of the cost of the war, an investment too great simply to abandon. But the French position at Dien Bien Phu was deteriorating rapidly. Air Force Chief of Staff Nathan Twining had a solution. He wanted to drop three small atomic bombs on the Vietminh around Dien Bien Phu 'and clean those Commies out of there and the band could play the Marseillaise and the French would come marching out . . . in fine shape'. Eisenhower was opposed to using atomic bombs for the second time in a decade against Asians, but he did consider a conventional air strike. Dulles flew to London a week before the Geneva Conference to get Churchill's approval. Churchill would not approve, and Eisenhower did not act. Brinksmanship had failed.

On 7 May 1954, Dien Bien Phu fell. Still there was no immediate progress in Geneva and the Americans withdrew from the conference. At the insistance of the N.A.T.O. allies Eisenhower eventually sent his close friend, Walter B. Smith, as an observer. Dulles himself refused to return and the negotiations dragged on. The break came when the French government fell and, in mid-June, the Radical-Socialist Pierre Mendès-France assumed the position of Foreign Minister as well as of Premier. On the strength of his pledge to end the war or resign by 20 July, he had a vote of confidence of 419 to 47. Mendès-France immediately met Chinese Premier Chou En-lai privately at Berne, which infuriated the Americans, and progress towards peace began. Eisenhower, Dulles, and Smith were helpless bystanders. On 20–21 July two pacts were signed, the Geneva Accords and the Geneva Armistice Agreement.

The parties agreed to a truce and to a temporary partition of Vietnam at the 17th parallel, with the French withdrawing south of that line. Neither the French in south Vietnam nor Ho Chi Minh in the north could join a military alliance or allow foreign military bases on their territory.

There would be elections, supervised by a joint commission of India, Canada, and Poland, within two years to unify the country. France would stay in the south to carry out the elections. The United States did not sign either of the pacts, nor did any South Vietnamese government. The Americans did promise that they would support 'free elections supervised by the United Nations' and would not use force to upset the agreements. Ho Chi Minh had been on the verge of taking all of Vietnam, but he accepted only the northern half because he needed time to repair the war damage and he was confident that when the elections came he would win a smashing victory. All Western observers agreed with his prediction on how the vote would go.

Desperate to save something from the débâcle, in July 1954 Dulles, Radford and Twining, along with others at the Pentagon, worked out an invasion scheme calling for a landing at Haiphong and a march to Hanoi, which American troops would then liberate. Again, Ridgway opposed, arguing that the adventure would require at least six divisions even if the Chinese did not intervene, and again Eisenhower refused to act.

The New Look had tied Dulles's hands in Vietnam, so after Geneva and Eisenhower's refusal to invade North Vietnam the Secretary of State moved in two ways to restore some flexibility to American foreign policy. One of the major problems had been the lack of allies for an intervention. Dulles tried to correct this before the next crisis came by signing up the allies in advance. In September 1954, he persuaded Britain, Australia, New Zealand, France, Thailand, Pakistan, and the Philippines to join the Southeast Asian Treaty Organization (S.E.A.T.O.), in which the parties agreed to consult if any signatory felt threatened. They would act together to meet an aggressor if they could unanimously agree on designating him and if the threatened state agreed to action on its territory. Protection for Cambodia, Laos, and South Vietnam was covered in a separate protocol. Thus quickly did the United States undermine the

Geneva Accords by implicitly bringing the former French colonies into an alliance system. The absence of India, Burma, and Indonesia was embarrassing, as was the presence of so many white men. Clearly this was no N.A.T.O. for Southeast Asia, but rather a Western – especially American – effort to regulate the affairs of Asia from the outside. Once again the hoary old Monroe Doctrine had been extended. The United States, as Dulles put it, had 'declared that an intrusion [in Southeast Asia] would be dangerous to our peace and security', and America would fight to prevent it.

Not, however, with infantry. Dulles assured a suspicious Senate that the New Look policies would continue, that the American response to aggression would be with bombs, not men. This solved one problem but left another. What if the aggression took the form of internal communist subversion directed and supported from without? In such an event, it would be difficult to get the S.E.A.T.O. signatories to agree to act. Dulles was aware of the danger and assured the Cabinet that in such an event he was ready to act alone. He took a different tack in the Senate Foreign Relations Committee, where he stated that 'if there is a revolutionary movement in Vietnam or in Thailand, we would consult together as to what to do about it . . . but we have no undertaking to put it down, all we have is an undertaking to consult.' Reassured, the Senate passed the treaty by a vote of 82 to 1.

Dulles's other major post-Geneva move was unilaterally to shore up the government of South Vietnam. In so doing, he revealed much about American attitudes towards revolution in the Third World. Dulles grew almost frantic when he thought about the colored peoples of the world, for he realized that the struggle for their loyalty was the next battleground of the Cold War and he knew that American military might was almost useless in the struggle. Russia had a tremendous initial advantage, since the Third World did not regard the Russians as white exploiters and colonists. Further, the Russian example of how a nation could build its economy through controlled production and consumption rather than by waiting for the slow accumulation of capital through the profits of free enterprise had great appeal to the emerging nations. Finally, the oppressed of the world were not overthrowing their white masters merely in order to substitute local rulers with the same policies. The revolutionaries were just what they said they were, men determined to change the entire social, political, and economic order. It was this radicalism that separated the post-World War II revolutions from the American Revolution and made the American talk about an identity between George Washington and the Third World just so much cant.

America could neither accept nor adjust to radicalism, either psychologically or economically. Dulles accused the Soviets of being the real imperialists of the modern world, but in East Europe at least the Russians encouraged industrial development and they were never shocked by, and in fact encouraged, radical action in the Third World. All the colored peoples had to do to see what America regarded as a proper role for the emerging nations was to look at the Mid-East or Latin America, where the Western-owned corporations retained their position, the economy was extractive, the rulers lived in splendor, and the masses of the people remained in poverty. Truman's Point Four ensured the continuation of these conditions.

Given the American emotional need to define social change as communist aggression, given the needs of American business to maintain an extractive economy in the Third World, and given the military desire to retain bases around Russia and China, the United States had to set its face against revolution. 'American policy was designed to create maximum change behind the Iron Curtain and to prevent it elsewhere,' Norman Graebner has written. 'On both counts, this nation placed itself in opposition to the fundamental political and military realities of the age.' In

1960 V. K. Krishna Menon of India invited the American delegation to the United Nations to read the Declaration of Independence. 'Legitimism cannot be defended,' he declared, 'and if you object to revolutionary governments, then you simply argue against the whole of progress.' But America did object to revolution. In 1958 Senator Fulbright summed up the Truman and Eisenhower approach when he said that the United States 'has dealt with princes, potentates, big business, and the entrenched, frequently corrupt, representatives of the past'.

Fulbright had accurately described Dulles's post-Geneva policy in South Vietnam. In September 1954, Dulles announced that henceforth American aid would go directly to the South Vietnamese and not through the French. In November, American military advisers began training a South Vietnamese Army. Fulbright had warned that 'there are few of the newly independent countries in the world in which we have an understanding of the motivations of the common man', but Dulles was sure that the United States could do what the French could not. The Americans gave power in South Vietnam to Ngo Dinh Diem, who drew his support from the landlords and had good relations with the French plantation owners, and Eisenhower pledged American economic aid to Diem. The President hedged by requiring social and economic reforms from Diem, but from the first it was understood that Diem could do as he wished as long as he remained firmly anti-communist.

By July 1955, the French had left Vietnam, where they were supposed to stay to supervise the elections promised at Geneva, and with American support Diem announced that the elections would not be held. Diem and Dulles both knew that Eisenhower was correct in predicting that in an election Ho Chi Minh would win 80 per cent of the vote. In May 1955, Dulles had told reporters that the United States would recognize an anti-Diem government in the south only if 'it seems to be expressive of the real will of the people and if it is truly representative'. Since the President himself had admitted that an overwhelming majority of the people wanted Ho, Dulles had to cover himself by arguing that the people of South Vietnam could not make a real choice since they did not understand the alternative to Ho and did not realize that Ho was an agent of international communism. Dulles was willing to abide by election results after the Vietnamese had learned how much more Diem had to offer. The Russians had used an identical argument to justify the absence of elections in East Europe.

American aid then began to pour into Diem's hands as the United States tried to promote South Vietnam as a model for Third World development. Brinksmanship had failed to prevent the loss of North Vietnam and was of little or no help in dealing with the problems of the underdeveloped nations, so Dulles offered the Diem example as a method of handling what he regarded as the most important problem of the era. Whether it would be a convincing example or not remained to be seen.

If brinksmanship failed to halt or even shape the revolution of rising expectations, it could still be used to protect what was already clearly America's. Dulles faced his third major challenge, and used brinksmanship for the third time, in the Formosa Straits, where he did succeed in achieving his objective.

In January 1953, Eisenhower had unleashed Chiang. The Nationalist Chinese then began a series of bombing raids, in American-built planes, against mainland shipping and ports. The pin-prick war was just enough to keep the Chinese enraged without injuring them seriously.* In January 1955, the Chinese were ready to strike back. They began by bombing the Tachen islands, 230 miles north of

---

* Eisenhower was once asked what the United States would have done in 1865 if Jefferson Davis, Robert E. Lee, and the Confederate Army had escaped to Cuba, if they had then mounted raids against Florida, and if the British Navy had stationed a fleet between Florida and Cuba to prevent the United States from overrunning the island and driving the Confederates off. Eisenhower replied that the analogy was not a good one, since the Confederate government had never been legitimate.

Formosa and held by a division of Chiang's troops. The Chinese also began to build up strength and mount cannon opposite Quemoy and Matsu, small islands sitting at the mouths of two Chinese harbors and garrisoned by Nationalist divisions. Eisenhower – although not some of his advisers – was willing to write off the Tachens, which were soon evacuated, but he was determined to hold Quemoy and Matsu as he believed they were integral to the defense of Formosa itself. His reasoning, as he explained during a 1958 crisis over the same issue, was that if Quemoy and Matsu fell, Formosa would follow, which would 'seriously jeopardize the anti-Communist barrier consisting of the insular and peninsular position in the Western Pacific, e.g., Japan, Republic of Korea, Republic of China, Republic of the Philippines, Thailand and Vietnam.' Indonesia, Malaya, Cambodia, Laos, and Burma 'would probably come fully under Communist influence'.

Summing up, Eisenhower declared, 'the consequences in the Far East would be even more far-reaching and catastrophic than those which followed when the United States allowed the Chinese mainland to be taken over by the Chinese Communists, aided and abetted by the Soviet Union.' The statement was not, it is important to note, campaign propaganda. It was not even intended for the public. It was a position paper drafted by Dulles and edited by Eisenhower, which indicated that it represented their honest opinion. Aside from revealing their astonishing attitude towards the reasons for Chiang's loss of China, it accepted for the purposes of policy the idea that if the Chinese were not fought on Quemoy and Matsu, America would have to fight them in San Francisco.

To avoid the 'catastrophic consequences' of the loss of Quemoy and Matsu, on 24 January 1955 Eisenhower went before Congress to ask for authority to 'employ the armed forces of the United States as he [the President] deems necessary for the specific purpose of protecting Formosa and the Pescadores against armed attack', the authority to include protection for 'related positions', which meant Quemoy and Matsu. Eisenhower feared that if the Chinese moved and he had to go to Congress for authority to act it would be too late, so he asked for a blank check on which he could draw at will. As the legal adviser of the Department of State who helped draft the resolution remarked, it was a 'monumental' step, for 'never before in our history had anything been done like that'. Nevertheless, there was hardly a debate. The House passed the Resolution by 409 to 3, while it went through the Senate by 85 to 3.

A major war scare then ensued. As the Chinese began to bombard Quemoy and Matsu, the Eisenhower administration seriously considered dropping nuclear weapons on the mainland. At no other time in the Cold War did the United States come so close to launching a preventive war. Had the Chinese actually launched invasions of the islands, it is possible, perhaps even probable, that the United States would have struck. In a speech on 20 March, Dulles referred to the Chinese in terms usually reserved for use against nations at war. The Secretary said the Chinese were 'an acute and imminent threat, . . . dizzy with success'. He compared their 'aggressive fanaticism' with Hitler's and said they were 'more dangerous and provocative of war'. To stop them, he threatened to use 'new and powerful weapons of precision, which can utterly destroy military targets without endangering unrelated civilian centers', which meant tactical atomic bombs. Eisenhower backed him up by saying he regarded the small atomic bombs as no different than bullets or any other military weapon.

On 25 March, the Chief of Naval Operations, Admiral R. B. Carney, briefed correspondents at a private dinner. He said the President was considering acting militarily on an all-out basis 'to destroy Red China's military potential and thus end its expansionist tendencies'. Dulles told the President that before the problem was solved, 'I believe there is at least an even chance that the United States will have to go to war.' Dulles thought that small air bursts, with minimal civilian casualties, would do the job quickly and 'the revulsion might not be long-lived'. Eisenhower, however, began to doubt that the operation could be limited in time or scope, and he set his face against preventive war. On 28 April, at a press conference, he said he had a 'sixth-sense' feeling that the outlook for peace had brightened and revealed that he had been in correspondence with his old wartime friend, Marshal Zhukov, one of the current Soviet rulers. Chinese pressure on Quemoy and Matsu lessened and the crisis receded. Brinksmanship had held the line.

In the process, however, it had scared the wits out of people around the globe, perhaps even members of the Eisenhower administration itself. The nuclear weapons of the fifties were at least a thousand times more destructive than the atomic bombs of the forties – one American bomber carried more destructive power than all the explosives set off in all the world's history put together – and everyone was frightened. The small, tactical atomic bombs Dulles was talking about were much larger than those dropped on Japan. Ever since the first American tests of the new fission bomb, Winston Churchill had been urging the United States and the Soviets to meet at the summit to try to resolve their differences. The Americans had consistently rejected his calls for a summit meeting, but by mid-1955, as the Russians began to improve both the size of their bombs and their delivery capabilities, and as the Formosa crisis made the United States face squarely the possibility of a nuclear exchange, Eisenhower and Dulles were more amenable.

Eisenhower's decision to go to the summit meant the end of any American dreams of winning the Cold War by military means. The Russians had come so far in nuclear development that Eisenhower himself warned the nation that an atomic war would ruin the world. There could be no 'possibility of victory or defeat', only different degrees of destruction. As James Reston reported in the *New York Times*, 'Perhaps the most important single fact in world politics today is that Mr Eisenhower has thrown the immense authority of the American Presidency against risking a military solution of the cold war '. Since Eisenhower would not lead the nation into a nuclear war, and since he did not have the troops to fight a limited war, nor could he get them from his allies, and since the Republicans were more determined to balance the budget and enjoy the fruits of capitalism than they were to support a war machine, the only alternative left was peace of some kind with the Russians. Eisenhower was not willing to give in on any of the crucial questions, like the unification of Germany or Vietnam or Korea, but he was willing to talk with the new Russian leaders.

Eisenhower's readiness to go to Geneva and sit down with the Russians – the first meeting in a decade between leaders of the two nations – also represented his and Dulles's assumption that between them Moscow and Washington could rule the world, which in turn rested on the American notion that revolutionary activities in the Third World were directed by the Kremlin. A good illustration of the attitude, held in Moscow as well as in Washington, came at the height of the Formosan crisis, when Dulles talked to Molotov about easing tensions. Dulles reported that America was putting pressure on Chiang to cool down and asked Molotov to do the same to Mao. The American Secretary said that 'we needed a situation where as in Germany, Korea and Vietnam, it was agreed that unification would not be sought by force', which was another way of saying that the Chinese – both in Peking and on Formosa – should forget their own aspirations, pride, and national interests because Washington and Moscow had decided the time had come to calm the waters, not in the interests of the Chinese but in the interests of America and Russia. Molotov more or less agreed and suggested a summit conference.

Events broke rapidly in the late spring of 1955, helping to drive Eisenhower and the Russians to the summit. On 9 May, West Germany became a formal member of N.A.T.O. On 14 May the Soviet Union and the Eastern European nations signed the Warsaw Pact, the communist military counter to N.A.T.O. The next day Russia and America finally solved one of the long-standing problems of World War II by signing the Austrian treaty, which gave Austria independence, forbade union with Germany, and made Austria a permanent neutral. Both sides had been responsible for various delays. The Russians signed because they wanted to ease tensions and advance to the summit while the Americans accepted it as a reasonable solution for the Austrian problem. Dulles was unhappy. As Eisenhower later recalled, 'Well, suddenly the thing was signed one day and [Dulles] came in and he grinned rather ruefully and he said, "Well, I think we've had it".'

What Dulles feared was misinterpretation. The fear was justified, for columnists and pundits began to advocate a similar solution for Germany. Actually, far from being a step towards German unity and neutrality, the Austrian treaty was a step towards making German division permanent. Russia and America in effect agreed that neither of the Germanies would get Austria.

On 19 May, in an air show, the Soviets displayed impressive quantities of their latest long-range bombers. A week later the new top Russian leaders, Nikita Khrushchev and Nikolai Bulganin, flew to Yugoslavia, where in true Canossa style they apologized for Stalin's treatment of Tito and begged Tito's forgiveness. The Soviets were also initiating an economic assistance program for selected Third World nations. Clearly Russia had emerged from the confusion that followed Stalin's death and was on the offensive.

Some ground rules for the Cold War, of spirit if not of substance, were obviously needed. America's N.A.T.O. allies were adamant about the need, insistently so after N.A.T.O. war games in June showed that if conflict started in Europe (and if the war game scenario were accurate), 171 atomic bombs would be dropped on West Europe. For the United States to continue to take a stance of unrestrained hostility towards Russia was intolerable.

This deeply felt sentiment in Europe, plus Eisenhower's personal dedication to peace, were the main factors in making the summit meeting at Geneva possible.

The Geneva meeting was not the result of any political settlement. Neither side was willing to back down from previous positions. Dulles made this perfectly clear when he drew up the American demands on Germany. His first goal was unification 'under conditions which will neither ''neutralize'' nor ''demilitarize'' united Germany, nor subtract it from N.A.T.O.'. There was not the slightest chance that the Russians would accept such a proposal. Neither would they ever agree to the only new American offer, Eisenhower's call for an 'open skies' agreement, for to them that was only another heavy-handed American attempt to spy on Russia. Bulganin, who fronted for Khrushchev at Geneva, was no more ready to deal than the Americans were. His position on Germany was to let things stand as they were.

On 18 July 1955 the summit meeting began. It had been called in response to the arms race and it was no surprise that there was no progress towards political settlements. What Dulles had feared most, however, did happen – there emerged a 'spirit of Geneva'. Before the meeting, Dulles had warned Eisenhower to maintain 'an austere countenance' when being photographed with Bulganin. He pointed out that any pictures taken of the two leaders smiling 'would be distributed throughout the Soviet satellite countries', signifying 'that all hope of liberation was lost and that resistance to communist rule was henceforth hopeless'. But the pictures were taken, and 'Ike' could not restrain his famous grin, and the photographs were distributed.

Dulles had been unable to prevent this symbolic recognition of the failure of Republican promises for liberation of communist satellites. The Soviets had almost caught up militarily and brinksmanship was dead. Geneva did not mean the end of the Cold War but it did put it on a different basis. The West had admitted that it could not win the Cold

War, that a thermonuclear stalemate had developed, and that the *status quo* in Europe and China (where tensions quickly eased) had to be substantially accepted.

Dulles was bitter but helpless. He was especially infuriated because the battleground now shifted to the areas of economic and political influence in the Third World, a battleground on which Russia had enormous advantages. Dulles warned the N.A.T.O. Foreign Ministers in December 1955 that the Soviets would hereafter employ 'indirect' threats 'primarily developed in relations to the Near and Middle East and South Asia'. To fight back, Dulles needed two things – money, and an American willingness to accept radicalism in the emerging nations. He had neither. Republicans who resented giving money to West Europe through the Marshall Plan were hardly likely to approve significant sums for non-white revolutionaries.

Like his spiritual ancestors, the nineteenth-century abolitionists, Dulles was forced to retreat to what the abolitionists used to call moral suasion. He would talk the Soviets out of East Europe. This provided emotional satisfaction but little else. His chances for success were indicated by the aftermath of Geneva. In September, the Soviets worked out formal diplomatic relations with West Germany and a week later they gave East Germany full powers in foreign affairs. In January 1956, East Germany entered the Warsaw Pact.

Adjusting to the new realities was not easy. Dulles had denounced containment but had been unable to go beyond Truman's policy. He had promised liberation and had failed. Neither brinksmanship nor moral suasion had freed a single slave or prevented North Vietnam from going communist. But despite Geneva and the new realities, Dulles would not quit without a fight. On Christmas day, 1955, the White House sent its usual message to the peoples of Eastern Europe to 'recognize the trials under which you are suffering' and to 'share your faith that right in the end will bring you again among the free nations of the world'.

When Khrushchev complained that this 'crude interference' was not in accord with the spirit of Geneva, the White House pointed out that the goal of liberation was permanent. The statement said, 'The peaceful liberation of the captive peoples is, and, until success is achieved, will continue to be a major goal of United States foreign policy.'

A Presidential election year had just begun. As in 1952, captive nations' pronouncements made good campaign material. Unfortunately, some of the captive people did not know how to distinguish between campaign bombast and actual policy. They were about to demand payment on the American liberation promises.

9

From Hungary and Suez to Cuba

THE overwhelming first impression of American foreign policy from 1956 to 1961 was one of unrelieved failure. Eisenhower and Dulles were unable to contain the Russians, who succeeded in their centuries-old dream of establishing themselves in the Mediterranean and the Middle East. America's inability to do anything at all to aid Hungary's rebels made a mockery of the Republican calls for liberation. Spectacular Soviet successes in rocketry, beginning with Sputnik, sent the United States into a deep emotional depression. Russia seemed to have won the arms race and in 1959 it was Khrushchev who played at brinksmanship from a position of strength. After Suez the French, and to a lesser extent the British, would never trust the United States again. In Southeast Asia, communist guerrillas in South Vietnam and Laos threatened to upset the delicate balance there in favor of the communists. In Latin America, the Eisenhower administration was helpless in the face of a revolution in Cuba, which soon allowed the Russians to extend their influence to within ninety miles of the United States. Only in Africa did the Soviets fail to gain new Third World adherents, although even there this was less because of American actions and more because the Russians, like the Americans, did not have a clear understanding of what was happening in black Africa.

Surface appearances, however, reveal only surface truths. After he retired, Eisenhower said his greatest disappointment was his failure to bring real peace to the world. Given his attitudes towards communism, peace – in the sense of mutual co-operation with the Soviets to solve the world's problems – was never a strong possibility. Eisenhower's outstanding achievement was the negative one of avoiding war. However irresponsible Republican emotional appeals to the anti-communist vote may have been, and despite the Russian shift to the offensive in the Cold War, Eisenhower refused to engage American troops in armed conflict. He was not immune to intervention, nor to provocative rhetoric, nor to nuclear testing, nor to the arms race (within strict limits), but he did set his face against war. It became the Democrats' turn to complain that the United States was not 'going forward', that it was not 'doing enough', that America was 'losing the Cold War'.

But despite the Democratic complaints, and although Dulles's sermonizing and moralizing and baffling shifts of position drove America's allies to distraction, the United States emerged from the Eisenhower years in a spectacularly good position. The American G.N.P. went up, without dangerous inflation. The Western European economy continued to boom. N.A.T.O. stood more or less intact. Anglo-American oil interests in the Middle East were secure. The Latin American economy remained under American domination. American military bases in the Pacific were safe. Chiang remained in control of Formosa. And the United States, although Eisenhower was spending only about two-thirds the amount that the Democrats wanted him to on defense, was in fact strategically superior to the Soviet Union.

Eisenhower had been unable to contain the communists, much less liberate East Europe, and he remained wedded to the clichés of the Cold War, but he was a man of moderation and caution with a clear view of what it would cost the United States to resist communist advances everywhere. He thought the American economy could not pay the price, which was the fundamental distinction between Eisenhower and his Democratic successors. Because of Eisenhower's fiscal conservatism, Dulles's hands were tied. The Secretary of State was reduced to vapid fulminations which provided emotional satisfaction but kept the budget balanced.

Eisenhower showed his reluctance to take aggressive action most clearly during the 1956 Presidential election campaign, in response to the events that preceded and accompanied it. The Democratic nominee, Adlai Stevenson, accused Eisenhower of not doing enough to stop the communists. For the party out of power to charge that the administration was too weak in dealing with the communists had become, apparently, a permanent part of the American political scene. Half of Indochina had become a 'new Communist satellite', Stevenson declared, and the United States 'emerged from that debacle looking like a "paper tiger"'. Stevenson was also upset at what he called N.A.T.O.'s decline, wanted the American Armed Forces strengthened, and charged that Eisenhower had rejected 'great opportunities to exploit weaknesses in the Communist ranks . . .'.

Eisenhower would not be stampeded into anything more than a tough verbal response, although the opportunities for action were certainly present. In the Middle East, ignoring ideology, the communists were extending their influence. Although Dulles had broken with Truman's policy of support for Israel and was trying to improve relations with the Arabs, he was either unable or unwilling to match communist aid programs for the area. In late 1955 he had a 'conniption fit' when he learned that the Egyptians had negotiated an arms deal with the Czechs. Dulles's initial response was to offer the Egyptian leader, Colonel Gamal Abdel Nasser, American aid for the Aswan Dam, a gigantic project designed to harness the power of the lower Nile. Technical experts then studied the project and pronounced it feasible. By February 1956, Nasser was ready to conclude the deal.

Dulles, however, had trouble selling the Aswan Dam in the United States. Pro-Israeli politicians denounced the dam. Southern Congressmen wondered why the United States should build a dam which would allow the Egyptians to raise more cotton. In the Cabinet, old-guard Republicans feared the cost of the dam would unbalance the budget. All the opponents agreed that the Egyptians could not possibly provide the technicians nor the industry to use the dam properly. Dulles himself began to back off when in April 1956 Nasser formed a military alliance with Saudi Arabia, Syria, and Yemen and refused to repudiate the Czech arms deal. The Secretary of State assumed that the Russians could not replace the Americans as backers of the Aswan Dam, an assumption based on the curious notion that the Russians did not have the technological know-how. When in May Nasser withdrew recognition from Chiang Kai-shek and recognized Communist China, Dulles had had enough. He decided to withdraw from the Aswan Dam project, although he did not make the decision public.

Finally, on 19 July 1956, at the moment the Egyptian Foreign Minister was arriving in Washington to discuss the project, Dulles announced that America was withdrawing its support from the Aswan Dam. What Dulles expected to happen next remains a mystery (eventually, the Russians built the dam; in the process their influence within Egypt became pervasive). Nasser's immediate response was to seize the Suez Canal, which at a stroke restored his lost prestige and gave him the $25 million annual profit from the canal operation. Now it was the British and French who were furious. They were absolutely dependent on the canal for oil to run their economies, they were certain that the Arabs did not have the skills to run the canal properly, they feared that Nasser would close it to their ships, and their self-esteem had suffered a serious blow. Long, complicated negotiations ensued. They got nowhere. Dulles's main concern was to protect American oil interests in the Middle East, while the British and French could be satisfied by nothing less than complete control of the canal. Dulles, fearing Arab reaction, was unwilling to restore the colonial powers.

It was, indeed, a mess. In a later investigation, Senator Fulbright charged that the Aswan Dam project was sound, that its repudiation was a personal decision by Dulles, that Dulles misjudged both Nasser's attitude toward the Soviet Union and the importance of the dam to Egypt, that he confused Egyptian nationalism and neutralism with communism, and that he never made any serious effort to persuade the Congressional opponents of the project. Dulles had damaged the American position in France, Britain, and N.A.T.O., lost all chance of tying Nasser to the West, allowed the Soviet Union to begin preparation for a naval base in the Mediterranean, which had since 1945 been an American lake, angered Israel and her supporters, and failed to gain any more Arab adherents.

The anger of the critics was justified, but it did not take everything into account. The Middle East contained 64 per cent of the world's known oil resources – even as late as 1969 the great discovery on the Alaskan North Slope was, by Middle Eastern standards, only a small pool. The leading producers were Kuwait, Saudi Arabia, and Iraq. During and after World War II, American oil companies, aided by the United States government, had forced concessions from both the British and the Arabs and now had a major interest in Middle Eastern oil. Despite Dulles's bumbling, these interests were secure.

Suez remained necessary to move the oil. Dulles, adamant as always about old-style European colonialism, began a complex series of negotiations designed to help Nasser run the canal without the British or French. The Europeans thereupon decided to take matters into their own hands. In conjunction with Israel, whose borders Nasser was constantly violating, the British and French began plans for an invasion of Egypt. They did not inform the United States.

Another development, in East Europe, complicated everything. At the 20th Party Congress in February 1956, Khrushchev shocked the world by denouncing Stalin for his crimes, confessing that there could be several roads to communism, and indicating that Stalinist restrictions would be loosened. Two months later the Russians dissolved the

Cominform. Ferment swept through East Europe. Riots in Poland forced Khrushchev to disband the old, Stalinist Politburo and allow Wladyslaw Gomulka, an independent communist, to take power (20 October 1956). Poland remained communist and a member of the Warsaw Pact, but it won substantial independence and set an example for the other satellites.

The excitement spread to Hungary, before the war the most fascist of the East European states and the one where Stalin's imposition of communism had been most alien. On 23 October Hungarian students took to the streets to demand that the Stalinist rulers be replaced with Imre Nagy. Workers joined the students and the riot spread. Khrushchev agreed to give power to Nagy, but that was no longer enough. The Hungarians demanded the removal of the Red Army from Hungary and the creation of an anti-communist political party. By 28 October the Russians had given in and begun to withdraw their tanks from around Budapest.

Liberation was at hand. Eisenhower was careful in his campaign speeches to use only the vaguest of phrases, although the Voice of America and Radio Free Europe did encourage the rebels. So did Dulles, who promised economic aid to those who broke with the Kremlin. At the decisive moment, however, just as it seemed that the European balance of power was about to be drastically altered, the Israeli Army struck Egypt. In a matter of hours it nearly destroyed Nasser's Army and took most of the Sinai peninsula. Britain and France then issued an ultimatum, arranged in advance with the Israelis, warning the Jews and the Egyptians to stay away from the Suez Canal. When Nasser rejected the note, the Europeans began bombing Egyptian military targets and prepared to move troops into Suez, under the cover of keeping the Jews and Arabs apart.

On 31 October, the day after the bombing in Egypt began, Nagy announced that Hungary was withdrawing from the Warsaw Pact. The Russians, certain that events in Egypt and the American Presidential campaign would paralyze the United States, and unwilling in any event to let the Warsaw Pact disintegrate, decided to move. Russian tanks crushed the Hungarian rebels, although only after bitter street fighting that left 7,000 Russians and 30,000 Hungarians dead. The emotional impact on the United States was exemplified by the angry tears of thousands of American students who met and passed resolutions in support of the Hungarians. Radio pleas for help from Hungary made the tragedy even more painful: 'Any news about help? Quickly, quickly, quickly!' And the last, desperate cry, on a teletype message to the Associated Press: 'Help! – help! – help! – SOS! – SOS! – SOS! They just brought us a rumor that the American troops will be here within one or two hours . . . . We are well and fighting.'

There would never be any American troops. Eisenhower did not even consider giving military support to the Hungarians and he would not have done so even had there been no concurrent Middle Eastern crisis. Under no conceivable circumstances would he risk World War III for East Europe. Liberation was a sham; it had always been a sham. All Hungary did was to expose it to the world. However deep Eisenhower's hatred of communism, his fear of war was deeper. Even had this not been so, the armed forces of the United States were not capable of driving the Red Army out of Hungary, except through a nuclear holocaust that would have left all Hungary and most of Europe devastated. The Hungarians, and the other Eastern European peoples, learned that there would be no liberation, that they could not look forward to tying themselves to the West, that their traditional policy of playing East against West was finished. They would have to make the best deal they could with the Soviets. The Russian capture and execution of Nagy made the point brutally clear.

In Egypt, meanwhile, the British and French had bungled. They blew their cover story almost immediately. The Israeli advance was so rapid that they could not pretend that their invasion was one by a disinterested third party designed to keep the Jews and Egyptians apart. Eisenhower was upset at their use of nineteenth-century colonial tactics; he was livid at their failure to inform him of their intentions. The Americans backed a resolution in the General Assembly urging a truce, then cut off oil supplies desperately needed in Britain and France. Khrushchev, meanwhile, rattled his rockets, warning the British and French on 5 November to withdraw before he destroyed them. Although they were only hours away from taking the canal, the Anglo-French governments agreed to a cease-fire and pullback.

It had been quite a week for lessons. The British and French learned that they no longer stood on the center of the world stage – they were second-rate powers incapable of independent action. Henceforth they could either operate within the American orbit or try to create European unity with Germany and without the United States, thereby allowing Europe to play a world role. American politicians learned to stop their irresponsible prattling about liberation. The Russians learned just how strong a force nationalism was in East Europe, while the Israelis saw that they would have to make it on their own in their conflict with the Arabs. United States and United Nations pressure soon forced the Jews to give up their gains in Sinai. The Egyptians learned to look at the Soviet Union for support – encouraged by Nasser, they believed that the Russian ultimatum, not the United States' action in the United Nations, had saved them.

Dulles seemed to be losing the Third World, but from his point of view things were not that bad. To be sure the Russians were taking over the great Western military base in Egypt, but the oil-rich countries stayed in the Anglo-American orbit. To solidify this hold, Dulles and Eisenhower pushed through Congress (January 1957) the Eisenhower Doctrine, which gave the President the right to intervene in the Middle East whenever a legitimate government said it was threatened by communism and asked for aid.

Simultaneously, Eisenhower broke all diplomatic precedents and went to the airport to meet King Saud of Saudi
Arabia (the mayor of New York City had just refused to
meet the King, who was violently anti-Israel), and in the
talks that followed gave the King extensive military aid in
return for an American air base at Dhahran. Eisenhower
went so far as to assure the King that no American Jew
would serve in the U.S. Air Force in Saudi Arabia.

In April 1957, when pro-Nasser officers tried to oust
King Hussein of Jordan, Eisenhower dispatched the U.S.
Sixth Fleet from the French Riviera to the Eastern Mediterranean and gave $20 million to Hussein in military aid.
There were sardonic references in Britain and France about
unilateral action and gunboat diplomacy, but it worked.
The three feudal Arab monarchies, Jordan, Saudi Arabia,
and Iraq, were now wedded to the United States. A year
later, when Russia began to move into Syria, and Iraq
moved towards Nasser, thereby threatening its neighbor,
Lebanon, Eisenhower rushed troops to that Christian Arab
country (14 July 1958). The Russians may have gained
bases in the Mediterranean, but the United States still had
the oil.

The intervention in Lebanon illustrated Eisenhower's
methods. It was a unilateral action that risked general war
in support of a less than democratic government threatened
by pro-Nasser Arabs. Eisenhower tried to tie the action into
great historic precedents by invoking Greece and the 1947
Truman Doctrine. He emphasized the danger by mention-
ing the communist takeovers in Czechoslovakia and China,
and he explained that the United States 'had no intention
of replacing the United Nations in its primary responsibility
of maintaining international peace and security'. The
United States had acted alone merely 'because only swift
action would suffice'.

The rhetoric was grand, the intervention itself less sweeping. The Joint Chiefs wanted American troops to overrun
all of Lebanon, but Eisenhower ordered the men to limit

themselves to taking the airfield and the capital. If the government could not survive even after American soldiers had secured the capital, Eisenhower said, 'I felt we were backing up a government with so little popular support that we probably should not be there.' The British used the occasion to send troops into Jordan to prop up King Hussein and to make sure their oil interests in Iraq were not damaged. The British then asked the Americans to join them in occupying Jordan. Although many administration officials wanted to take advantage of the request in order to extend American influence, Eisenhower flatly refused. As always, he wanted to limit the risks and America's commitment.

The Russians, too, were unwilling to take drastic action. Nasser flew to Moscow to beg for aid; Khrushchev turned him down. The Soviet ruler knew that Eisenhower acted to protect Western oil holdings and he knew how vital those holdings were to the West. As long as Eisenhower was willing to hold down the scope of the intervention, Khrushchev would not interfere.

Khrushchev's caution surprised many observers, since the Russians were generally believed to have achieved military superiority. On 4 October 1957, the Soviet Union successfully launched the world's first man-made satellite, Sputnik. Two months earlier they had fired the world's first intercontinental ballistic missile (I.C.B.M.). Americans were frustrated, angry, ashamed, and afraid all at once. As Walter LaFeber puts it, '"gaps" were suddenly discovered in everything from missile production to the teaching of arithmetic at the preschool level'. Eisenhower dispersed Strategic Air Force units and installed medium-range ballistic missiles in Turkey and Italy, but this was hardly enough to assuage the sudden fear. When the Russians began trumpeting about their average increase in their G.N.P. (7 per cent, nearly twice the American rate), the pressure on Eisenhower to 'get the country moving again' became almost irresistible.

Eisenhower refused to panic, even when in late 1957 the

newspapers discovered and published the findings and
recommendations of a committee headed by H. Rowan
Gaither, Jr, of the Ford Foundation, which painted an
exceedingly dark picture of the future of American security.
The Gaither Report, as Eisenhower typically understated
it, included 'some sobering observations'. It found that the
Soviet G.N.P. was indeed increasing at a much faster rate
than that of the United States, that the Russians were
spending as much on their armed forces and heavy industry
as the Americans were, that the Soviets had enough fission-
able material for 1,500 nuclear weapons, with 4,500 jet
bombers, 300 long-range submarines and an extensive air
defense system, that they had been producing ballistic
missiles with a 700-mile range, that by 1959 the Soviets
might be able to launch an attack against the United States
with 100 I.C.B.M.'s carrying megaton-sized nuclear warheads, and that if such an attack should come the civilian
population and the American bombers in S.A.C. would be
vulnerable.

The Gaither Report was similar to N.S.C. 68 in its findings, and like N.S.C. 68 it recommended a much improved
defense. The committee wanted fallout shelters built on a
massive scale, an improvement of America's air defense
capability, a vast increase in S.A.C.'s offensive power, a
build-up of conventional forces capable of fighting limited
war, and another reorganization of the Pentagon. As a
starter, the Gaither Report (and a somewhat similar study
done by the Rockefeller Foundation) urged an increase in
defense spending to $48 billion.

Eisenhower said no. 'We could not turn the nation into a
garrison state,' he explained in his memoirs, adding as an
afterthought that the Gaither Report was 'useful; it acted
as a gadfly . . .'. He kept the Defense budget under $40
billion, quietly rejected the demands for fallout shelters and
increased conventional war capability, and dropped one
more Army division and a number of tactical air wings from
active duty. He did disperse S.A.C. bombers and he speeded

up the ballistic missile programs, although Congress had to appropriate more funds than the administration requested for the I.C.B.M. and Polaris to get those programs into high gear.

Democrats charged that the Republicans were allowing their Neanderthal fiscal views to endanger the national security, but Eisenhower knew what he was doing. The C.I.A., in one of the great intelligence coups of all time, had in 1956 inaugurated a series of flights over the Soviet Union in high-altitude airplanes, called U-2s. The photographs that resulted from the flights revealed, as Eisenhower later put it, 'proof that the horrors of the alleged ''bomber gap'' and the later ''missile gap'' were nothing more than imaginative creations of irresponsibility'. The United States still had a substantial lead in strategic weapons.

One of the most important points about the U-2 flights was that Khrushchev knew they were taking place (none of the Russian fighter airplanes could reach the altitude the U-2s flew at, so they could not knock them down), which meant that Khrushchev knew that Eisenhower knew how hollow were the Soviet boasts about strategic superiority. The fact that Eisenhower made no strong statements about Soviet inferiority during the American domestic controversy about the missile gap tended to reassure the Soviets and convince them that the President really was a man of moderation who was sincerely interested in some sort of *modus vivendi*. The flights, the information they produced, and Eisenhower's rejection of the Gaither Report, all indicated to the Soviets that Eisenhower had accepted the fundamental idea that neither side could win a nuclear war and that both would lose in an arms race.

The events in the year following Sputnik had the effect of establishing ground rules for the Cold War. By staying out of the Lebanon situation the Soviets indicated that they recognized and would not challenge the West's vital interests. By refusing to take the easy way out of the missile gap controversy, Eisenhower indicated that he did not want an

arms race and was eager to establish a *modus vivendi*. Through their negative signals, both sides showed that they would keep the threshold of conflict low. The years of Eisenhower's second term marked the height of bipolarity, for as the British, French, Israelis, and Egyptians could testify, what the Big Two wanted, they got. Whether they could continue to control their allies, especially France and China,* much less the Third World, was an open question. Indeed, it was not at all clear that Eisenhower and Khrushchev could control the hard-liners in their own countries.

A major test soon came in divided Berlin. However much Khrushchev had learned to trust Eisenhower, or perhaps precisely because he had come to trust the President, he could not continue to allow the situation in Berlin to go unchallenged. Eisenhower's desire for a *modus vivendi* was based on a continuation of the *status quo*, which Khrushchev could not accept everywhere and certainly could not accept in Berlin. West Berlin was a bone in his throat. Each year 300,000 East Germans defected to the West via Berlin, most of them young, talented, educated, and professional people. Since 1949 East Germany had lost 3,000,000 people through the West Berlin escape hatch. West Berlin also contained the largest combination of espionage agencies ever assembled in one place, 110 miles deep in communist territory, as well as radio stations that constantly beamed propaganda into East Europe.

Equally important was the West Berlin economic miracle. The Americans had poured $600 billion into the city, which the Bonn government had matched. West Berlin was turning out nearly $2 billion worth of goods per year. It had become the greatest manufacturing city in Germany and its G.N.P. exceeded that of more than half the members of the United Nations. The glittering social, intellectual, and economic life in West Berlin stood in sharp contrast to the

* Much to the Americans' displeasure, France was pushing forward the development of its own nuclear weapons; China, in August 1958, inaugurated the second Quemoy crisis.

drab, depressed life of East Berlin. What made the situation especially intolerable for Khrushchev was the steady flow of American propaganda about Berlin. Americans used the refugees and the economic contrast between the two Berlins throughout the world as the ultimate proof of the superiority of capitalism to communism.

The situation had, however, existed for over a decade. Why did Khrushchev decide to move against West Berlin in late 1958, during a period of relative calm in the Cold War? He may have reasoned that since Eisenhower would not build up conventional forces, and since the President would obviously do everything possible to avoid a nuclear exchange, a diplomatic solution was now possible. More immediately, Khrushchev feared the growing rearmament of West Germany. The Americans had sent artillery capable of firing nuclear shells and airplanes that could carry nuclear bombs to West Germany. Konrad Adenauer, the West German leader, was increasing the pace of rearmament. Finally, the Bonn government was on the verge of joining with France, Italy, and the Benelux in the Common Market, which would tie West Germany more firmly than ever into the Western bloc. Within the Kremlin, Khrushchev was under intense pressure to do something about the German situation.

On 10 November 1958, Khrushchev declared that the Soviet Union was ready to turn over control of Berlin to East Germany. Then the West would have to negotiate rights of access to West Berlin with the East German government (which none of the Western governments recognized). The West was in Berlin only on the basis of pre-surrender occupation agreements; if Khrushchev signed a peace treaty with the East Germans, the occupation would have to come to an end. Khrushchev warned that any attack against East Germany would be considered an attack on the Soviet Union. He set a time limit of six months and said that if agreement were not reached by then, the West would have to deal with the East Germans. In later speeches, he indicated that the only satisfactory resolution of the Berlin situation was to turn West Berlin into a free city with the British, French, and Americans withdrawing their 10,000 troops. He also wanted the West Berlin economy integrated into that of East Germany and the Soviet Union. But if the demands were extreme, Khrushchev made it clear that he was anxious to talk. On 30 November he said 'we would like to drink toasts again with war time allies. We want a peaceful solution. We would like to discuss things around a table.'

The idea of a free city, possibly followed by a loose confederation of the two Germanies after all foreign troops had withdrawn, had a certain appeal in the West. George Kennan had advocated a policy of disengagement a year earlier, touching off a long debate in the United States. Kennan and his supporters argued that the only realistic hope for liberation of East Europe lay in disengagement. If the two superpowers could agree to withdraw from Germany, they might eventually pull out of all of Europe. N.A.T.O. and the Warsaw Pact could be simultaneously dismantled and an integration of the whole European economy, along Common Market lines, might then take place. In any case, if there were some disengagement, American soldiers would not be glaring at Red Army troops across divided Berlin, risks and tensions would be lower, and a halting step would have been made towards solving the German problem.

Cold Warriors within the United States denounced Kennan's proposal as hopelessly idealistic. Dean Acheson gave the authoritative answer. 'Mr Kennan has never, in my judgment, grasped the realities of power relationships, but takes a rather mystical attitude toward them. To Mr Kennan there is no Soviet military threat in Europe.' Acheson saw no reason to change the decade-old policy of keeping the powder dry and the barricades in good repair.

Acheson was extreme, but the toughness of his statement hid as much as it revealed. He was not merely looking at the world through military binoculars. Kennan assumed that the United States wanted a strong, vibrant, independent Europe. This was not necessarily the case. American leaders wanted a Europe tied to the United States, and since the Red Army made it impossible to bring all of Europe into the American economic orbit, they would settle for Western Europe. A unified, independent Europe would set its own policies in the Cold War, carry on extensive trade with Russia, and offer strong competition in America's overseas markets. The Russians, too, were more interested in continuing their exploitation of East Europe than they were in moving towards Kennan's dream.

Eisenhower took a middle course. He rejected the free city proposal but at the same time he refused to follow Acheson and those who wanted no change at all. He also rebuffed those Americans who wanted to increase the Armed Services dramatically as a prelude to taking a hard line over Berlin. In March 1959, as Khrushchev's deadline approached and Democrats, along with some Republicans, urged him to mobilize, he told Congress that he did not need additional money for missiles or conventional warfare forces to deal with the crisis. At a press conference on 11 March, with considerable emotion, he dismissed demands that he refrain from carrying out plans to further reduce the size of the Army. He wanted to know what in heaven's name the United States would do with more ground forces in Europe. Thumping the table, he declared, 'We are certainly not going to fight a ground war in Europe' and pointed out the elementary truth that a few more men or even a few more divisions in Europe would have no effect on the military balance there. He thought the greatest danger in the Berlin crisis was that the Russians would frighten the United States into an arms race that would bankrupt the country. The contrast between what Eisenhower did and what the Democrats wanted (and did a few years later in a similar Berlin crisis) could not have been greater.

Khrushchev, who wanted to reduce his own armed forces and who was no more anxious to exchange nuclear strikes than Eisenhower, began to back down. He denied that he had ever set a time limit, agreed to visit the United States (September 1959), and arranged with Eisenhower for a summit meeting in Geneva, scheduled for May 1960.

During private talks with Khrushchev at Camp David, Maryland, in the fall of 1959, Eisenhower admitted that the situation in Berlin was abnormal and that some modification would be necessary. Although by no means ready to take up Kennan's disengagement proposal, Eisenhower was prepared to make concessions in order to normalize the situation. Dulles had resigned, due to a fatal illness, and Eisenhower became noticeably friendlier to the Russians than any American leader had been since 1945. The West Germans were furious but there was little they could do. Great changes in Europe were not in the immediate future, but for the first time since the beginning of the Cold War it was possible to imagine some shifts in basic positions.

In a limited and halting but nevertheless real way, Eisenhower had opted for peace. Throughout his second term he warned of the danger of turning America into a garrison state and of the need to learn to live with the communists. As a professional soldier of the old school, Eisenhower felt his first responsibility was the nation's security, which he realized could never be enhanced by an arms race in the nuclear age. If the United States built more bombers and missiles, the Russians also would build more. American security would be lowered, not increased. Negotiation with the Russians was a more effective way to enhance the nation's security. Democrats thought the primary reason for Eisenhower's concern was his commitment to a balanced budget, and it was true that he had decided the cost of the Cold War was more than America could bear, but there was something else. By 1958 Eisenhower realized that he had only two more years on the world stage, that if he were to leave any lasting gift to the world he would have to do it soon. His deepest personal desire was to leave mankind the gift of peace.

Eisenhower and Khrushchev were anxious to solidify the concept of peaceful coexistence, each for his own reasons, but by 1959 the Cold War had gone on for so long that calling it off was no easy task. Both men had to fend off hardliners at home, both had troubles with their allies, and both were beset by Third World problems that they could neither understand nor control. Eisenhower had trouble with the Democrats, who were unhampered by orthodox fiscal views and who did want an arms race. In their view, government spending would help, not hurt, the economy. The Democrats, led by Senators John F. Kennedy, Lyndon B. Johnson, and Hubert H. Humphrey, were impatient with Eisenhower's conservatism, yearned for a dynamic President, and talked incessantly about America's loss of prestige. They wanted to restore America to world leadership, which in practice meant extending American commitments and increasing American arms. On the other side, Eisenhower was beset by Republicans who wanted to hear more about liberation and getting tough with the communists, and the President himself had by no means escaped fully from the patterns of thought of the Cold War.

Neither had Khrushchev, who also had hardliners in Moscow pushing him towards the brink. In addition, Mao had become as much a problem for Khrushchev as Chiang was for Eisenhower. Khrushchev's refusal to support Mao's call for wars of national liberation, a basic cause of the Sino-Russian split, signified to Mao that the Russians had joined the have powers against the have-nots. There was other evidence, such as Khrushchev's trip to the United States, his willingness to go to Geneva again, and the cooling of the Berlin crisis. As the Chinese saw it, the Soviets were selling out both communism and the Third World. They accused Khrushchev of appeasement. Mao's propaganda increasingly warned of winds blowing from the east instead of the west and of a world-wide revolt of the rural peoples against the urbanites, among whom the Chinese counted the Russians. Mao's radicalism, heightened by his emphasis on racism, appealed strongly to the Third World and made it almost as difficult for the Soviets to influence development in Southeast Asia and Africa as it was for the United States. Mao challenged, directly and successfully, Khrushchev's leadership of the communist world. Indirectly, he challenged bipolarity. The world was simply too large, with too much diversity, to be controlled by the two super powers, no matter how closely together they marched (Mao would soon discover, in Africa, that the world could not be controlled by three powers either).

Khrushchev and Eisenhower, in short, had gone too far towards co-existence for the Cold Warriors in their own countries and for their allies. Khrushchev was in the weaker position at home, since Eisenhower was almost immune to criticism, especially on military matters. When the Air Force and certain Congressmen demanded that one-third of S.A.C.'s bombers be airborne at all times, for example, Eisenhower dismissed the proposal as too costly and not necessary. As one Senator, who was an Air Force supporter, put it, 'How the hell can I argue with "Ike" Eisenhower on military matters?' Khrushchev did not have such prestige and he found it increasingly difficult to ward off those in the Kremlin who wanted more arms and something done about Berlin. He also had to face the Chinese challenge for communist leadership.

Khrushchev badly needed a Cold War victory, for internal political reasons and to compete with China for followers. He may have felt that Eisenhower, who would shortly be leaving office and who had no pressing need for a resounding triumph, would be willing to allow him a victory. Whatever his reasoning, Khrushchev announced on 5 May 1960, on the eve of the Geneva summit meeting, that a Russian surface-to-air missile (S.A.M.) had knocked down an American U-2 spy plane inside Russia.

The event illustrated more than Khrushchev's flair for

the dramatic, for it also showed how entrenched Cold War interests could block any move towards peace. Having finally achieved the ability to knock down the U-2s, the Soviets could have waited for the results of the Geneva meeting to actually do it. On the other side, the C.I.A. could have suspended the flights in the period preceding the meeting. Or Khrushchev could have kept quiet about the entire affair, hoping that the C.I.A. had learned the lesson and would cease and desist thereafter. Instead, he deliberately embarrassed the President. Khrushchev boasted about the performance of the S.A.M.s but concealed the pilot's survival in order to elicit an American explanation that could be demolished by producing the pilot. When Eisenhower fell into the trap, Khrushchev crowed over his discomfort and demanded an apology or a repudiation of presidential responsibility. He had misjudged the man. Eisenhower stated instead that the United States had the right to spy on the Soviet Union and took full personal responsibility for the flight. The summit conference was ruined. The best hope for an agreement on Berlin was gone, although Khrushchev did abandon his effort to change the *status quo* there. He said he would wait for the new President to take office before he brought it up again.

Khrushchev had improved his position at home, and with the Chinese, but not much. Eisenhower had tried but in the end he was unable to bring the Cold War to a close. Despite the U-2 and the wrecked summit meeting, he had improved Russian–American relations. He had failed to liberate any communist slaves – had indeed been forced to acquiesce in the coming of communism to Indochina and in the establishment of a Russian base in the Mediterranean – but he had avoided war and kept the arms race at a low level. He had tried, insofar as he was capable, to ease the policy of permanent crisis he had inherited from Truman.

Eisenhower's major weakness was that he was an old man, head of an old party, surrounded by old advisers. He dealt with old problems. His image, deliberately promoted by the

Republicans, was that of a kindly grandfather. He could not anticipate new problems, nor adjust to the winds of change that Mao always talked about and which were, indeed, blowing across the world. Domestically as well as abroad, the revolution of rising expectations more or less escaped notice.*

Cuba illustrated Eisenhower's limited view best, but it also showed the constraints within which any President would have to operate in dealing with Third World revolution. The United States had given verbal support to the colonial revolutions in the immediate post-war period, but it found it much more difficult to adjust to, much less welcome, the thoroughgoing social and economic revolutions that followed. When African and Asian states achieved their independence, they found themselves in the same position as the Latin Americans. Their economy remained extractive, their principal sources of income were owned or controlled by the West, and their masses continued to live in poverty. They needed to change the nature of their economies. To do that, they needed money. To get money, since neither the United States nor Russia would loan it on anything like the scale required, they had to nationalize the major foreign holdings, as Nasser had done. They also had

* In 1960, while Eisenhower was touring Latin America, he received a long letter from the President of the Federation of Students in Chile. The student, in respectful but firm words, charged that American policy was to favor the rich in Latin America. All the private and federal aid programs were designed to maintain the 'prevailing order in this starved and illiterate [South] America' and allow the few to 'enjoy a standard of living which would be envied by the multimillionaires of the United States'. Eisenhower was so shocked and upset by this information, which did not fit at all into his idea of how the United States related to Latin America, that in the middle of a speech he delivered the afternoon he received the letter he discarded the prepared text and replied to the student. He said in effect that he had not realized what the situation was and assured the audience that the United States did not intend to ignore the masses of Latin America. Eisenhower's startling admission of ignorance about the way Point Four worked indicated how little he understood the Third World or America's role in it.

to have state planning and control in order to use their limited resources most effectively, for their people would not wait for the slow process of economic advance via capitalism, which in any case would only enrich a few and leave the masses where they had always been.

The underdeveloped nations, in short, needed to change their entire relationship with the West, which posed a continuing problem for the United States. On the simple economic level, American citizens and corporations lost money when plants, mines, or plantations were expropriated. Most emerging nations did not pay for what they seized, partly out of principle – they had been exploited so long they felt they deserved whatever they took, and more – and partly because they did not have the funds. Beyond the immediate loss, the Americans also lost the opportunity for further profits and an area of potential further investment. Within the United States, whenever an American investment was nationalized, there were cries of anguish and Congressional demands for action, which made it extraordinarily difficult for a President to deal effectively with the Third World.

Ideology also got in the way, for even if no American investments were involved the idea of socialism sent some Americans – especially in Congress – into a near panic. As an example, Eisenhower's successor wanted to give aid to India in its efforts to industrialize, thereby showing the Third World that the Americans were ready to accept neutralism and, far more important, to build a counter to China in Asia. But because India's steel industry was nationalized, the President had to drop the proposal.

All of America's difficulties in dealing with the underdeveloped world came to a head in Cuba. Throughout the nineteenth century, Americans had looked with undisguised longing towards the island. In 1898 they drove the Spanish out and occupied it. After the Cubans wrote a constitution that gave the United States the right to intervene on the island whenever Washington felt it was necessary, the American troops left. Investors stayed behind. Three times after 1902 the United States intervened in Cuba to protect the investments, which by the end of World War II had grown to impressive proportions. Americans owned 80 per cent of Cuba's utilities, 40 per cent of its sugar, 90 per cent of its mining wealth, and occupied the island's key strategic location of Guantanamo Bay. Cuban life was controlled from Washington, for almost the only source of income was sugar, and by manipulating the amount of sugar allowed into the United States, Washington directed the economy. As Ambassador Earl Smith later confessed, 'Senator, let me explain to you that the United States ... was so overwhelmingly influential in Cuba that ... the American Ambassador was the second most important man in Cuba; sometimes even more important than the [Cuban] President.'

Fulgencio Batista was the Cuban dictator. He had come to power as a revolutionary but had adjusted to the realities of leading a small nation in which the United States had a large investment. Postponing land reform and other promised improvements, by the fifties he had become a fairly typical Latin American ruler. His sole support was the Cuban Army, which was equipped by the United States, and his policies were repressive. In January 1959, after a long struggle, Fidel Castro, who had placed himself at the head of the various anti-Batista guerrilla movements, drove Batista from power. At first the general public in the United States welcomed Castro, casting him in a romantic mold and applauding his democratic reforms. Castro helped by putting leading Cuban liberals in important posts on his Cabinet. American supporters of Castro expected him to restore civil liberties, introduce gradual and compensated land reform, look to the United States for leadership, maintain Havana as the swingingest city in the New World, and not tamper with the fundamental source of Cuba's poverty, American ownership of the mines and sugar plantations.

Within the American government, however, Castro did

not receive an enthusiastic welcome. Allen Dulles, the C.I.A. chief, told Eisenhower that 'Communists and other extreme radicals appear to have penetrated the Castro movement'; Dulles warned that the communists would probably participate in the government. 'When I heard this estimate,' Eisenhower later said, 'I was provoked that such a conclusion had not been given earlier.' The limitations on American policy then became apparent. Someone suggested that the United States help Batista return to power. Eisenhower refused – Batista was too much the dictator. Since Castro was too close to the communists to deserve American support, the administration began working on a third alternative. 'Our only hope,' Eisenhower said, 'lay with some kind of non-dictatorial "third force", neither Castroite nor Batistiano.' The statement summed up the entire American relationship to the underdeveloped world – find a liberal who would not disturb the existing economic arrangements but who would rule in a democratic manner. It was a self-defeating program, for in Cuba – and elsewhere – there was little point to having a revolution if the basic economic structure were not changed, beginning with expropriation of foreign-owned property.

In Cuba, meanwhile, the forces in the Castro movement combined with the realities he faced to push him to the left. His own inclination was towards radicalism anyway, and there was no possibility of improvement in Cuba as long as the profits continued to flow back to the United States. Castro therefore began an extensive land reform program and a nationalization of American-owned property, without compensation.* The United States turned down his requests for loans and relations steadily worsened. Cuban liberals began to flee the country; Cuban com-

---

* Castro did offer to pay for what he took, on the basis of the value of the property stated by the owners themselves in response to an early Castro request for a reassessment for taxation purposes. American investors denounced this as a fraud and refused – they demanded full value, not what they had said the property was worth when the question was taxation by the Cuban government.

munists rose to power under Castro. Khrushchev, not adverse to a little liberation himself, welcomed Castro as a new force in Latin America, pronounced the Monroe Doctrine dead, and in February 1960 signed a trade agreement to exchange Cuban sugar for Soviet oil and machinery. Four months later the United States eliminated the Cuban sugar quota; in the first days of 1961 Eisenhower formally severed diplomatic relations with Cuba. The mass media explained that Castro had 'betrayed' the Cuban revolution by his radical measures, a line that revealed only how little newsmen understood conditions in Cuba, but a line that was nonetheless accepted.

The search for a liberal alternative went on. Eisenhower gave the C.I.A. permission to plan an invasion of Cuba and to begin training Cuban exiles to carry it out, with American support. Some of Castro's original liberal Cabinet members participated in the invasion scheme. Preparations were not complete when Eisenhower left office and whether to go forward with the invasion or not became his successor's problem.

By the time Eisenhower left office, he knew that the United States was in deep trouble in Cuba. He was also clear in briefing his successor on the situation in Berlin, Formosa, N.A.T.O., and the Middle East. He never mentioned Vietnam in the briefings, however, and the American press and government continued to present Diem as the liberal model on which the Third World could base its revolution.

Eisenhower's lack of foresight was hardly unusual. The young Democrats who had taken over the party by nominating John F. Kennedy for the Presidency, and who were urging dynamism in foreign relations and a major increase in America's armed forces, as well as a totally new American relationship to the Third World, did not know that there was a problem in Vietnam either. Kennedy and his advisers, like Eisenhower, were most concerned with finding a liberal alternative to Castro. During the campaign Kennedy said his policy would be to give American support to 'non-

Batista democratic anti-Castro forces'. The major foreign policy issue in the Nixon–Kennedy campaign of 1960 was Quemoy and Matsu. Kennedy doubted that the islands were worth defending, although he never suggested anything approaching a reorientation of American policy *vis-à-vis* China. Nixon insisted that Quemoy and Matsu had to be held. Kennedy also stressed the missile gap, which Nixon denied existed. There were no other significant differences on foreign policy issues. Kennedy won by a narrow margin.

In January 1961, Eisenhower delivered his farewell address to the people. He was concerned about the internal cost of the Cold War. His ideals were those of the small town in the Middle West where he grew up. He was afraid that big government and the regimentation of private life were threatening the old American values. He had no precise idea of what could be done about the dangers, for he knew that both were necessary to carrying on the Cold War, but he did want to warn his countrymen. He pointed out that the 'conjunction of an immense military establishment and a large arms industry, . . . new in American experience', exercised a 'total influence . . . felt in every city, every state house, every office of the federal government. . . . In the councils of government, we must guard against the acquisition of unwarranted influence, whether sought or unsought, by the military-industrial complex.'

The Democrats paid no attention. In the campaign, and in his inaugural address, Kennedy emphasized that a new generation was coming to power in America. Hardened by the Cold War, it was prepared to deal with all the tough problems. He promised to replace Eisenhower's tired, bland leadership with new ideas and new approaches. Since these generalities were not reinforced by any specific suggestions, it was difficult to tell what the new directions would be. What was clear was that a forward-looking, offensive spirit had come to America. Action was about to replace inaction. Kennedy promised to get the country moving again. Where to, no one knew precisely.

10

Kennedy

'Let every nation know, whether it wishes us well or ill, that we shall pay any price, bear any burden, meet any hardship, support any friend, oppose any foes, in order to assure the survival and success of liberty. This much we pledge – and more.'

JOHN F. KENNEDY, *Inaugural Address*

JOHN KENNEDY had a vision of America. He thought the United States was the last, best hope of mankind. He wanted prosperity and happiness for all the world's people and believed the United States was capable of supplying the leadership necessary to achieve those goals. He surrounded himself with the very best minds America had to offer, appointing men who had the techniques and the brains that would enable the new administration to solve any problem, indeed to go out and find new problems so that they could solve them.

Kennedy and the men around him had been impatient with Eisenhower's leadership. Eisenhower had not been aggressive enough, he tended to compromise, he could not stir the nation to great deeds. Fundamentally, Eisenhower had rejected the idea that there could be a military solution to Cold War problems or that America could shape the world's destiny. He had accepted limitations on America's role. Kennedy did not. Where Eisenhower had been passive, Kennedy would be active. Where Eisenhower had been cautious, Kennedy would be bold. Kennedy and his aides were especially interested in restoring the prestige and primacy of the Presidency, which they felt had fallen under Eisenhower.

Kennedy's energy was almost boundless. He was interested in every area of the world, anxious to bring the benefits of cost analysis and rational planning to everyone. Khrushchev caught this spirit best when in mid-1961 he responded to a toast Kennedy gave at a luncheon table in Vienna. In his toast Kennedy recalled that Khrushchev had remarked that when he was the President's age he had been a member of the Moscow Planning Commission and was looking forward to becoming chairman. Kennedy said that when he was Khrushchev's age he hoped to be head of the Boston Planning Commission. Khrushchev interjected that perhaps Kennedy would like to be head of a planning commission for the whole world.

Kennedy was dynamic, good-looking, youthful. He exuded confidence. He got on easily with the intellectuals who flocked to Washington to help the new administration and he was by far the most sophisticated President America had had since the Cold War began. His wit and charm seemed to place him light years ahead of his predecessor. Republican rhetoric had consisted of unrestrained hostility to the Soviet Union and emphasized permanent war with communism. It was filled with Cold War clichés. Republican action, however, revealed restraint and caution. The Democratic rhetoric, under Kennedy, favored coexistence. Kennedy abandoned the clichés of the Cold War, especially with regard to the Third World, where he claimed to be ready to accept neutralism and even socialism. He was sympathetic to the non-white peoples, believed himself to be free of any taint of racism, showed an interest in black Africa unique to American politicians, and in general spoke of an entirely new relationship between America and the Third World. But Democratic actions revealed a dynamic militancy, which traditional Cold Warriors like Acheson and Truman could and did applaud.

On the domestic front, Kennedy had the reputation of being a coldly calculating, ruthless politician. He probably would have substituted rational and tough as the adjectives. but in general he rather agreed with this assessment of his style. He thought of himself as being especially capable of crisis management, the man who could keep his head while others around him were losing theirs. When he was not grappling with a difficult problem, he seemed almost bored. Kennedy was far too sophisticated to talk about liberation or brinksmanship or to deliver turgid sermons on the immorality of neutrality, but that did not mean that he had changed Dulles's goals. The chief difference was that, where the Republicans had crept, Kennedy drove at breakneck speed.

The new President deeply believed that the United States was not doing nearly well enough in the Cold War. 'Are we doing as much as we can do?' he asked during the campaign. The answer was no. And if the United States failed, 'then freedom fails'. He said he was 'not satisfied as an American with the progress that we are making'. Kennedy wanted the people of Latin America and Africa and Asia 'to start to look to America, to what the President of the United States is doing, not . . . Khrushchev or the Chinese Communists'. Freedom was under the 'most severe attack it has ever known'. It could be saved only by the United States. The recurring theme, therefore, was, 'I think it's time America started moving again.'

If anyone thought Kennedy was merely indulging in campaign rhetoric, he quickly dispelled that idea. In his first State of the Union address, on 30 January 1961, he warned, 'Each day the crises multiply . . . . Each day we draw nearer the hour of maximum danger.' He felt he had to tell the Congress the truth: 'The tide of events has been running out and time has not been our friend.' Finally, the grim prophecy. 'There will be further setbacks before the tide is turned.'

Kennedy wanted the United States to take the initiative. This sounded suspiciously like Dulles's talk about liberation, but Kennedy emphasized that 'a total solution is impossible in the nuclear age'. He did not expect to 'win' in any traditional sense. The military realities precluded victory, while America's view of the nature of the change and of communism precluded peace. This tended to lock the nation into a policy of containment. Since stalemate was no more satisfactory to Kennedy than it had been to Dulles, however, Kennedy had to hold out a long-range hope. 'Without having a nuclear war,' he said, 'we want to permit what Thomas Jefferson called "the disease of liberty" to be caught in areas which are now held by the Communists.' Sooner or later freedom would triumph. How? Partly by waiting, partly through the example of American vitality. Kennedy told the American people to expect a long, slow process of evolution 'away from Communism and toward national independence and freedom'.

The Third World provided the key. 'The great battleground for the defense and expansion of freedom today,' Kennedy said, 'is the whole southern half of the globe . . . the lands of the rising people.' Kennedy, like the communists, believed in the inevitable victory of his system in the long run. Again like his enemies, however, he was not averse to speeding up the process. Fittingly, his first great opportunity, and his first crisis, came in a Third World revolutionary nation. For all the President's speeches about willingness to tolerate differences in the world, he was no more ready to accept a communist regime off the tip of Florida than Eisenhower had been. In late 1960 the C.I.A., with Eisenhower's approval, had begun training anti-Castro Cuban exiles in the arts of guerrilla warfare. The plan was to land the counter-revolutionaries in a remote section of Cuba, with covert American assistance, so that they could set up a base of operations to overthrow Castro. Some members of the C.I.A. even dreamed of a huge anti-Castro uprising, one that would begin when word reached the Cuban people that the liberators had arrived.

It all proved to be hot air. In mid-April 1961, the invasion began. Cuban exiles, carried in American ships and covered by American airplanes, waded ashore at the Bay of Pigs. Castro completely crushed them. He proved to be far stronger than the Americans had thought, the Cuban people showed no inclination to revolt against him (the truth, in fact, was the other way around), and the exiles were unable to find support in the Cuban mountains. Kennedy had played a delicate game, trying to give enough support to make the invasion work but not enough to make the American involvement obvious. He had failed on both counts.

Later, in analyzing the failure, Kennedy muttered that 'all my life I've known better than to depend on the experts. How could I have been so stupid, to let them go ahead?' That the fault lay with the C.I.A. and the Joint Chiefs became the standard explanation. The President, young and inexperienced, had depended on their expert judgement and had been let down. He would, thereafter, know better.

The explanation was patent nonsense. The Bay of Pigs was hardly an operation carried out against the President's wishes or in opposition to his policy. He had advocated such activity by exile forces during the 1960 campaign, and the fact was that it fitted perfectly into his general approach. The C.I.A. had been wrong in predicting an uprising against Castro, but the prediction was exactly what Kennedy wanted to hear. He, too, believed that Castro had betrayed the Cuban revolution; he, too, believed that the Cuban people were groaning under the oppressor's heel. Kennedy's assumptions about the Cuban people were no different than those Dean Rusk had held in the early fifties about the Chinese people. The President believed there was a liberal alternative between Castro and Batista and that the exile counter-revolutionary group would supply the liberal leadership around which the Cuban people would rally. It was not the experts who got Kennedy into the Bay of Pigs; it was his own view of the world.

Before he gave the final go-ahead, Kennedy had consulted with Senator Fulbright. On 29 March, the Senator sent a memorandum to the President. 'To give this activity even covert support,' Fulbright warned, 'is of a piece with the hypocrisy and cynicism for which the United States is constantly denouncing the Soviet Union.' The Bay of Pigs, the Senator said, would compromise America's moral position in the world and make it impossible for Kennedy to protest treaty violations by the communists. Kennedy ignored Fulbright, partly because he felt that success would provide its own justification, more because to back down on the invasion would compromise Kennedy's position more than the invasion would compromise America's morality. Kennedy believed, as he later explained, that 'his disapproval of the plan would be a show of weakness inconsistent with his general stance'.

One of Kennedy's great fears was to appear weak. And, like most Cold Warriors, he thought the only way to deal with the Russians and their associates was from a position of strength. How much strength became the great question. The man Kennedy picked to answer it, Robert S. McNamara, the Secretary of Defense, maintained that 'enough' meant great superiority. He set out to give America that superiority. McNamara, whose brilliance and ability to use the new technological tools to solve old problems epitomized the Kennedy administration, described the result in some detail in a 1967 speech to the editors of United Press International. McNamara recalled that when he took office, the Soviets possessed 'a very small operational arsenal of intercontinental missiles', but they had the ability to 'enlarge that arsenal very substantially'. The Americans had 'no evidence that the Soviets did in fact plan to fully use that capability', but the possibility existed that they intended to so expand. McNamara and Kennedy decided that 'we had to insure against' a Soviet build-up by dramatically increasing American strength. After two years in office, Kennedy had the Defense budget up to $56 billion; with the coming of war in Vietnam it would skyrocket even higher. By 1967, America had 41 Polaris submarines carrying 656 missile launchers and 600 long-range bombers, 40 per cent of which were always in a high state of alert. In the area that counted most, I.C.B.M.s, Kennedy and McNamara had increased the American force level by a factor of 5. They had inherited 200 I.C.B.M.s from Eisenhower; by 1967 the United States had 1,000 I.C.B.M.s. N.S.C. 68 had finally become firm national policy.

The Kennedy–McNamara team had launched the greatest arms race in the history of mankind. It extended far beyond nuclear delivery weapons. The White House and the Pentagon co-operated in vastly increasing America's conventional war capability and, as a Kennedy favorite, guerrilla warfare forces. Eisenhower had backed away from involvement in Dien Bien Phu because, unless he wished to inaugurate a nuclear exchange, he did not have the forces required. Kennedy was determined that he would never have his hands tied so tightly. He wanted, and got, an ability to intervene anywhere. The new strategy was called flexible response.

As a reaction to the enormous American build-up, the Russians increased their I.C.B.M. forces. As McNamara put it in 1967, the Soviets had had no intention of engaging in an arms race and would have been satisfied to accept the *status quo* of 1960, under which America had superiority but not enough to launch a first-strike. The Kennedy–McNamara program, however, apparently convinced the Kremlin that America did in fact aim at achieving a first-strike capability, which left the Soviets with no choice. They increased their missile forces, which forced the United States to begin another round of expansion. But, as McNamara confessed, the whole thing had been a terrible mistake. America had been unwilling to take the risk of allowing the Soviets to achieve parity in nuclear delivery systems, but by building more missiles the Americans only increased their own danger. Given the inevitable Soviet response, the more missiles America built, the less secure America was. McNamara himself recognized this when he admitted that 'the blunt fact is that if we had had more accurate information about planned Soviet strategic forces [in 1961], we simply would not have needed to build as large a nuclear arsenal as we have today.' The heart of the matter was that Kennedy and McNamara probably did not aim at achieving a first-strike capability, and even if they had they quickly realized that such a goal was impossible. Therefore, as McNamara concluded, American superiority in I.C.B.M.s by 1967 was 'both greater than we had originally planned, and is in fact more than we require'.

The political response to the Kennedy build-up was even more important than the military reaction. Where the Republicans had been content to make general, vague statements to the effect that there was no missile gap, and to rest their military policy on the grounds that General Ike knew best, the Democrats made specific statements in insistent tones about American superiority. Coupled with the Bay of Pigs, the new American military policy demonstrated conclusively to the Soviets that they had to deal with an aggressive, outward-looking administration. The 'hards' in the Kremlin found their direst predictions fulfilled and they gleefully charged Khrushchev with having neglected Soviet military security. Even Khrushchev and his followers, committed to the possibility of détente, had to alter their view, for it seemed to them that the United States was trying to shift the military balance in its favor before reaching a world-wide settlement, part of which would be an agreement to keep military forces at the existing levels. Kennedy was always talking about arms limitation talks, and at the end of his first year in office said his greatest disappointment was the failure to secure a nuclear test ban treaty. The Russians saw Kennedy's expressed desire for arms limitation as a deliberate propaganda lie, coming as it did concurrently with the American military build-up, and believed it was a cover for the continuation of the *status quo* throughout the world, especially in Berlin, Vietnam, Korea, and Formosa. Kennedy, the Russians charged, would use superior American arms to block all change.

Kennedy said as much in the summer of 1961, when he

met Khrushchev in Vienna. Again and again the President urged the Premier to preserve the existing balance of power – which obviously favored the United States – in arms and geography. Kennedy insisted that the entry of additional nations into the communist camp, or the loss of Formosa or Berlin, would alter the equilibrium and force the United States to react. Khrushchev rejected the conception. Even if he wanted to, he said, he could not stop change, and in any case the Soviet Union could hardly be expected to co-operate in enforcing stability on a world that was predominantly colonial and capitalist. Khrushchev complained that Kennedy 'bypassed' the real problem. 'We in the U.S.S.R. feel that the revolutionary process should have the right to exist,' he explained. The question of 'the right to rebel, and the Soviet right to help combat reactionary governments . . . is the question of questions'. It was, he said, 'at the heart of our relations' with the United States. He was sorry that 'Kennedy could not understand this'.

Since Kennedy had just tried to upset the equilibrium at the Bay of Pigs, Khrushchev must have been somewhat startled at the young President's insistence that the communists could not do so elsewhere. To explore the subject further, Khrushchev asked about Formosa. Kennedy said that withdrawal of American forces from Formosa would impair the American strategic position in Asia and would therefore be resisted. Khrushchev shook his head. That meant that the Chinese communists would have to fight for Formosa, which was a 'sad thing'. It forced him to doubt America's sincerity about peaceful co-existence. If he were in the Chinese shoes, he added, he would already have fought for Formosa. Kennedy urged him to restrain Peking, for America would fight back. However abnormal the Formosan situation, however just China's claim to the island, Kennedy was as determined as Truman and Eisenhower to maintain Chiang and the American military bases on the island.

Kennedy wanted the struggle for the Third World to take place without violence, which was to say without changes in the governments and thus without changes in the relationship between the Third World and the West. In his conception, the Cold War would turn on which side could pour the most money and arms into former colonies and thus buy the greatest support. What he did not recognize was how completely his policy ignored the hopes and needs of the Third World masses. The Alliance for Progress, for example, which Kennedy launched with great fanfare as an alternative to Castro in Latin America, was merely a dressed-up version of Truman's Point Four. The major revenue-producing properties in Latin America remained in the hands of American corporations, which meant that the profits returned to the United States. In addition, the Alliance for Progress loans carried strings, the most important of which was that the money had to be spent on American-made goods, which cost far more than the European or Japanese equivalent.* The 'question of questions' was exactly what Khrushchev said it was, the nature of change. The United States, like Europe in the nineteenth century and the first four decades of the twentieth, had no intention of allowing any real change in the exploitive relationship that existed in its dealing with Asia, Africa, and especially Latin America.

The American military build-up indicated that the United States would stop, by force if necessary, revolutionary movement in the Third World. It also indicated that the United States was willing to use force to maintain the *status quo* in Europe. But just as Khrushchev could not forfeit the Soviet Union's right to aid revolutions, neither could he accept the situation in Berlin as permanent. The bone continued to catch in his throat. By the summer of 1961, however, he had to move soon if he wished to do

---

* When Latin American governments complained, they were told – in this case by the Ambassador to Brazil, Lincoln Gordon – that the 'struggle for freedom in Vietnam' required the practice.

anything about it before the Kennedy–McNamara program gave the United States the capability of matching the Red Army on conventional terms.

Kennedy, for his part, seemed open to reasonable accommodation. He was impatient with Third World leaders who continued to squabble with each other over what he considered to be irrational issues. He urged India and Pakistan to get together and jointly solve the problems of Asia; he thought the Arabs and the Jews should settle their differences, forgetting prestige and other non-rational factors. He wanted everyone to be open-minded, prepared to offer and accept alternatives, ready to advance the cause of peace and prosperity. Yet in Berlin he showed that he could be just as stubborn, just as committed to old positions, just as unwilling to consider compromise as the most extreme Arab or Asian nationalist. As if to underscore the point, when Khrushchev started another crisis in Berlin, Kennedy turned to Dean Acheson for advice. Acheson, as always, recommended keeping the powder dry and standing firm. The gist of his stance was, Do not negotiate.

Kennedy agreed. All through the summer of 1961 Khrushchev insisted that there had to be some settlement in Berlin before the end of the year. Kennedy's response was cold and firm: nothing could be changed. He explained the rationale to the Finnish President. Soviet policy, Kennedy said, 'is designed to neutralize West Germany as a first step in the neutralization of Western Europe. That is what makes the present situation so dangerous. West Germany is the key as to whether Western Europe will be free.' By Kennedy's definition, in short, a neutral Europe could not be free.* To make the domino theory more explicit, Kennedy added, 'If we don't meet our commitments in Berlin, it will mean the destruction of N.A.T.O. and a dangerous situation for the whole world. All Europe is at stake in West Berlin.'

* It is worth noting that Kennedy made this observation to the Finns, who were neutral and who thought of themselves as free.

Khrushchev had raised the issue of Berlin for many reasons; one that played a large role was the American military build-up. The Russians wanted a satisfactory settlement in Germany before the effects of Kennedy's policies were complete. Kennedy, meanwhile, raced ahead. He put a $3.2 billion additional military budget through Congress, tripled the draft calls, extended enlistments, and mobilized 158,000 Reserves and National Guardsmen. Altogether he increased the size of the Armed Forces by 300,000 men, sending 40,000 of them to Europe and making six 'priority divisions' in the Reserves ready for quick mobilization.

The two sides were now on a collision course. Khrushchev could not allow West Berlin to remain as an escape hatch; Kennedy could not accept any change in its status. Walter Ulbricht announced that after he signed a peace treaty with the Russians, he would close West Berlin's access to the Western world. The President prepared the American people for the worst. In a television address on 25 July 1961, Kennedy showed how determined he was to stay in Berlin by invoking heroic deeds from the past. 'I hear it said that West Berlin is militarily untenable,' he began. 'And so was Bastogne. And so, in fact, was Stalingrad. Any dangerous spot is tenable if men – brave men – will make it so.' He again said that if Berlin went Germany would follow, then all of Western Europe. Berlin was essential to the 'entire free world'.

Khrushchev regarded the speech as belligerent and called Kennedy's arms policy military hysteria. Kennedy had made no new offers; indeed, he had made no offers at all to adjust the Berlin situation. East Germans continued to escape via Berlin; Western propaganda continued to embarrass the communists by loudly proclaiming that the flow of refugees proved the superiority of capitalism. By early August both world leaders had so completely committed themselves that no solution seemed possible. The crisis seemed destined to end in war.

The refugees were the sticking point. Khrushchev and the East Germans could accept the Western spy apparatus in West Berlin, and they could even live with the propaganda that emanated from the city. But they could not afford to continue to lose their best human resources to the West, nor continue to give the West such an ideal propaganda advantage. For his part, Kennedy could hardly be expected to shut the doors to West Berlin or to refrain from using the refugee issue.

On 13 August 1961, Khrushchev suddenly and dramatically solved the Berlin problem. He built the Wall, presenting America and the West with a *fait accompli* and permanently dividing Berlin. The flow of refugees was shut off and – after an initial reaction of outrage – the tension visibly eased. The Soviet building of the Wall, and the eventual Western acceptance of it, signified the end to all serious attempts to reunify Germany. The great powers had decided that Berlin, and beyond it Germany, were not worth a nuclear exchange. Khrushchev lost prestige in the world, and the West lost the refugees, but both sides were able to accept the result because nothing vital had been sacrificed. Khrushchev was willing to live with West Berlin as long as it was isolated and did not drain East Germany. Kennedy was willing to live with the Wall as long as West Berlin stayed in the Western orbit. Khrushchev's Wall was a brilliant stroke. The only question left was whether the Germans, East and West, would accept the solution. Throughout the sixties, they did.

The compromise solution in Berlin did not lead to a permanent end to tension. It could not, since Berlin was but one of the unsettled issues remaining from World War II and since the American military build-up continued, after being expanded during the crisis. Kennedy had looked weak to many Cold Warriors in the United States because he had not torn down the Wall. Khrushchev looked weak to the Cold Warriors in the communist world for building it. Khrushchev was in deeper trouble, however, because the

Kennedy administration insisted on boasting about American military superiority. Kennedy officials and American strategic intellectuals were publicly sketching scenarios in which the United States would strike first. They justified the exercise by expressing their skepticism of Soviet missile credibility.

Khrushchev had to react. He could allow the United States its strategic nuclear superiority, and there was little he could do about it in any case, since the United States could and would out-build him. But he could not allow the United States to be both superior and to boast about its superiority. He needed a dramatic strategic victory, one that would focus world attention on Soviet military capability and satisfy his own armed services. He found the answer with increased megatonnage. On 30 August 1961, he announced that he was breaking the three-year Russian–American moratorium on nuclear testing with a series of tests that climaxed with the explosion of a 58-megaton weapon, 3,000 times more powerful than the bomb used against Hiroshima and many times more powerful than anything the United States had developed. The big bomb was good for propaganda, but it had little if any military use, as both sides already had bombs far larger than they needed to destroy any city in the world.

Khrushchev's series of tests did have the effect, however, of leading to strident demands that Kennedy begin his own series of tests. The President had given top priority to achieving a nuclear test ban treaty and was despondent when he could not get it. He was furious with Khrushchev for breaking the moratorium, but he refused to be stampeded into a new series of tests. Kennedy was greatly worried about the fall-out problem and he realized that no matter how big Russian bombs grew the United States would remain strategically superior because of American delivery capability. He tried to compromise with a series of underground tests that began in September 1961. It was not enough, however, to satisfy his domestic critics and by April 1962 Kennedy gave in to those who warned that the

Soviets might have made important discoveries by ordering a series of American tests (thirty in all) in the atmosphere.

Khrushchev, frustrated in the nuclear field, unable to push the West out of Berlin, incapable of matching the United States in I.C.B.M.s, and increasingly irritated by the Chinese harping about Soviet weakness, began to look elsewhere for a Cold War victory and an opportunity to alter the strategic balance. He found it in Cuba. Since the Bay of Pigs, Russia had increased her aid to Castro and had begun to include military supplies. Kennedy had warned the Soviets not to give offensive weapons to the Cubans; Khrushchev assured the President that he had no intention of doing so. But in August 1962 the Soviet Union began to build medium-range ballistic missile sites in Cuba.

What did Khrushchev hope to accomplish? He could not have expected to attain a first-strike capability. The American delivery system was far too vast for the Russians ever to expect to be able to destroy it. Nor could Khrushchev have wanted to expand the arms race, for the Russians would not be able to match the American productive capacity. Putting missiles in Cuba would not make Castro any more of a communist, but it was possible that Khrushchev thought the missiles were necessary to protect Cuba from invasion. The American Congress, military, and popular press were all talking openly of invading Cuba again, and the Russians insisted after the event that the missiles had been in response to the invasion talk. If this was his motive, however, Khrushchev badly miscalculated, for the missiles practically invited Kennedy to invade.

As with the 58-megaton bomb, Khrushchev may have been seeking military parity on the cheap. His medium-range missiles in Cuba would match America's I.C.B.M.s. Even this explanation, however, although the most probable, is unsatisfactory. The Kennedy administration, once it learned of the presence of the Soviet missiles, never doubted that one way or another it had to get them out of Cuba, even at the risk of a nuclear war. This would seem to indicate

that in the best judgement of the J.C.S. and the C.I.A. the missiles in Cuba did make a strategic difference. But the same officials had already decided that American medium-range missiles in Turkey were obsolete; more important, they believed that if all-out war came, the United States would be destroyed. If the United States could be destroyed before the missile sites in Cuba were operational, what did the Cuban sites matter?

From the first, the issue in Cuba was prestige. Kennedy had taken from Khrushchev the fiction of the missile gap. The 58-megaton bomb had not been sufficiently impressive. The hardliners in the Soviet Union and the Chinese continued to pressure Khrushchev to stand up to the United States. The Kennedy administration continued to boast about American military superiority. As Theodore Sorensen, Kennedy's chief speech writer, later put it, 'To be sure, these Cuban missiles alone, in view of all the other megatonnage the Soviets were capable of unleashing upon us, did not substantially alter the strategic balance *in fact* . . . but that balance would have been substantially altered *in appearance*; and in matters of national will and world leadership . . . such appearances contribute to reality.' The most serious crisis in the history of mankind, in short, turned on a question of appearances. The world came close to total destruction over a matter of prestige.

On 14 October 1962, American U-2s photographed in Cuba a launch pad under construction which, when completed, could fire missiles with a range of 1,000 miles. Kennedy was already under pressure from the Republicans, led by New York Senator Kenneth Keating, for failing to stop the Soviet military build-up in Cuba. Congressional elections were less than three weeks away. The pressure to respond was overwhelming. When a high official in the Pentagon suggested that Kennedy do nothing and ignore the missiles, as they constituted no additional threat to the United States, the President replied that he had to act. If he did not, he would be impeached.

How to respond became the great question. The President set the general goals: get the missiles out of Cuba; avoid a nuclear exchange; prepare for Russian moves elsewhere, as in Berlin; do not lose face. He appointed a special committee of a dozen or so members, which called itself the Executive Committee (Ex Comm), to give him advice. The leading figure on the Ex Comm was the President's younger brother, Attorney General Robert F. Kennedy. The committee debated a wide range of alternatives, which soon narrowed down to launching a nuclear strike against the missile sites, launching a conventional air strike, followed by an invasion, or initiating a naval blockade that would prevent the Soviets from sending any further material into Cuba. Fear of Russian reprisal soon eliminated the talk of a nuclear strike; support for a conventional attack and an invasion grew. The missiles were a heaven-sent opportunity to get rid of Castro once and for all. Invasion forces gathered in Florida and Kennedy had the State Department proceed with a crash program for civil government in Cuba to be established after the occupation of that country.

Robert Kennedy, however, continued to insist on a less belligerent initial response. He refused to countenance a surprise attack, repeating over and over, 'My brother is not going to be the Tojo of the 1960s.' He wanted to begin the response with a partial naval blockade, one that would keep out Soviet military goods but not force Khrushchev to react immediately. The great advantage of the blockade, as he saw it, was that the pressure could be stepped up if it did not work. Dean Acheson, who was called in for advice, vigorously opposed the blockade and voted for the air strike, as did the Joint Chiefs, but in the end Kennedy chose the blockade as the initial American response.

Having decided on what to do, Kennedy sent Acheson to Europe to inform the N.A.T.O. allies. Although somewhat surprised at the extreme American reactions – the Europeans had lived under the shadow of Soviet medium-range missiles for years – de Gaulle, Adenauer and the others supported the President. So did the Organization of American States. Then at 7:00 P.M., 22 October 1962, Kennedy went on television to break the well-kept secret to the American people. He explained the situation, then announced that the United States was imposing 'a strict quarantine on all offensive military equipment' being shipped into Cuba. He had placed American military forces on full alert and warned Khrushchev that the United States would regard any nuclear missile launched from Cuba against any nation in the Western Hemisphere as an attack by the Soviet Union on the United States, requiring a full retaliatory response upon the Soviet Union. He appealed to Khrushchev to remove the offensive weapons under United Nations supervision.

Kennedy had seized the initiative. It was now up to Khrushchev to respond. His first reaction was belligerent. In a letter received in Washington on 23 October, Khrushchev said the Soviet Union would not observe the illegal blockade. 'The actions of U.S.A. with regard to Cuba are outright banditry or, if you like, the folly of degenerate imperialism.' He accused Kennedy of pushing mankind 'to the abyss of a world missile-nuclear war' and asserted that Soviet captains bound for Cuba would not obey the orders of American naval forces. The United States Navy meanwhile deployed 500 miles off Cuba's coast. Two destroyers stopped and boarded a Panamanian vessel headed for Cuba carrying Russian goods. It contained no military material and was allowed to proceed. Soviet ships continued to steam for Cuba, although those carrying missiles turned back. Work on the missile sites in Cuba continued without interruption, however, and they would soon be operational.

The threat of mutual annihilation remained high. Kennedy stood firm. Finally, at 6:00 P.M. on 26 October, Khrushchev sent another message. Fittingly, considering the stakes, it was long and emotional. The Premier wanted the President to realize that 'if indeed war should break out, then it would not be in our power to stop it'. He said once again that the missiles were in Cuba for defensive purposes only. 'We are of sound mind and understand perfectly well that if we attack you, you will respond the same way. But you too will receive the same that you hurl against us . . . . Only lunatics or suicides, who themselves want to perish and to destroy the whole world before they die, could do this.' He said he did not want an arms race. 'Armaments bring only disasters. When one accumulates them, this damages the economy, and if one puts them to use, then they destroy people on both sides. Consequently, only a madman can believe that armaments are the principal means in the life of society.'

Then came the specific proposal. Khrushchev said he would send no more weapons to Cuba and would withdraw or destroy those already there if Kennedy would withdraw the blockade and promise not to invade Cuba. He urged Kennedy to untie the knot rather than pulling it tighter.

The following morning, 27 October, the Ex Comm met to consider Khrushchev's proposal. Before they could decide whether or not to accept, a second letter from the Premier arrived. More formal than the first, it raised the price. Khrushchev, perhaps bowing to pressure from his own military, said he would take out the Cuban missiles when Kennedy removed the American missiles from Turkey. 'You are worried over Cuba,' Khrushchev stated. 'You say that it worries you because it lies at a distance of ninety miles across the sea from the shores of the United States. However, Turkey lies next to us . . . . You have stationed devastating rocket weapons . . . in Turkey literally right next to us.'

The Ex Comm was thunderstruck, even though as Robert Kennedy later put it, 'The fact was that the proposal the Russians made was not unreasonable and did not amount to a loss to the United States or to our N.A.T.O. allies.' The President had actually already ordered the missiles out of Turkey, but due to a bureaucratic foul-up and Turkish resistance they were still there. To remove them now, however, under Soviet pressure, he regarded as intolerable. The blow to American prestige would be too great. The possibility of a nuclear exchange continued to hang in the balance.

The Joint Chiefs recommended an air strike the next morning against Cuba. The generals and admirals said they had always been against the blockade as being too weak and now they wanted immediate action. Their position was strengthened when a Soviet S.A.M. knocked down an American U-2 flying over Cuba. At this point a majority on the Ex Comm agreed on the necessity of an air strike the next morning. The President demurred. He wanted to wait at least one more day. The State Department drafted a letter from Kennedy to Khrushchev, informing the Premier that the United States could not remove the missiles from Turkey and that no trade could be made.

Robert Kennedy then stepped forward. He suggested that the Ex Comm ignore Khrushchev's second letter and answer his first, the one that offered to trade the missiles in Cuba for an American promise not to invade the island. Bitter arguments followed, but the President finally accepted his brother's suggestion. He sent an appropriate letter to Khrushchev.

Far more important than this famous incident, however, was an oral promise Robert Kennedy gave to the Soviet Ambassador to the United States, Anatoly Dobrynin. Although the President would not back down in public on the Turkish missile sites, he evidently had begun to see the absurdity of the situation – the United States was on the verge of bombing a small nation with which it was not at war, and risking in the process a nuclear exchange with the Soviet Union, over the issue of obsolete missiles in Turkey that he had already ordered removed. Kennedy discussed the issues with his brother and asked him to talk to Dobrynin. On Saturday night, 27 October, Dobrynin came to Robert Kennedy's office. The Attorney General first presented the Russian Ambassador with an ultimatum: If the United

States did not have a commitment by the next day that the missiles would be removed, 'we would remove them'. Dobrynin then asked what kind of a deal the United States was prepared to make. Kennedy summarized the letter that had just gone to Khrushchev, offering to trade the missiles for an American promise not to invade Cuba. Dobrynin turned to the sticking point – what about the American missiles in Turkey?

Robert Kennedy's answer, as given in his own account of the crisis, was: 'I said that there could be no quid pro quo or any arrangement made under this kind of threat or pressure, and that in the last analysis this was a decision that would have to be made by N.A.T.O. However, I said, President Kennedy had been anxious to remove those missiles from Turkey and Italy for a long period of time. He had ordered their removal some time ago, and it was our judgement that, within a short time after this crisis was over, those missiles would be gone.'

The statement was sufficient. The Russians had their promise. The next day Dobrynin informed Robert Kennedy that the missiles in Cuba would be withdrawn.

The world settled back to assess the lessons. Everyone learned something different. The Chinese, for example, told the Third World that the Cuban crisis proved one could not trust the Russians. Europe, led by de Gaulle, learned that in emergencies the United States would act on its own, without N.A.T.O. consultation, on matters affecting not only American security but world survival. The Russians learned that they could not have military parity with the United States, or even the appearance of it. Kennedy, having been to the brink and having looked into the yawning chasm of world holocaust, learned to be a little softer in his pronouncements, a little less strident in his assertions. His administration took on a more moderate tone, at least with regard to the Soviet Union, and the need for peace and arms reductions replaced boasts about American military power.

Kennedy now began to push for a nuclear test ban treaty as a start to halting the arms race. 'Mr Khrushchev and I are in the same boat in the sense of both having this nuclear capacity and both wanting to protect our societies,' he said in one speech. 'He realizes how dangerous a world we live in. If Mr Khrushchev would concern himself with the real interests of the people of the Soviet Union, their standard of living . . . there is no real reason why we should not be able to live in peace.' This was almost, but not quite, a return to Kennedy's position in Vienna – the Soviet Union should call off the arms race on the basis of permanent American military superiority and the *status quo*. What was new was Kennedy's growing recognition that the American system could not be universally imposed or accepted in a world where most of the people 'are not white . . . are not Christians . . . and know nothing about free enterprise or due process of law or the Australian ballot'. Without specifically contradicting Woodrow Wilson's phrase of 'a world made safe for democracy', Kennedy spoke increasingly in 1963 of 'a world made safe for diversity'.

Khrushchev, two years earlier, had accused Kennedy of not seeing 'the question of questions'. Kennedy now began to see it, to realize that in the Third World land distribution, literacy drives and central planning were reforms to be encouraged, not communist plots to be resisted. 'These countries are poor,' Kennedy stressed in his last press conference, 'they are nationalist, they are proud, they are in many cases radical. I don't think threats from Capitol Hill bring the results which are frequently hoped . . . .' He summed up his new attitude rather simply: 'I think it is a very dangerous, untidy world. I think we will have to live with it.' The real test of how deeply Kennedy meant what he said would come in Vietnam, but at least he was saying what the Third World peoples wanted to hear.

The message to Khrushchev was that the two super-powers should stop rattling their nuclear sabers at each other, stop testing bigger and bigger bombs, and concentrate on their domestic economies. Kennedy would not stand in the way of change in the Third World, although he would do his utmost to influence it. Khrushchev could not agree to all of the program – he certainly was not going to make the Soviet Union inward-looking while Kennedy expanded the American frontiers – but he could accept a partial test ban. Kennedy sped the negotiations for the treaty when at American University, on 10 June 1963, he made a dramatic appeal for peace, which he characterized as 'the necessary rational end of rational men'. The Partial Test Ban Treaty was signed a few weeks later, prohibiting nuclear tests in the atmosphere. As Herbert S. Dinerstein notes, 'the test ban treaty symbolically recognized that the accommodation between the Soviet Union and the United States would be made on the basis of American superiority'. It was symbolic only, however, for the reality of Soviet inferiority had long been known to military men on both sides.

The Chinese, nevertheless, were furious. They called Khrushchev foolish for putting the missiles into Cuba and cowardly for removing them. Within the Kremlin, opposition to Khrushchev mounted. For all his dramatics, he had been unable to deliver enough meaningful victories in the Cold War, while his brinksmanship had frightened nearly everyone. Within a year he was out of power.

The easing of tensions that followed the Cuban missile crisis allowed de Gaulle, and other Europeans, to begin to think in serious terms about revising their relationship with the United States. De Gaulle wanted to restore European independence, if not European primacy; to do so, he realized, he had to break with N.A.T.O. After Cuba, he knew that the United States would not consult with its N.A.T.O. partners before acting; he was convinced that the United States would not risk its own existence for the sake of protecting Europe; he doubted that the old bogeyman, the Red Army, would ever march across the Elbe. He believed that the time had come for Europe to drop out of the Cold

War and assert herself. He therefore prepared a Franco-German friendship treaty, moved to establish better relations with the Warsaw Pact nations, quickened the pace of French nuclear development, and decided to keep Britain out of the Common Market.

On 14 January 1963, de Gaulle announced his program. He vetoed British participation in the Common Market because it would transform the character of the European Economic Community and 'finally it would appear as a colossal Atlantic community under American domination and direction'. Kennedy had been pushing for a multi-lateral nuclear force within N.A.T.O., which supposedly would give the Europeans some say in the use of nuclear weapons while blocking any West German move to develop their own bombs. The trouble with the proposal was that under no circumstances would the United States give up its ultimate veto on the bombs. De Gaulle, therefore, denounced the plan. 'France intends to have her own national defense,' he declared. 'For us, . . . integration is something which is not imaginable.' He concluded about the French nuclear force, 'It is entirely understandable that this French enterprise should not seem very satisfactory to certain American quarters. In politics and strategy, as in economics, monopoly naturally appears to him who enjoys it as the best possible system.'

De Gaulle then proceeded to withdraw French naval forces from N.A.T.O. and would soon request N.A.T.O. headquarters to leave France. His bold bid for European independence was not an immediate success, as West Germany decided to maintain her close ties with the United States, but the long-term effects remained unknown. Certainly his general goals had enormous appeal. From Yalta, in 1945, to Vienna in 1961, the Soviet Union and the United States had presumed to settle the affairs of Europe without any European leaders at the conference table. Those days were rapidly coming to an end. Europe was unwilling to be burned to a cinder because Russia and

America disagreed about an island in the Gulf of Mexico, or to continue to be an investment and market area for American corporations and Russian managers. The possibilities of a European withdrawal from Cold War were vastly increased as a result of the Cuban missile crisis and as the superpowers increasingly turned their attention to the Third World.

The greatest lesson from Cuba was the perils of brinksmanship. Henceforth, Russia and America would strive to keep some kind of a lid on their disputes, to avoid actions that could lead to escalations, to limit their commitments so that they could limit the other side's response. Struggle would continue, most obviously in the Third World, but hopefully at a lower level. American goals remained the same, and Kennedy would continue to pursue them energetically, but he would try to do so with less military force and within the confines of the realization that the Third World had its own hopes and programs. Whether or not he could achieve what remained relatively unlimited goals through limited means remained to be seen.

He had learned. An ability to grow was his most impressive asset and he was surely the honor graduate of the Cuban missile crisis class. 'In the final analysis,' he said in his American University speech, 'our most basic common link is the fact that we all inhabit this planet. We all breathe the same air. We all cherish our children's future. And we are all mortal.'

11

Extending the Frontiers to the Mekong

'[McGeorge] Bundy said he had come to accept what he had learned from Dean Acheson – that, in the final analysis, the United States was the locomotive at the head of mankind, and the rest of the world the caboose.'

McGeorge Bundy, *in an interview with Henry F. Graff*

IN the field of counter-insurgency, as nowhere else, Kennedy found full scope for his imagination and drive, a challenge worthy of his energies and of his nation's greatness. He would prove to the world that wars of national liberation, carried on as he saw it by armed minorities, did not work. Through counter-insurgency, the West would win the battle for the Third World.

Kennedy set out to build a force – the Green Berets – that could put down an insurrection or revolution anywhere. He relied heavily on technology to overcome the manpower problem, giving the Berets first call on all the Army's latest equipment. The whole concept appealed strongly to the elitist strain in Kennedy, for the Berets consisted of the best young officers and enlisted men in the Army. They received extra training, better equipment, and additional privileges. As the military equivalent to the Peace Corps, the Berets would apply American techniques and know-how in guerrilla warfare situations and solve the problems that had baffled the French and other Europeans. As Kennedy told a West Point commencement, he would apply 'a wholly new kind of strategy'. One of the great appeals of counter-insurgency, especially after the Cuban crisis, was that it avoided direct confrontation with the Soviet Union. The risks of an escalation to nuclear war were small, which meant that in this area at least America could use her enormous military power for political gains.

Americans would be able to do what other white men had failed at partly because America's motives were pure, partly because America had mastered the lessons of guerrilla warfare. The United States would not try to overwhelm the enemy or fight a strictly conventional war, as the French had done in Vietnam. Instead the Berets would give advice to local troops while American civil agencies would help the young governments to institute political reforms that would separate the guerrillas from the people. Kennedy's counter-insurgency would show the people that there was a liberal middle-ground between feudal colonialism and totalitarian communism. Like Dulles, Kennedy never doubted that when Asians or Africans realized that a liberal alternative existed they would reject communism.

Kennedy read Mao Tse-Tung and Che Guevara on guerrilla warfare and ordered the Army's generals to do the same. He put all his influence into the development of a dedicated, high-quality elite corps of specialists, capable of training local troops in guerrilla warfare, equipped to perform a wide range of civilian as well as military tasks, able to live in the jungle behind enemy lines. Kennedy personally supervised the selection of new equipment. He replaced the Army's traditional heavy but noisy combat boots with sneakers and when the sneakers proved vulnerable to bamboo spikes he had them reinforced with flexible steel inner soles. Kennedy gave the Green Berets lighter field radios and more helicopters. When all was ready, he sent them out to save the world.

The first great opportunity came in South Vietnam. It had numerous advantages. Diem was more a low-grade despot than he was a ruthless dictator. He was relatively honest and a sincere nationalist. He had introduced a land reform program that, on paper at least, was a model for others to follow. The Americans were already in Vietnam, with military and economic advisers, which was a great plus, for in the Cold War whoever got to a territory first had in effect staked it out. If the Russians challenged the Americans in Vietnam, they would be escalating the conflict and risking a nuclear exchange, just as the Americans would have done had Eisenhower challenged Khrushchev in Hungary. Finally, Vietnam was an ideal battleground for the Green Berets. Small unit actions in the jungle or rice paddies suited them perfectly, as did the emphasis on winning the hearts and minds of the people through medical and technical aid. From Kennedy's point of view, Vietnam was an almost perfect place to get involved. There he could show his interest in the Third World, demonstrate conclusively that America lived up to her commitments (the S.E.A.T.O. Treaty had extended protection to South Vietnam if it were attacked from without), and play the exciting new game of counter-insurgency.

The only major difficulty was the fuzzy legal situation. South Vietnam was a sovereign nation only because Diem and the United States said it was. Under the terms of the Geneva agreements, which America had not signed but which it promised not to upset by force, South Vietnam was merely a territory to be administered by the French until nation-wide elections were held. The 1954 agreements had also stipulated that neither Ho in North Vietnam nor Diem in South Vietnam should allow the introduction of foreign troops into their territories. The United States got around this stumbling-block by redefining the Geneva agreements, deliberately creating the fiction that Geneva had set up two Vietnams, North and South. The Secretary of State, Dean Rusk, made the redefinition complete in 1963 when he claimed that 'the other side was fully committed – fully committed – in the original Geneva settlement of 1954 to the arrangements which provided for South Vietnam as an independent entity, and we see no reason to modify those in the direction of a larger influence of North Vietnam or Hanoi in South Vietnam.'

The second major problem was the nature of the struggle.

After Dulles wrote the S.E.A.T.O. Treaty and extended protection to South Vietnam, he assured the Senate that under no circumstances would the United States be required to put down an internal uprising or get involved in a civil war. Assuming that South Vietnam was a sovereign nation, the question then became one of ascertaining whether the opposition to the government came from within or without. The question was almost impossible to answer. After 1956 the North Vietnamese had taken a Stalinist route, concentrating on building socialism in one country. There were thousands of southerners in the North, men who had fought with Ho and the Vietminh and then left their homes when the French gave power in the South to Diem. There were, in addition, thousands of Vietminh still in the South who had stayed in 1954 to prepare for the elections that were scheduled for 1956. Both groups seem to have felt that Ho's failure to do anything about Diem's refusal to hold elections amounted to a sell-out. The Vietminh in the South grew increasingly restive. Beginning in 1957 they carried on a systematic campaign to assassinate village chiefs and thus destroy Diem's hold on the countryside. They suffered from political persecution, as did all Diem's opponents, for Diem was incapable of distinguishing between communist and anti-communist resistance to his government. In early 1960 eighteen national figures, including ten former ministers under Diem, took their lives in their hands by issuing a public manifesto protesting Diem's nepotism and the 'continuous arrests that fill the jails and prisons to the rafters'. They called for free elections. Diem threw them all into jail.

In March 1960, full-scale revolt began. Diem labeled his opponents Viet Cong, or Vietnamese Communists, although many of the Viet Cong were anti-communist and included a number of former Diem supporters. The Viet Cong established the National Liberation Front (N.L.F.) as its political arm. The struggle intensified, possibly without Ho's approval and almost certainly without his active support in the form of manpower. Some 2,000 men did go south in

1960, but nearly all were old Vietminh who had lived there before 1954. The great bulk of the Viet Cong were recruited in South Vietnam and captured most of their arms and equipment from Diem's army. But as the war mounted, Ho either had to support the Viet Cong or lose all chance of controlling the movement. In September 1960, the Communist Party of North Vietnam bestowed its formal blessing on the N.L.F. and called for the liberation of South Vietnam from American imperialism.

Under the circumstances it was exceedingly difficult to prove that South Vietnam was the victim of outside aggression. The American Secretary of State, however, had no doubts that North Vietnam was committing aggression, nor did he doubt what was at stake. Rusk's views had changed not at all since 1950, when he decided that the Chinese communists were 'not Chinese'. As he saw it, the war in South Vietnam was sponsored by Hanoi, which in turn was acting as the agent of Peking. If the United States allowed the Viet Cong to win in South Vietnam, the Chinese would quickly gobble up the rest of Asia. Again and again he warned his countrymen of the dangers of a Far Eastern Munich, thereby equating Ho Chi Minh with Hitler and raising the dreaded specter of appeasement.

Rusk warned of the dangers of another Munich so often, however, and the idea of Ho being the Asian Hitler was so silly, that the Secretary became almost an embarrassment to the administration. Nevertheless he persisted. In their memoirs, Kennedy's aides had great fun at Rusk's expense, pointing to the slowness and shallowness of his mind, his supercilious personality, and the rigidity of his views. Arthur Schlesinger and Theodore Sorensen presented Rusk as a figure out of the past, a man still caught in the clichés of the late forties, a Secretary of State whose prime aim was to encircle Communist China just as Acheson had encircled Russia. They were amused by his emphasis on military force and argued that Rusk never understood the new sophistication of the Kennedy foreign policy.

What Schlesinger and Sorensen ignored was that Kennedy had picked Rusk for the job – after a strong recommendation from Acheson – knowing that Rusk was the leader of those who wanted to hem in China militarily. Rusk had never hidden his beliefs. Kennedy, and anyone else who bothered to look at Rusk's record, knew perfectly well that the Secretary believed there was a life and death struggle going on between freedom and slavery in Asia and that he would respond to it along the same lines Acheson had laid out in Europe.

In any case Rusk was hardly alone in recommending the American involvement in Vietnam, nor was the decision to save Diem an aberration or the result of a conspiracy. Everything in the Kennedy record pointed to increased aid to Diem and nearly everyone in the Kennedy administration supported the decision. The Joint Chiefs went along, but they did not push Kennedy into Vietnam, nor did American corporations with Asian interests, nor did the Asia-firsters in the Republican Party.*

Vietnam was the liberals' war. It was the logical extension of a policy of military containment of communism and it was based on the same premisses that Truman and Acheson had used. The United States, as Sorensen put it – in words that Acheson might have used in speaking of the

* By 1969, when the war had become widely unpopular, various interpretations of where the original mistake had been made enjoyed a certain popularity. The New Left tried to show that America went to Vietnam as a part of a general pattern of imperialism and in response to certain immediate needs of the American corporate structure, principally for raw materials unique to Southeast Asia. But Southeast Asia's economic importance was so minimal that it was difficult to sustain the argument, especially since one of the most consistent opponents of the war had been the financial community and its semi-official spokesman, *The Wall Street Journal*. Liberals, led by Kennedy's younger brother and the former President's friend John K. Galbraith, lay the blame at the foot of the military–industrial complex, an equally difficult argument to sustain and one that ignored completely the actions of such men as Walt Rostow and his brother Eugene, McGeorge Bundy, and Kennedy himself.

1947 Greek policy – 'could supply better training, support and direction, better communications, transportation and intelligence, better weapons, equipment and logistics' to Vietnam. With American skills and Vietnamese soldiers ('South Vietnam will supply the necessary men,' Kennedy said), freedom would prevail.

After making the basic decision to support Diem, whatever happened, Kennedy began sending his experts to South Vietnam. Their mission was to report to him on what was needed and to teach Diem how to get the job done. The first to go was the Vice President, Lyndon Johnson. He returned in May 1961 and reported that time was running out. 'The basic decision in Southeast Asia is here. We must decide whether to help these countries to the best of our ability or throw in the towel in the area and pull back our defenses to San Francisco and a "Fortress America" concept.' Rusk and the intellectuals Kennedy had brought into the White House agreed with Johnson's analysis. They never explained how the fall of Diem (and the probable consequence of a reorientation in Laos, Cambodia, Thailand, and even Malaya) could drive the United States from its major Asian bases in the Philippines, Formosa, Okinawa, and Japan.

The Kennedy team, like that of Truman and Acheson, felt that America could not afford to back down anywhere. As Johnson put it in his report, if America did not stand behind Diem 'we would say to the world that we don't live up to our treaties and don't stand by our friends,' which were almost the same words Kennedy was using with respect to the concurrent Berlin crisis. The Kennedy administration also assumed that if America set her mind to it there was no limit to what the nation could do, which made Johnson's conclusions inevitable: 'I recommend that we move forward promptly with a major effort to help these countries defend themselves.' American combat troops would not be needed and indeed it would be a mistake to send them because it would revive anti-colonial emotions throughout

Asia. Johnson thought the South Vietnamese themselves could do the fighting, aided by American training and equipment.

Shortly after Johnson's trip Professor Eugene Staley, an economist from Stanford University, went to Saigon to advise Diem. Staley made a number of suggestions, the most important of which was that Diem institute a strategic hamlet program. The idea was that by bringing the peasants together it would be easier to protect them from the Viet Cong. In practice, however, the strategic hamlets amounted to concentration camps. Diem's troops forced villagers to leave land their families had lived on for generations and thereby turned thousands of Vietnamese against the government. The war continued to go badly. Although the Viet Cong were concentrated in the least populated districts, they controlled nearly half the countryside.

In October 1961, Kennedy sent another mission to Saigon. It was headed by two men widely regarded as among the best in America, Walt Rostow and Maxwell Taylor, and thus reflected Kennedy's ability to attract men of proven competence to his service. Rostow was a Rhodes scholar, an M.I.T. professor, and an internationally famous economic historian. Taylor was a war hero, former Superintendent of the U.S. Military Academy, and one of the leading critics of Eisenhower's reliance on massive deterrence. Between them, the professor who enjoyed making policy decisions and the soldier who moved easily in intellectual circles made a team that represented the very best America had to offer. Rostow had no immediate ties to the military–industrial complex, Taylor was not a professional anti-communist, neither were trapped by the clichés of the Cold War. Whatever judgements and recommendations they made, Kennedy had to regard as authoritative.

The Rostow–Taylor mission reported that South Vietnam had enough vitality to justify a major United States effort. Taylor said the major difficulty was that the South Vietnamese doubted that the Americans really would save them and he recommended an increased American intervention. He wanted the South Vietnamese Army (A.R.V.N.) to take the offensive, with American troops supplying the air lift and reconnaissance. Taylor also urged Kennedy to send a small combat unit of 10,000 or so men to South Vietnam. The unit should be capable of conducting combat operations if A.R.V.N. was hard pressed. Rostow thought that Diem, if pressed by the United States to reform, would be satisfactory. Both Rostow and Taylor agreed that the key to victory was stopping infiltration from the North. If it continued, they could see no end to the war. Rostow argued forcibly for a policy of retaliation against the North by bombing, graduated to match the intensity of Hanoi's support for the Viet Cong. Kennedy accepted the main conclusions (although he refused to bomb North Vietnam) and stepped up the shipment of troops and equipment to Diem. When Eisenhower left office there were a few hundred American advisers in South Vietnam; at the time of the Rostow–Taylor mission there were 1,364; by the end of the following year, 1962, there were nearly 10,000, and by November 1963 there were 15,000. Equipment came in at a faster rate, especially helicopters.

The American commitment to Diem was so strong that, as David Halberstam reported in the *New York Times*, Saigon 'became more convinced than ever that it had its ally in a corner, that it could do anything it wanted, that continued support would be guaranteed because of the Communist threat and that after the commitment was made, the United States could not suddenly admit it had made a vast mistake.' The entire emphasis of the Rostow–Taylor report had been on a military response and Kennedy concentrated on sending military hardware to Saigon. The American Ambassador did try to put pressure on Diem to institute political and economic reforms, but Diem ignored him and even launched anti-American campaigns in the Saigon press. When the Viet Cong liberated a village, they immediately told the peasants that the land was now theirs; when A.R.V.N. took a village they brought the landlords along with them, and the landlords collected back rents, often covering the past five years.

Even so, the war seemed to be going well. McNamara visited Vietnam in June 1962 and reported, 'Every quantitative measurement we have shows we're winning this war.' In March of 1963 Rusk declared that the struggle against the Viet Cong had 'turned an important corner' and was nearly over. A month later he said there was 'a steady movement in South Vietnam toward a constitutional system resting upon popular consent'. The American generals on the spot made similar statements. The Buddhist uprisings against Diem, in May of 1963, brought on by religious persecution, dampened the official optimism, but even the Buddhist display of dissatisfaction with Diem only caused embarrassment, not a re-evaluation of policy. Kennedy continued to increase the size of the American military contingent and in one of his last press conferences declared, 'Our goal is a stable government there, carrying on a struggle to maintain its national independence. We believe strongly in that . . . . In my opinion, for us to withdraw from that effort would mean a collapse not only of South Vietnam but Southeast Asia. So we are going to stay there.'

Kennedy's statement was a concise summary of the continuity of policy. Vietnam was Greece and South Korea all over again. The C.I.A. was soon involved in plots in Saigon to overthrow Diem and bring an efficient, honest government to power – in short, as in Cuba, to find a liberal alternative to both repressive dictatorship and communism. Kennedy's belief that such an alternative existed, and that the United States had the power to hold the line until it emerged, remained as firm as ever. America would stave off the enemy while Diem (or someone else if Diem proved recalcitrant), with American help, wrote a constitution, instituted land reforms, and granted civil liberties. America would help remake South Vietnam in America's image.

Kennedy was prepared to do whatever was necessary to prevent a Viet Cong victory. Just as Truman had blamed Greece and Korea on the Russians and Eisenhower had blamed Castro on international communism, Kennedy blamed Vietnam on the Chinese. In each case, acceptance of the thesis of external aggression made it possible for the President to believe that there was little or no indigenous support for the revolt, which in turn led to the belief that if the United States could cut off the sources of supply the uprising would die. The inevitable response to the challenge, then, was a military one, which ultimately led to the curious notion that Saigon could win its civil war if the United States bombed North Vietnam.*

Kennedy and the men around him recognized that there were important social and political aspects to the war, but the insight was hazy. Like the owners of an American baseball team, they decided to fire the manager while retaining the team. Diem was an international embarrassment. A Catholic aristocrat, he had little support in his own army and no real ties with the non-Catholic majority of his people. His repressions were too blatant, his strategic hamlet and land reform programs had too obviously failed. He had to go. In November 1963, A.R.V.N. — with covert

---

* In an interview in 1969 General William Westmoreland, commander of the American military effort in South Vietnam from 1964 to 1968, said that before 1967 he had discussed South Vietnam with every top official in the White House, the State Department, and the Pentagon. All agreed that the United States had to stand up to the aggressors from the North, using whatever means were necessary. He could not recall a single dissenter. There was also universal agreement on the need to prove to the Chinese that wars of national liberation did not work and to show the Third World that America stood by her commitments. These views were held most strongly by Kennedy's personal advisers, led by Rostow and McGeorge Bundy. Westmoreland emphasized that America did not get into Vietnam, or stay there, because of a military conspiracy, or a military-industrial complex conspiracy, or any other conspiracy. America fought in Vietnam as a direct result of a world-view from which no one in power dissented and as a logical culmination of the policy of containment.

American support – overthrew and then killed Diem and his brother. The trouble was that the new managers came from the old organization and could not institute a new policy. A military regime that could only promise some efficiency in the conduct of the war – nothing more – took over.

Three weeks later Kennedy himself was assassinated and Lyndon Johnson became President. In Vietnam, as elsewhere, Johnson continued Kennedy's policies. When A.R.V.N. eliminated Diem, the N.L.F. had contacted the generals in Saigon and proposed negotiations 'to reach a cease-fire and solve important problems of the nation . . . with a view to reaching free general elections . . . to form a national coalition government composed of representatives of all forces, parties, tendencies, and strata of the South Vietnamese people'. Important elements of the A.R.V.N. officer corps supported the idea of a coalition government and a neutral South Vietnam (Diem himself may have been in contact with the Viet Cong at the time of his death), but the Americans in Saigon, backed by the government in Washington, refused to have anything to do with it.

In a New Year's message to South Vietnam, Johnson strengthened the hands of the hardliners in A.R.V.N. by declaring, 'neutralization of South Vietnam would only be another name for a Communist take-over. The United States will continue to furnish you and your people with the fullest measure of support in this bitter fight. We shall maintain in Vietnam American personnel and material as needed to assist you in achieving victory.' In July 1964, Moscow, Hanoi, and Paris joined together to issue a call for an international conference in Geneva to deal with an outbreak of fighting in Laos and with the war in Vietnam. China, the N.L.F., and Cambodia supported the call, as did U.N. Secretary General U Thant. Johnson replied that 'we do not believe in conferences called to ratify terror', and the next day announced that the American military advisers to South Vietnam would be increased by 30 per cent, from 16,000 to 21,000.

America continued to believe that it could win the war by applying a limited amount of force, primarily through A.R.V.N. Throughout the summer of 1964 high American officials continued to issue optimistic statements. Faith in the Kennedy–McNamara program of flexible response, counter-insurgency techniques, and the new theories of limited war remained high. Years later, when almost everyone was unhappy with the war, the American military and their supporters would charge that the failure in South Vietnam resulted from an inadequate application of force. America could have won the war, some generals and admirals claimed, had it put in more men sooner. The fact that North Vietnam could match American escalation step by step, and did (at least up to a point), made the logic questionable, and in any case the claim only showed that as late as 1970 the critics continued to suffer from the myopic view that got America into trouble in the first place – that the struggle in South Vietnam was a purely military one.

The real point was that at each step along the path the American military, intelligence community, and State Department all believed that enough was being done. Ten thousand more troops, or 100,000 more, or 500 more helicopters, or three more bombing targets, would do the trick. The restraints on American action in Vietnam were self-imposed, to be sure, and such factors as the public's unwillingness to pay a high cost for the war or fear of Chinese intervention played a role in limiting the use of force. But by far the most important reason for the gradualism was the deep belief in the Kennedy–Johnson administrations that enough was being done. All the old myths, such as the idea that communism could never inspire genuine support or the notion that Asians could not stand up to Western military techniques, led to a consistent underestimation of the enemy.

Barry Goldwater, Republican candidate for the Presidency in 1964, was one of the few politicians who disagreed. He thought that more, much more, had to be done, and soon. Goldwater said he was prepared to go to the Joint

Chiefs and tell them to win, using whatever measures were necessary, including nuclear weapons. He also wanted to carry the war to North Vietnam, starting with bombing raids.

Johnson gleefully took up the challenge. In the 1964 campaign he ran on a platform promising major social reforms at home and peace abroad. He presented himself as the reasonable, prudent man who could be trusted to win in Vietnam while keeping the war limited. Johnson scornfully rejected Goldwater's bellicose suggestions. Bombing the North, the President said, would widen the war and lead to committing American troops to the battle. He was especially insistent about the last point: 'We are not going to send American boys nine or ten thousand miles away from home to do what Asian boys ought to be doing for themselves.'

In the by now familiar pattern of American Presidential campaigns in the Cold War, Goldwater was accusing Johnson of not being tough enough with the communists. Johnson had to cover himself, had to show that he could be firm as well as patient, hard as well as reasonable. He therefore seized the opportunity that came on 2 and 3 August 1964, when he received reports that American destroyers had been attacked by North Vietnamese torpedo boats in the Gulf of Tonkin. At the time few doubted that the attacks had actually taken place, although the *New York Times* and others suggested that the U.S. Navy had provoked the attacks by escorting South Vietnamese commando raids into North Vietnam. Later, in 1968, Senator Fulbright's Senate hearings convinced millions that the entire Tonkin Gulf affair was a fraud. In any case Johnson, without an investigation, charged North Vietnam with committing 'open aggression on the high seas', adding that 'we Americans know, although others appear to forget, the risk of spreading conflict'. He decided to respond by ordering American air attacks on North Vietnamese ports to destroy the torpedo boats. This marked the first victory for Walt Rostow's concept of matching reaction to provocation.

TONKIN

The more important result was the Gulf of Tonkin Resolution. Like Eisenhower in the Mid-East, Johnson wanted and got a blank check that would allow him to expand the war as he saw fit without consulting Congress. The President asked Congress for authority to use 'all necessary measures' to 'repel any armed attack' against American forces. In addition, Congress gave the President the power to 'prevent further aggression' and take 'all necessary steps' to protect any nation covered by S.E.A.T.O. which might request aid 'in defense of its freedom'. The Resolution sailed through the House on 7 August by a vote of 416 to 0. In the Senate, Fulbright steered the Resolution through. He insisted that the Congress had to trust the President and turned back an amendment to the Resolution that would have explicitly denied to the President authority to widen the war. The election was only three months away and Fulbright did not want to embarrass Johnson. The Senate then voted 88 to 2 in favor of the Resolution (Wayne Morse and Ernest Gruening were the lone dissenters).

Hanoi, meanwhile, had sent out peace feelers. Perhaps encouraged by Johnson's charges that Goldwater was reckless, perhaps frightened by the Gulf of Tonkin Resolution, Ho Chi Minh secretly offered to negotiate, which only showed that he misunderstood the Americans as completely as they misunderstood the Vietnamese. Neither Johnson nor his advisers nor the A.R.V.N. generals in Saigon were remotely prepared to accept a compromise solution to the war, for it would have meant a coalition government in South Vietnam with close ties to Hanoi. Elections almost surely would have eliminated the A.R.V.N. generals altogether. The new Saigon government would then order the American troops out of South Vietnam. These prospects were much too painful to contemplate and Johnson certainly did not want to make it possible for Goldwater to charge him with appeasement. Washington refused to negotiate, the war went on, and the American voters overwhelmingly approved Johnson's middle-ground of limited war in Vietnam.

The key to victory remained hidden. Indeed, as the war turned increasingly against Saigon the real question was whether the South Vietnamese government could hang on, much less prevail. The American military advisers before 1960 had trained A.R.V.N. to fight a conventional war, under the theory that if Hanoi decided to move against Saigon it would launch a North Korean-type assault. This was subsequently cited as a major factor in A.R.V.N.'s difficulties, but it only hid the deeper malaise. The officer corps had no real connection with the troops. Half were Catholics, many from North Vietnam. Corruption was rampant. The desertion rate was the highest in the world. The truth was that in the face of a conventional assault, A.R.V.N. probably would have scattered even more than it did when faced with guerrilla warfare. The South Korean Army had also been a shambles in 1950 when the war began, but with American help Rhee had eliminated corruption in his officer corps and built a respectable fighting force. A.R.V.N., with much greater American support and far more time to work with, never matched the South Korean achievement. There was simply no will to fight, for there was nothing to fight for.

A.R.V.N.'s failure made Johnson's dilemma clear. He had to either negotiate or introduce American combat troops to retrieve the situation. If he continued Kennedy's policy of all-out material support plus Green Beret advisers, the Saigon government would collapse and the Viet Cong take control of all South Vietnam, a development no one in the administration could bring himself to accept.

The main debate in Washington after the Gulf of Tonkin and the election, then, was whether to escalate American involvement in the war or to negotiate. Either option was open. Hanoi had indicated in various ways its willingness to talk, but although Ambassador Stevenson at the United Nations and a few other American officials were interested,

Johnson and Rusk and the Kennedy aides who had stayed with Johnson consistently refused to negotiate. In the words of David Kraslow and Stuart Loory, 'In 1964 the dominant view in official Washington was that the United States could not entertain the idea of talks or negotiations until after it applied more military pressure on the enemy. As a former White House aide later described the mood of that period: "The very word 'negotiations' was anathema in the Administration".' Rostow, Taylor, and others argued that the military imbalance would have to be redressed before negotiations could be considered, which really meant that they wanted and expected victory. As Rostow explained the policy, in a statement almost anyone in the Administration could have made, 'It is on this spot that we have to break the liberation war – Chinese type. If we don't break it here we shall have to face it again in Thailand, Venezuela, elsewhere. Vietnam is a clear testing ground for our policy in the world.'

Since Americans thought in world terms, it seemed to them that everyone else did too. Thus they could really believe that Mao was plotting to start another war in Venezuela after he had won the conflict in South Vietnam. China had to be hemmed in, a line had to be drawn in the Third World, just as Truman had drawn one in Europe. South Vietnam was important for Asian containment not only because it was a 'testing ground', but because its strategic position was crucial to a continued American presence in Southeast Asia. Thus although at every stage in the escalation Johnson declared that the United States had no long-term interest in South Vietnam and did not plan to maintain a permanent military base there, the American intention was quite the opposite.

The history of the Cold War clearly showed that the Americans would build military installations wherever they could. In 1950, when Truman sent the Seventh Fleet to protect Formosa, the Chinese and Russians had charged that the United States planned to build a military base on the island. Truman vehemently denied it, but nevertheless Formosa became the site of American bases. The process was repeated in South Korea. And in 1969, when the Americans began to reduce their combat commitment in South Vietnam, the Secretary of Defense announced that when hostilities ended America planned to maintain a permanent base of 7,000 or so men in South Vietnam.

There could be no permanent base, however, until the war was won. Johnson's great problem, after he rejected negotiation, was how to win it. The Air Force had the answer. Undaunted by the failure of strategic bombing in Germany and ignoring the failure of interdiction bombing in North Korea, strategic airpower advocates told the President they could stop Hanoi's aggression in a month. When a civilian aide asked the generals what would happen if Hanoi did not quit in a month, they answered that then another two weeks would do the trick. More specifically, Secretary of Defense McNamara, who also advocated taking the air war to North Vietnam, believed it would improve the morale of the South Vietnamese forces, reduce the flow and increase the cost of infiltration of men and equipment from North to South Vietnam, and hurt morale in North Vietnam. The net result would be to 'affect their will in such a way as to move Hanoi to a satisfactory settlement'. The third point was sometimes described as 'ouch warfare'. Sooner or later Ho Chi Minh would decide that his potential gain was not worth the cost, say 'ouch', and quit. Another advantage to bombing was its peculiarly American flavor – the United States would win the war by expending money and material, of which it had an abundance, and avoid manpower losses.

Indeed while the debate within the administration on whether or not to bomb North Vietnam was going on, the State Department gave an official explanation as to why no American combat units were committed to South Vietnam. The statement read in full: 'The Viet Cong use terrorism and armed attacks as well as propaganda. The Government forces must respond decisively on all appropriate levels, tasks that can best be handled by Vietnamese. U.S. combat units would face several obvious disadvantages in a guerrilla war situation of this type in which knowledge of terrain, language, and local customs is especially important. In addition, their introduction would provide ammunition for Communist propaganda which falsely proclaims that the United States is conducting a "white man's war" against Asians.'

How bombing the North would solve the problem of terrorism and propaganda (i.e. political activity) was unclear, but bombing had the clear advantage of saving American lives. Moreover, bombs were impersonal. Americans would hurl only their machines and industrial products, not their young men, against the Asian enemy. Thus, the Johnson administration convinced itself, America would not be fighting a white man's war against Asians.

Sometime in late 1964 or early 1965 Johnson decided to initiate a bombing campaign against North Vietnam. The Air Force and the Navy made the necessary preparations. But to bomb a country with whom the United States was not at war, which had committed no aggressive actions against the United States, and against whom no one in Washington intended to declare war, was a serious step. Johnson decided to make one last move to be certain the air campaign was really necessary to save the situation in the South, and in late January he sent a delegation headed by McGeorge Bundy, his special assistant for national security affairs and a Kennedy confidant, to Saigon to investigate.

Events were moving rapidly. U Thant was involved in one of his efforts to bring the North Vietnamese and the Americans together to talk and had received word from North Vietnam that they would appear at Rangoon if the Americans would send a representative. On 30 January Johnson rejected the possibility of negotiation. U.N. Ambassador Stevenson informed Thant that Washington felt such a meeting could not be concealed and that when the news leaked out it would demoralize the Saigon government. On 6 February, meanwhile, Soviet Premier Alexei Kosygin arrived in Hanoi. His purpose, according to one interpretation, was to persuade Ho Chi Minh to begin peace discussions. The next day, 7 February 1965, Viet Cong troops broke through the defense perimeter around the big American air base at Pleiku in South Vietnam and mortared the flight line and some American military barracks. Eight American soldiers died, six helicopters and a transport plane were destroyed. McGeorge Bundy went to the scene to inspect the damage. As a White House official later recalled, 'a man from the ivory tower was suddenly confronted with the grim horror of reality. Mac got mad and immediately urged a retaliatory strike.' The Ambassador to South Vietnam, Maxwell Taylor, and the American military commander, General William Westmoreland, joined Bundy in recommending instant retaliation. Within twelve hours what the Americans called a retaliatory raid began. The first major escalation had started.

On his way back to Washington, Bundy prepared a memorandum urging a steady program of bombing the North. He felt that within three months of the start of the bombing Hanoi would give up and seek peace. Bombing, he asserted, was the way to avoid the unpleasant decision to send combat troops. In Washington, planning went forward for a program of regular bombing of the North. The State Department, meanwhile, prepared the political justification, a White Paper intended to document North Vietnam's domination of the N.L.F. It was issued on 27 February. The theme of the 64-page Paper was that 'above all the war in Vietnam is *not* a spontaneous and local rebellion against the established government .... In Vietnam a Communist government has set out deliberately to conquer a sovereign people in a neighboring state .... North Vietnam's commitment to seize control of the South is no less total than was the commitment of the regime in North Korea in 1950.' The evidence presented to prove the point was less than massive. The Paper stated, for example, that 179 weapons of communist bloc manufacture had been captured from the Viet Cong, but I. F. Stone showed that this was only 2.5 per cent of the total weapons captured in the period covered. The rest had been taken from Diem's troops.

On 2 March 1965, three days after publication of the White Paper, American bombers hit an ammunition dump ten miles inside North Vietnam and a harbor fifty-five miles north of the demilitarized zone. The raids were the first launched without any alleged specific provocation by the North Vietnamese. Others quickly followed. Johnson himself picked the targets at luncheon meetings every Tuesday with McNamara, Rusk, and Rostow. Representatives of the Joint Chiefs and the C.I.A. were sometimes present. They set limits based on a check list of four items: (1) the military advantage of striking the proposed target; (2) the risk to American aircraft; (3) the danger of widening the war by forcing other countries into the fighting; (4) the danger of heavy civilian casualties. The third point was the most important, for it was imperative to keep Russia out of the conflict and Soviet ships were usually docked at Haiphong, which was therefore not bombed. The last limitations – civilian casualties – became less and less important as time went on.

Simultaneously with the bombing offensive in the North, American airmen drastically stepped up their activity in South Vietnam. Indeed, according to Bernard Fall, 'what changed the character of the Viet-Nam war was *not* the decision to bomb North Viet-Nam; *not* the decision to use American ground troops in South Viet-Nam; but the decision to wage unlimited aerial warfare inside the country at the price of literally pounding the place to bits.' The sheer magnitude of the American effort made the entire campaign almost unbelievable, just as Hitler's extermina-

tion camps had been unbelievable. The statistics boggled the
mind. First the headlines proclaimed that America had
dropped more bombs on tiny Vietnam than in the Pacific
Theater in World War II. By 1967 it was more bombs than
in the European Theater. Then more than in the whole of
World War II. Finally, by 1970, more than had been
dropped on all targets in the whole of human history.
Napalm poured into the villages while weed-killers defoli-
ated the countryside. Never had even America, much less
any other nation, relied so completely on industrial production and material superiority to wage a war.

Yet it did not work. Hanoi did not quit or lose its morale,
the infiltration of men and supplies continued (indeed
increased, thus making Rusk's charges of external aggression a self-fulfilling prophecy), the Viet Cong still fought,
and the political situation in Saigon got worse. Johnson had
rejected negotiation and given the Air Force its opportunity.
The Air Force had failed. New decisions had to be made.

Despite the bombing offensive the option to negotiate
remained and Johnson came under heavy pressure from the
N.A.T.O. allies and the neutral nations to talk to Hanoi.
Johnson gave his answer in a speech on 7 April at the Johns
Hopkins University. The address became famous for his
promise to launch a massive economic rehabilitation program in Southeast Asia once the conflict ended, a sort of
Marshall Plan for the area, and for his assertion that he
would go anywhere to discuss peace with anyone. But far
more important than the olive branch the President waved
was the sword he flourished. The central lesson of the
twentieth century, he proclaimed, was that 'the appetite
of aggression is never satisfied'. There would be no appeasement in South Vietnam as long as he was President. 'We
will not be defeated. We will not grow tired. We will not
withdraw, either openly or under the cloak of a meaningless
agreement.' The next day American bombers launched a
particularly severe series of air raids on North Vietnam, and
15,000 additional American troops started for South Vietnam.

Hanoi, meanwhile, set forth four points as the basis for a settlement. This proposal differed from earlier N.L.F. pronouncements on the subject, most notably by ignoring the N.L.F. demand that as the 'sole genuine representative of the South Vietnamese people' the N.L.F. had to be given a 'decisive voice' in any settlement. Hanoi's four points were: (1) recognition of the basic national rights of the Vietnamese people: peace, independence, sovereignty, unity, and territorial integrity; (2) no foreign bases, troops, or military personnel in North or South Vietnam. The wording seemed to indicate that Hanoi was *not* demanding an American withdrawal before negotiations began; (3) settlement of South Vietnam's internal affairs 'by the South Vietnamese people themselves . . .'; (4) no foreign interference in settling the eventual peaceful reunification of all Vietnam.

Washington made no response until 15 May 1965, when the administration announced that a pause in the bombing had begun two days previously. Rusk secretly informed Hanoi that the United States would be watching for 'significant reductions' in armed action on their part as an indication of a real desire to negotiate. Ho Chi Minh then informed the French that he was ready to talk on the basis of the four points. On 18 May the Americans terminated the bombing pause. Rusk expressed disappointment 'at the fact that there was no reaction' from Hanoi. Almost a year later he admitted that there had been a response, but dismissed it as a 'polemical rejection' of the American offer.

The point was that America was no more ready to negotiate in May than it had been in February, despite the fact that the military situation in South Vietnam daily grew more unsatisfactory. Bombing had not brought the Viet Cong or Hanoi to their knees, but there were other options available. America could still prevent a Viet Cong victory and perhaps even bring about a communist defeat by introducing her own ground combat troops. Any negotiated peace would mean, at the best, a neutral South Vietnam, which would lead to an expanded influence for Hanoi and, as Washington saw it, for China. There would be no permanent American bases in Saigon. Thailand might reorient her policy. China would become more aggressive and start a whole series of wars of national liberation. Other adverse developments might begin. The Johnson administration was not going to allow all this to happen by default.

On 8 June 1965, the President announced that he was authorizing U.S. troops, formerly confined to patrolling, to search out the enemy. Three days later Saigon's last civilian government fell and Air Vice-Marshal Ky, who had fought for the French against the Vietminh and who later became famous for his praise of Adolf Hitler and his advocacy of invading North Vietnam, became Premier. Ky soon announced that 'support for neutralism' would henceforth be punishable by death. Despite the hard line in Washington and Saigon, however, the war was not going well. The Viet Cong had completely destroyed the railway system in South Vietnam. Acts of terrorism increased in the cities and more territory fell into communist hands. Hanoi, meanwhile, working from its position of increasing strength, again attempted to open discussions by explicitly stating that approval in principle of American withdrawal, rather than withdrawal itself, was all that was needed to get the negotiations started.

In a major policy speech of 28 July Johnson repeated the untenable but customary claim that 'there has been no answer from the other side' to America's search for peace. He, therefore, was compelled to send an additional 50,000 men to South Vietnam, bringing the total commitment to 125,000 men. It was clear that the American forces would actively engage in ground combat. America had decided to win in Vietnam by overwhelming the enemy. Johnson had already (10 July) declared in a press conference that there would be no limit on the number of troops sent to General Westmoreland if he requested them.

From MacArthur onwards, every responsible American

military officer who had commented on the subject had warned against American involvement in a land war in Asia, yet the nation was now fully involved in one. Time and again Johnson had declared during the 1964 Presidential campaign that he did not want American boys dying in South Vietnam, doing what Asian boys ought to be doing for themselves, yet now the American boys were dying there. The State Department had repeated over and over that the United States should never allow the communists to claim that America was fighting a white man's war against Asians, but that was exactly what had happened. John Kennedy and his aides had repeatedly pointed out that counter-insurgency was primarily a political task and that no guerrilla war could be won without an appropriate political response, yet 90 per cent or more of the material America was sending to South Vietnam was military and U.S. troops were the only force that stood between a reactionary dictatorship and total collapse.

Why had the Americans not heeded their own warnings? Primarily because they were responding to even greater fears. Their view of the nature of international communism had not, at bottom, changed in twenty years, nor had they questioned the wisdom of a policy of military containment. Johnson explained the basis of the policy most succinctly in his Johns Hopkins address: 'Over this war – and all Asia – is another reality: the deepening shadow of Communist China. The rulers in Hanoi are urged on by Peiping . . . . It is a nation which is helping the forces of violence in almost every continent. The contest in Vietnam is part of a wider pattern of aggressive purpose.' No sacrifice was too great to stop such aggression. Johnson had committed himself, and his nation, to do whatever had to be done.

12

Vietnam: Paying the Cost of Containment

'I want to leave the footprints of America there. We're going to turn the Mekong into a Tennessee Valley.'

LYNDON B. JOHNSON

JOHN KENNEDY's build-up of American's conventional warfare capacities had enabled Lyndon Johnson to escalate the American involvement in Vietnam without declaring a national emergency or even calling up the reserves. Kennedy's program had been so successful, in fact, that Johnson was able to intervene in the Dominican Republic while escalating in Vietnam. The action in the Dominican Republic worked, in the sense that the administration achieved its objectives, which may have encouraged Johnson to plunge ahead in Vietnam. The Dominican intervention, in the eyes of the administration, was the pay-off for the entire Kennedy–McNamara strategy of flexible response. America had both the forces and the will to move immediately and decisively, to keep the conflict limited in scope and time, and to prevent the rise of another Castro in the Western Hemisphere. Although the police action in the Dominican Republic cost Johnson some support from the liberals and intellectuals who had responded favorably to his domestic program, the President was proud of what he had accomplished. For him, the Dominican affair proved that the policy of intervention was right. The results in the Dominican Republic represented what Johnson hoped and expected would happen in Vietnam.

The Dominican intervention also illustrated the continuity of policy from Kennedy to Johnson; indeed, Johnson's actions had even deeper roots in the American past. From 1916 to 1940 U.S. Marines and customs officers had controlled the Dominican Republic, where American corporations had large investments in plantations that provided fresh fruits and vegetables to American markets during the winter. President Roosevelt eliminated an overt American presence in 1940 when Rafael Trujillo won a rigged presidential election and established a ruthless, efficient dictatorship. Roosevelt characterized Trujillo as 'an s.o.b.' but 'our s.o.b.'. In May 1961 Trujillo was assassinated.

With Trujillo gone, Kennedy saw three possibilities. In 'descending order of preference', they were: 'a decent democratic regime, a continuation of the Trujillo regime, or a Castro regime. We ought to aim at the first, but we really can't renounce the second until we are sure that we can avoid the third.' This typified Kennedy's – and America's – approach to the Third World. Kennedy wanted a democracy, but if the revolutionary government had socialistic elements in it and there was consequently a threat that the country would go communist, he would take a dictator and see what could be done about restoring civil liberties. Above all he was determined to keep out Soviet influence and retain American economic and political influence.

Kennedy did not have to make a choice between a Castro and a Trujillo, for on 20 December 1962, following a series of transitory provisional governments, the Dominican people elected Juan Bosch as their president. Bosch was a leftist but non-communist visionary and writer who had spent years as an anti-Trujillo exile and who seemed to represent the liberal alternative Kennedy was searching for. But Bosch was no match for the Dominican military and their conservative partners. Ten months after his election, the military overthrew him in a coup which the United States did nothing to prevent. Donald Reid Cabral took over but, although he was a member of the Dominican oligarchy, he could not command the wholehearted support of the military and had almost no following among the masses. By early April the Republic was ready to explode again, even though the United States had sent $5 million to Reid Cabral to prop up his regime.

On 24 April 1965, young Boschist officers in the army launched a coup that drove Reid Cabral from office, but they were unable to restore order. Angry masses poured into the streets of Santo Domingo. A junta of the regular military, described in Washington as the Loyalists, decided to take power for themselves. The rebels armed thousands of civilians and fighting began. The American Ambassador, W. Tapley Bennett, warned that a sudden communist takeover was one likely result of the civil war.

Johnson immediately decided that the revolt was part of a larger conspiracy, probably masterminded by Castro, and that the challenge to American interests in the Dominican Republic was a challenge to American interests throughout Latin America. He decided to intervene. On 28 April, in direct violation of the O.A.S. Charter (which prohibits intervention 'directly or indirectly, for any reason whatever, in the internal or external affairs of any other State'), Johnson sent in the Marines, to be followed by the Army's 82nd Airborne Division. His initial rationale was to protect the lives of American citizens in Santo Domingo, but on 30 April he announced a quite different reason: 'People trained outside the Dominican Republic are seeking to gain control.' The American Embassy in Santo Domingo issued a documented list of fifty-eight 'identified and prominent Communist and Castroite leaders' in the rebel forces, a list that was obviously, even outrageously, false – it came from one initially prepared years earlier by Trujillo. Bosch's assessment was more widely accepted: 'This was a democratic revolution smashed by the leading democracy in the world.'

Johnson had acted unilaterally, partly because of the need for speed, partly because of his opinion of his partners in the Alliance for Progress. 'The O.A.S.,' he remarked, 'couldn't pour piss out of a boot if the instructions were written on the heel.' Once the Marines had restored some order and prevented Bosch from taking over, however, it was necessary to deal with the O.A.S. Johnson was able to persuade the Latin Americans to join him in the Dominican Republic and by 28 May an O.A.S. peace-keeping force had reinforced and taken control from the U.S. troops. The search for a middle-ground in the government went on – according to Johnson's sympathetic biographers, Rowland Evans and Robert Novak, 'Johnson spent literally hours examining the credentials of various coalition governments which his agents in the field were desperately trying to establish with the approval of the two warring sides.' Eventually, in September, a government was formed, and in June 1966 moderate rightist Joaquin Balaguer defeated Bosch in a presidential election.

Johnson had won. The intervention had been limited in time, number of troops involved, cost, and lives lost. American Marines and paratroopers had prevented the rise of either a Castro or a Trujillo in the Dominican Republic, American corporations retained their plantations, Dominican laborers continued to pick cantaloupes for the New York market at $.25 an hour, and the O.A.S. had been mollified.

At the height of the crisis, Johnson had been besieged by liberal critics. The *New York Times* editorialized: 'Little awareness has been shown by the United States that the Dominican people – not just a handful of Communists – were fighting and dying for social justice and constitutionalism.' Even Robert Kennedy protested, although his complaint was that Johnson had failed to notify the O.A.S. before acting. Johnson ignored the critics and his eventual success proved justification enough. He may have concluded that he could do the same in Vietnam, and that success there would also silence the critics.

For it was Vietnam that provided the setting for Lyndon Johnson's agony, indeed for the agony of an entire nation.

From 1965 on, Vietnam brought up all the old questions about America's position in the world, questions that had lain dormant since Senator Taft had first raised them in response to the Truman Doctrine. America had been called upon to pay up on an insurance policy written in 1947 for Europe and extended from 1950 to 1954 to Asia. The price proved to be higher – far higher – than anyone had expected, and the circumstances surrounding the claim were not at all clearcut. Eventually the almost universal commitment within the United States to the policy of containment began to give way. Senators, intellectuals, businessmen, and millions of citizens launched a massive attack on some of the fundamental premisses of American foreign policy during the Cold War, especially the definition of America's vital interests and the domino theory. The tendency had been to define the nation's vital interests as any area in which the United States had political, economic, or military influence, which meant that America's vital interests were always moving outward. There had been little serious opposition to this trend, however, until Vietnam. By 1968, for the first time since the late forties, the State Department had to defend the definition of vital interests.

In Vietnam the American people had been forced to face up to the cost of containment. In 1965 most Americans agreed that it was necessary to hem in China and Russia militarily, that America had a vital interest in Western Europe, Japan, Latin America, and certain sections of the Mid-East, that the United States would have to do whatever was required to prevent any of these areas from going communist, and that to protect these areas it was necessary to defend the regions around them. This was the original escalation – the escalation of what America considered its vital interests. It was also assumed that America's needs included world-wide stability and order, which in practice meant the preservation of the *status quo*. These had been the broad general aims of all the Cold War Presidents and although there had been differences in degree, Truman and

Eisenhower and Kennedy had been prepared to take the risks and pay the cost involved in maintaining them. It was Johnson's bad luck that he got stuck with Vietnam.

At bottom, Vietnam differed from the Dominican Republic only in the cost. The Vietnamese intervention was not, in Johnson's view, the misapplication of an otherwise sound policy but one possible outcome which had always been implicit in the policy of containment. On every possible occasion the President emphasized that he was only following in the footsteps of Truman, Eisenhower, and Kennedy, and he never saw any good reason to question the basic assumptions.   *Following Foot Steps*

Others did. As the American commitment mounted, from $10 to $20 to $30 billion a year, from 150,000 to 300,000 to 500,000 and more men, as the casualties mounted, as the bombs rained down on the women and children of both North and South Vietnam, and as the Great Society faded out of existence, Johnson's critics began to wonder not just about Vietnam but about containment itself. Riots in America's cities, air and water pollution, the persistence of racism coupled with the refusal of American black men to stay in their place, the revolt of young people against the draft – all added to the persistence of the questioning. For many reasons the college students of the fifties had not questioned the policy of containment, but the most important probably was that, except for the Korean War, containment did not entail the slaughter of thousands of civilians, the death of thousands of young American men, the squandering of billions of dollars. In the late sixties, as the war in Vietnam went on and on and on, students and others began to ask about not only the war in Vietnam but – more significantly – to ask what kind of a society could support such a war. This led to an examination of all aspects of American life. As a result, students across the land came to believe that they lived in an evil, repressive society that exploited not only foreigners but Americans as well.

The campus revolt, however, was not as immediately significant as the broader questions raised by older men who had a stake in the society and a commitment to preserving it. Many came to believe that containment, and the specific expression of that policy in Vietnam, was not saving America but destroying it. They returned to an older vision of America, best expressed by Lincoln at Gettysburg, which saw America's mission as one of setting an example for the world. 'America can exert its greatest influence in the outer world by demonstrating at home that the largest and most complex modern society can solve the problems of modernity,' Walter Lippmann wrote. 'Then, what all the world is struggling with will be shown to be soluble. Example, and not intervention and firepower, has been the historic instrument of American influence on mankind, and never has it been more necessary and more urgent to realize this truth once more.' Senator Fulbright added, 'The world has no need, in this age of nationalism and nuclear weapons, for a new imperial power, but there is a great need of moral leadership – by which I mean the leadership of decent example.' The ultimate question raised by Vietnam, according to Robert Tucker, was whether America chose to be an empire or a nation.

Johnson chose empire, and for all the criticism it was clear that he had a majority with him. There was a heated debate over tactics within the ranks of Johnson's supporters, but not over the policy. For the bulk of the American people, it was in America's self-interest – and it was her duty – to stop the spread of communism, whether in the Dominican Republic or in Vietnam.

Johnson's foreign-policy advisers, almost to a man Kennedy appointees, concurred. Secretary Rusk took the lead. In private as well as in public Rusk argued that China was actively promoting and supporting the war in Vietnam, which in his view did not differ in any significant way from Hitler's aggression in Europe. 'In his always articulate, sometimes eloquent, formulations,' as Townsend Hoopes,

Under Secretary of the Air Force, put it, 'Asia seemed to be Europe, China was either Stalinist Russia or Hitler Germany, and S.E.A.T.O. was either N.A.T.O. or the Grand Alliance of World War II.' Johnson echoed Rusk's theme. 'The backstage Johnson,' Philip Geyelin reported, 'was quite capable of telling one of the Senate's more serious students of foreign affairs that "if we don't stop the Reds in South Vietnam, tomorrow they will be in Hawaii, and next week they will be in San Francisco".' This view of the universal nature of the threat continued to command majority support, even after a change in administration. In a speech in November 1969, President Nixon explained that American boys were fighting the communists in Vietnam so that they would not have to fight them in the Western Hemisphere.

There was an obvious difficulty with the approach, a difficulty inherent in the policy of containment. If the threat were really as pervasive as Johnson and Rusk said it was, if the stakes were actually as cosmic as they claimed, it made little sense to fight the tail of the snake and leave the head alone. The only possible justification for the death of 40,000 American soldiers and twenty times or more that many Vietnamese was to win, which meant cutting off the head of the snake, Peking. But no one dared risk taking the war to China, or even to Hanoi (except in the air). The Vietnamese War differed from the Korean War in many ways, but one of the most important was that the administration never attempted to liberate North Vietnam. Yet unless Hanoi itself were occupied by American troops, the North Vietnamese and the Viet Cong could carry on the war for a very long time. Bombing could not harm their source of strategic materials, since the source was in China and even more in Russia, and the U.S. Air Force could not seriously disrupt a line of communications that depended in large part on trails and men on bicycles. Nor could the United States impose an unacceptable toll on the enemy's manpower or material resources on the battlefield, for whenever the Viet Cong wished to cut their losses they could withdraw into the jungle or across the Cambodian or Laotion borders and avoid further combat.

The war could not be won. The influx of American combat troops meant it would not be lost. Hanoi would not negotiate until the bombing ended, nor until America promised to withdraw her troops, nor on the basis of elections held under the auspices of the Saigon government. America would not negotiate until Hanoi 'stopped her aggression' by withdrawing her troops and material support for the Viet Cong, nor would America withdraw until she was assured that the Saigon government would remain in power. Since who ruled in Saigon was what the war was all about, and since neither side would surrender, America was committed to a seemingly permanent war in the East.

When the bombing campaign in the North began, the U.S. Air Force promised a response from Hanoi in a matter of weeks. By December 1965, it was clear that the airmen had been wrong. Pressure to call the campaign off, meanwhile, was mounting. After Defense Secretary McNamara joined foreign governments and domestic critics in urging Johnson to announce at least a bombing pause to give Hanoi time to think and – hopefully – come to the peace table, the President gave in, beginning a pause that lasted thirty-seven days. In a bravo performance, he also initiated a gigantic peace campaign, sending Averell Harriman, U.N. Ambassador Arthur Goldberg, McGeorge Bundy, and others on jet flights around the world to ask the support of leaders in various national capitals to use their influence to bring Hanoi to the peace table. When Hanoi did not respond in a manner agreeable to the administration – i.e., by admitting that it was supporting the Viet Cong and by agreeing to withdraw all material and manpower aid – Johnson resumed the bombing, with an extended list of targets. For the next two years the bombs fell in increasing quantity on both North and South Vietnam, while General Westmoreland stepped up the ground campaign in an effort to kill all the Viet Cong and drive all of North Vietnam's troops out of the South. America continued to pursue the will-of-the-wisp of military victory.

The Kennedy liberals, meanwhile, turned against the President, although as much because they were offended by his style as because they disagreed with the policy. The Senate doves began holding frequent meetings to complain about the President. At the meetings, as in their public statements, they tended to personalize the issues. At one of the private sessions, Senator Eugene McCarthy of Minnesota was reported to have said, 'We've got a wild man in the White House, and we are going to have to treat him as such,' and Senator Albert Gore of Tennessee called Johnson 'a desperate man who was likely to get us into war with China, and we have got to prevent it'.

Much of the criticism missed the point. Johnson was flamboyant, he did overreact to events, and he was as guilty of personalizing everything as the doves were, but his policies were simply a logical outgrowth of those pursued by his predecessors, as he himself pointed out on every possible occasion.

By 1967, however, style seemed to be the issue. The doves called Johnson a monster. He called them 'chickenshit'. 'I'm the only President you have,' he was fond of declaring, with the implication that any criticism was unpatriotic. 'Why don't you get on the team?' he would demand of the few critics who got through Walt Rostow to see him. Whenever a dove was about to make a major speech, Johnson would fly off to the Pacific, taking the White House press corps with him, in an effort to steal the headlines. In November 1966, on the eve of Congressional elections, he visited the Officers' Club in Camranh Bay on the South Vietnamese coast. 'Come home with the coonskin on the wall,' he told the assembled officers. Dean Rusk kept on talking about Munich and appeasement, a theme Johnson picked up, thereby linking the doves with Chamberlain and the administration with Churchill. Fulbright's private rejoinder was, 'We go ahead treating this little piss-ant country as though we were up against Russia and China put together.'

The opposition mounted, but Johnson was probably right in asserting that its strength was overstated. America had never fought a war without some internal dissension and it would be impossible to prove that the doves' dissatisfaction with Vietnam was deeper or more vocal than the Whig dissatisfaction with the Mexican War or the Copperheads' opposition to Lincoln, or even than the opposition Roosevelt had faced before Pearl Harbor. There was not, in any case, a straightforward dove position. All Johnson's critics on the left agreed on the need to halt the bombing of the North, but beyond that they could not rally behind a program. Some wanted to get out of Vietnam altogether, admitting defeat, but continuing the general policy of containment. Their criticism was tactical – America had overextended herself. Other doves wanted to struggle on in South Vietnam – they remained wedded to all-out containment and objected only to the bombing of the North. A growing number wanted not only to get out of Vietnam but to go further and re-examine the entire containment policy. The deep divisions within the opposition allowed Johnson to hold to his course.

As the public criticism mounted, Johnson fought back with predictions that victory was just around the corner. Rostow was in the vanguard of the effort. He fed the press carefully selected figures from the American computers in Vietnam that proved the administration was on the high road to victory. The 'weapons loss ration' was 4.7 to 1 in favor of the Americans, as opposed to the unfavorable 1 to 2 in 1963. Enemy desertions were up from 20,000 in 1966 to 35,000 in 1967. A.R.V.N. desertions were down from 160,000 to 75,000. The Viet Cong were incapable of mounting any large-scale attacks. The number of people under Saigon's control had jumped from 8 to 12 million, or nearly 75 per cent of the South's population.

Prediction of victory for Vietnam

The overwhelming application of American power, the Johnson administration insisted, was having a cumulative effect that would, in time, bring Hanoi and the Viet Cong to their knees. The enemy's losses in the South were little short of catastrophic, yet Hanoi was not sending more troops from North Vietnam to the South to make up the losses because the bombing campaign in the North tied down enormous numbers of workers and troops. Captured documents indicated that Viet Cong morale was low. There was light at the end of the tunnel. America was winning the war of attrition. Rostow and the administration were beginning to sound like French or British or German generals in 1915 and 1916 and 1917 – they seemed to be saying that the side that hung on for the last fifteen minutes would win, thereby justifying all the sacrifices.

When Rostow's brave analysis failed to silence the critics, Johnson tried a harder sell. He brought Westmoreland back to the states to explain how and when the victory would be won. At the National Press Club, Westmoreland said, 'I am absolutely certain that whereas in 1965 the enemy was winning, today he is certainly losing.' On national television the General predicted victory within two years. Johnson, meanwhile, to give the one last shove needed to force Ho Chi Minh to surrender, again expanded the bombing. In mid-November 1967, the heaviest attacks yet against the Hanoi–Haiphong complex began.

Through it all ran a single threat – military victory was possible and necessary. Although the administration presented the war as limited in scope and purpose, in fact the only satisfactory outcome for America was the maintenance in power of the Saigon regime, which meant the total frustration of Hanoi and the Viet Cong. America was committed, as Townsend Hoopes put it, 'to the preservation and anchoring of a narrowly based government in the South, which could not survive without a large-scale U.S. military presence, whose constitution ruled out all political participation by the main adversary, and which was diligently throwing in jail even those non-Communists who advocated opening a dialogue with the National Liberation Front.'

It could not have been otherwise. Containment meant containment. Any compromise solution would lead to an N.L.F. participation in the politics of South Vietnam, which would have carried with it the very great risk of an eventual communist victory, which would have meant that the communists had not been contained, which would have meant that all the sacrifices had been made in vain. As Dean Rusk put it in 1966, 'If the Viet Cong come to the conference table as full partners, they will in a sense have been victorious in the very aims that South Vietnam and the United States are pledged to prevent.' Hoopes sums it up nicely: 'In short, President Johnson and his close advisers had so defined our national purposes and so conducted the war that a compromise political settlement would be tantamount to a resounding defeat for U.S. policy and prestige. Accordingly, it could not be faced. Military victory was the only way out. Throughout 1967, and into 1968, the administration insisted that the victory was possible.

Then came Tet. The communist offensive in February 1968 showed in a direct, if painful, fashion that everything Rostow had said and everything the computers had reported was hog-wash. The Viet Cong drove the Americans and A.R.V.N. out of the countryside and into the cities, thereby making a shambles out of the pacification program, and even took some of the cities. The Americans, it turned out, did not control the situation. They were not winning. The enemy retained enormous strength and vitality.

Tet revealed more than past errors. The American response illustrated much about the American view of the war and of the American attitude toward the people of Vietnam. As one example, the Viet Cong took control of the ancient cultural capital of Hue. David Douglas Duncan, a famous combat photographer with long experience in war, was appalled by the American method of freeing the city.

'The Americans pounded the Citadel and surrounding city almost to dust with air strikes, napalm runs, artillery and naval gunfire, and the direct cannon fire from tanks and recoilless rifles – a total effort to root out and kill every enemy soldier. The mind reels at the carnage, cost, and ruthlessness of it all.'

Hue's destruction highlighted the racist attitudes of the Americans in Vietnam, especially when contrasted with the difference in the American approach to combat in Europe in World War II. In 1944, on the eve of D-Day, Eisenhower warned his air commanders to remember that the coming battle would be fought over friendly territory. He ordered the airmen to avoid French civilian casualties at all costs and to restrict themselves to strictly military targets. On the ground, Eisenhower was even more explicit. He told Bradley, Patton and the other generals that in the coming campaign 'in the path of our advance will be found historical monuments and cultural centers which symbolize to the world all that we are fighting to preserve.' He made it the commanders' responsibility 'to protect and respect these symbols'. His orders were obeyed. In Vietnam, the American forces hardly even thought about what they were doing as they demolished the most cherished Vietnamese cultural center. The main reason for the difference was that while the Americans respected European cultural centers, they neither understood nor respected the cultural monuments in Asia. Eisenhower said the historical sites in Europe symbolized what the Allies were fighting for. Hue hardly filled the same role in Vietnam. Freedom for the Vietnamese people, under the American definition, meant nothing more than freedom from Ho Chi Minh. America was evidently ready to destroy all of Vietnam, and all its people, to assure that freedom. The point-blank shooting of hundreds of women and children at My Lai, shortly after Tet, illustrated the point.

The administration tried to pretend that Tet represented a last-gasp effort by the enemy, but that interpretation found few adherents. Senator McCarthy, meanwhile, challenged the President in a Presidential primary campaign in New Hampshire and almost defeated him. The junior Senator from New York, Robert Kennedy, then announced that he was entering the campaign. McNamara had left the Cabinet after failing to persuade Johnson to stop the bombing, but to Johnson's great surprise the new Secretary of Defense, Clark Clifford, widely considered to be a hawk, also wanted to stop the bombing. Faced by the crisis in confidence in his administration, informed by the polls that he faced almost certain defeat in the up-coming Wisconsin Presidential primary, deserted by all but a small handful of the most extreme hawks within his own administration, shocked by a request from Westmoreland for 200,000 additional troops for Vietnam (which would have required calling up the reserves and expanding the draft), Johnson finally decided to change his military policy. On Sunday evening, 31 March 1968, Johnson announced on national television that he was stopping the bombing in North Vietnam, except for the area immediately north of the Demilitarized Zone. To everyone's astonishment, he then withdrew from the Presidential race.

In the summer, the Republicans nominated Nixon for the Presidency. He said he had a plan to end the war honorably but could not reveal it. The Democrats nominated Vice-President Hubert Humphrey, rejecting a major effort by the doves to take control of the party, and pledged in general to continue Johnson's policies. Late in the campaign, when the polls showed Humphrey trailing badly, Johnson called off all bombing in North Vietnam. Nixon nevertheless won a tightly contested election.

Hanoi, meanwhile, had come to the peace table. After many false starts, the four sides in the war – the Viet Cong, Saigon, Hanoi, and the United States – sat down together to discuss peace. They quickly discovered that there was no basis for a compromise, since none of the parties were ready to surrender. The issue remained, Who will rule in Saigon?

Nixon declared that the United States did not seek a military victory, but that statement only meant the Americans had abandoned the Westmoreland policy of trying to kill all the communist troops, not that the United States was ready to accept a complete reorientation of the Saigon government.

Nixon's plan to end the war, he finally declared after ten months in office, was to turn it over to the Vietnamese. He would withdraw American combat troops while continuing to give naval and air support to A.R.V.N., meanwhile rearming A.R.V.N. with modern weapons. American policy had come full circle. Three decades earlier, when Franklin Roosevelt began his third term as President, he had declared that the United States would serve as the great arsenal of democracy. America would supply the tools of war so that others could contain the Axis aggressors. Now Nixon was proposing to contain the communist aggressors by extending lend-lease to the South Vietnamese.

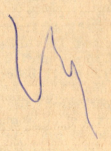

13

Nixon and the Debacle in Vietnam

'Give us six months, and if we haven't ended the war by then, you can come back and tear down the White House fence.'

HENRY KISSINGER *to a group of Quakers, March 1969*

'Let me speak to you honestly, frankly, openheartedly. You are a liar.'

LE DUC THO *to Henry Kissinger, 1972*

PRESIDENT Richard Nixon counted on the prestige of his office in carrying out his Vietnam policy. For Nixon, and for millions of citizens, the value of Vietnam was proved by the simple fact that his four predecessors had all thought it important. The President was the Great Captain to whom everyone should rally in times of crisis and in whom everyone should believe. As Nixon asked his close adviser H. R. Haldeman at the height of the Watergate mess, 'They still want to believe out there, don't they?' Haldeman assured him that indeed the American people did still want to believe in the President and were supporting him.

Johnson had relied on that same sentiment, of course, in support of his war-making policy, but by 1969 Nixon needed more than just the prestige of his office to continue the war, because he and all the world realized that short of using nuclear weapons the United States had done its best and was still not in a position to win. For economic and political reasons Nixon had to cut back on the American commitment in Vietnam. The best he could hope for – and this was his aim – was a gradual U.S. withdrawal, complemented by a huge increase in A.R.V.N.'s fighting qualities. By cutting down and then eliminating American combat losses, Nixon expected to be able to carry on until Saigon could stand on its own feet. He brushed aside warnings that this could not be accomplished until the Saigon regime was broadened and instituted meaningful economic and social reforms.

Nixon really had no choice, however. Any true reform by the Saigon regime would alienate the only groups supporting President Nguyen Van Thieu (the Catholic Church, A.R.V.N., and the landlords), and no reform Thieu might be willing to promise could possibly compete with the reforms already instituted by the Viet Cong in the areas it held. For Nixon, there was no alternative to Thieu; for Thieu, there was no alternative to continued suppression; for the Viet Cong and the North Vietnamese, there was no alternative to continued struggle.

Richard Nixon rode into office on a wave of popular dissatisfaction with the war, caused primarily by the Tet offensive of 1968. Voters evidently expected him to follow Eisenhower's example and to end the war within half a year of taking office, but Nixon's problems were not as easily solved as Eisenhower's had been in Korea. The basic difference was that by 1953 the South Korean government had been able to create an effective army to defend itself, while by 1969 A.R.V.N. had made little progress despite arms shipments four times as great as the Korean troops had received. Nixon's major objective, therefore, was to build up A.R.V.N. Since the easiest way to do that – improve morale through massive and permanent reform, most especially in land ownership – was impossible given the realities of Thieu's politics, the President tried to substitute arms for morale. He also desperately needed to gain time, so miserable was A.R.V.N.'s condition in 1969.

To buy time, Nixon had to moderate the domestic dissatisfaction with the war. Hawks, although seldom as vocal as doves, were still in a majority (as they almost surely were

right to the end). Nixon himself had thoroughly established his credentials as a hawk, and his major supporters
and advisers were, if possible, even more determined than
he was to stop the communist tide. Nixon and his chief
associates continued to believe in the dogma of falling
dominoes, in the faith that the United States had a mission
to uphold freedom around the world, and in the doctrine
that the President cannot allow policy to be made in the
streets by mobs of young people protesting the war. Most
of all, they held that a disaster for the United States in
Vietnam would be a disaster for the free world. In short,
the aims, goals, and assumptions of the Nixon administration were no different from those of the Johnson
administration.

Nixon recognized, however, as even the Pentagon seems
to have realized, that the war could not be won, whatever
the price the United States was willing to pay. Inflation
was already getting out of control. The common wisdom
held that the inflation was due to Johnson's refusal to raise
taxes to fight the war, but Nixon seems to have seen the
broader truth, that all wars produce inflation and that the
longer a war lasts, the worse inflation becomes.

Although inflation was a long-term worry in 1969, Nixon
had three other problems affecting his efforts to buy time
to build up A.R.V.N.; these problems centered around the
antiwar movement, the seemingly endless nature of the
war, and the absence of any cause worth fighting for. In a
bravura performance, one of the great triumphs of his
long political career, Nixon managed to solve all three
problems.

The antiwar movement, as a political event, was essentially a student movement. Nixon hoped to time the with-
drawals of troops from Vietnam with a reduction in the
size of the army, seeking to return to an all-volunteer army,
something the United States had not had since 1939. Such
an army would represent a return to America's traditional
practice. It also figured to save money. Best of all, it would

seriously weaken the political impact of the doves by robbing them of their major support, male college students.

So while constantly proclaiming that he would not allow policy to be dictated in the streets, Nixon seemed to allow just that to happen, giving the protesting students exactly what they had been demanding: no more conscription. Nixon believed that there was not enough idealism in the antiwar movement to sustain it once college students were no longer threatened with the draft, and he was right. Except for a brief period following the Cambodian invasion (May 1970), Nixon had less trouble with the antiwar movement than did his predecessor.

Ten months after taking office, Nixon took care of the problem of the seemingly endless nature of the war, simultaneously redeeming his pledge to produce a plan to end the war. He called it Vietnamization. This policy called for a gradual reduction in American ground strength in Vietnam and an improvement in A.R.V.N. It also meant, although Nixon did not say so, a marked increase in the American air offensive in Indochina. Soon Nixon was outbombing Johnson, but the great bulk of the American people did not object to killing Vietnamese from the skies with machines, not so long as American casualties were reduced from 200 to 100 per week and there was an end to the war in sight. People hoped, and Nixon believed, that the result in Vietnam would be the same as in Korea – a country divided – with Thieu holding on to his power in South Vietnam, supported by American arms.

Nixon brilliantly handled the third problem interfering with his efforts to maximize time to rebuild A.R.V.N. Although he needed to produce a cause to fight for, Nixon recognized that he could no longer rely on a consensus that every communist everywhere had to be shot, nor could he fall back on the hoary old thesis that Vietnam was a vital national interest to the United States – almost no one would swallow that argument by 1970. So he used a series of different justifications. He said he had inherited the war and was fighting on only to extract American troops safely, or he argued that an American defeat in Vietnam would seriously affect American interests elsewhere. At times he referred to America's treaty commitments and the overwhelming need to prove to friend and foe alike that America stood by her word.

Nixon also warned the American people that if they quit and the Viet Cong won, there would be a terrible bloodbath in Saigon, with all America's supporters losing their heads, and the blame would rest with the United States. In his foreign-policy message to Congress in January 1970, Nixon declared, 'When we assumed the burden of helping South Vietnam, millions of South Vietnamese men and women placed their trust in us. To abandon them would risk a massacre that would shock and dismay every one in the world who values human life.' Besides insisting that there had been no massacre in Hanoi in 1954, doves pointed out that the American military had already killed more Vietnamese than the Viet Cong ever could, and that listening to Richard Nixon – the Commander in Chief of the greatest offensive air attack in history, mostly directed against civilian targets – talk about the value of human life was hard to take.

Most of all, Nixon justified the continuation of the war by raising the issue of the P.O.W.'s held by Hanoi. We will fight on until we get them back, he cried again and again, and it was a rallying cry with enough emotional content to convince most Americans that the war must go on.

The P.O.W. issue could not, however, win the war for Thieu. Vietnamization meant, first of all, vastly increased military aid for the Government of South Vietnam (G.V.N.). Backed by the sudden, massive inflow of money and arms, Thieu ordered a general mobilization. By inducting all men between eighteen and thirty-eight into the service, Thieu expanded the G.V.N. armed forces from 700,000 to 1,100,000, which meant that over half the able-bodied male population of South Vietnam was in uniform.

As Frances Fitzgerald points out in her award-winning *Fire in the Lake,* counting the militia, the civil service, and the 110,000-man police force, 'the United States was arming and, in one way or another, supporting most of the male population of Vietnam – and for the duration of the war.'

Coupled with the 'search and destroy' policy of the American combat troops, the sudden expansion of A.R.V.N. produced a temporary but real military advantage for the U.S.–G.V.N. side. Fitzgerald describes the results: 'Now all, or most, of the Vietnamese were swept up into the American war machine. "Vietnamization" pre-empted the manpower base of the country and brought it into a state of dependency on the American economy. And the results were spectacular. The major roads were open to traffic; the cities flourished on American money and goods; those peasant families that remained in the fertile areas of the Delta grew rich on bumper crops of "miracle" rice. The country was more "pacified" than it had ever been before.'

From the American (and Thieu's) point of view, Vietnamization seemed to be working. By 1972, 50 per cent of the population lived in cities (Saigon's population alone had jumped in ten years from 300,000 to 3,000,000), where the refugees from the countryside became dependent upon the Americans. South Vietnam had the population distribution of an industrialized state, but it had no industry, except for the war and the Americans. Vietnamese refugees made their living either in the army of the G.V.N. (where they were paid by the Americans) or by working directly for the Americans – on construction jobs, unloading (and stealing) at the docks, as shoeshine boys or pimps, as cleaning women or prostitutes. In the cities the refugees were safe, certainly better off than they had been when living in the notorious 'free-fire zones' the Americans designated, and they were fed, more or less, by the American government – but they had no real economy.

From 1961 onward, American Presidents never tired of

proclaiming that the United States was making such huge
sacrifices in Southeast Asia only for the good of the people
of the region. The United States had no territorial objectives, nor did it wish to replace the French as the colonial
masters of the Vietnamese. It was true that the United
States took no wealth out of Vietnam; in fact, it poured
money in. 'And yet,' Fitzgerald points out, 'it has produced
much the same effects as the most exploitative of colonial
regimes. The reason is that the overwhelming proportion
of American funds has gone not into agricultural or industrial development but into the creation of services for the
Americans – the greatest service being the Saigon government's army. As a whole, American wealth has gone into
creating and supporting a group of people – refugees,
soldiers, prostitutes, secretaries, translators, maids, and
shoeshine boys – who do not engage in any form of
production.'

   The G.V.N. was a government without a country. The
people were dependent on it – or rather on the Americans – but they felt no loyalty to it. South Vietnam, once
a major world exporter of rice, now produced almost
nothing. The G.V.N. had guns and money. The other side
had a cause. Viet Cong and North Vietnamese morale went
up and down over the decade of active American involvement, as would be true in any army in such a long war, but
even at its lowest point, communist morale was so much
higher than A.R.V.N.'s that no comparison was possible.
The Americans talked incessantly about 'pacification' and
'winning the hearts and minds of the people' while Nixon
dropped new record tonnages of bombs on the people.
Those who escaped the bombing offensive went to the
cities to become unwilling conscripts in A.R.V.N. or re-
sentful servants to the Americans. In the army they would
not fight, for the good reason that they had nothing to
fight for. Meanwhile the Viet Cong and the North Vietnamese held on against the world's most powerful military
machine, thereby providing – in Fitzgerald's words – 'an

example of courage and endurance that measures with any in modern history.'

Throughout 1969 and into 1970, the Americans regularly released figures to prove that Vietnamization was working. A.R.V.N., according to the Pentagon, could 'hack it.' Body counts were higher than ever; A.R.V.N. had more troops, more and better leaders and equipment. Then, in late April 1970, Nixon made a surprise announcement that a large force of U.S. troops, supported by major air strikes and backed by a huge A.R.V.N. force, had invaded Cambodia. Nixon said the purpose was to gain time for the American withdrawal. His objective was C.O.S.V.N., which he described as the command headquarters of the entire North Vietnamese and Viet Cong effort. The capture of C.O.S.V.N., according to Nixon, would be as decisive as the capture of Hitler's Berlin bunker. This revealed only how little Nixon and the Pentagon and the generals in the field understood the nature of the war. The North Vietnamese and Viet Cong had nothing like the sophisticated military headquarters common to Western armies. C.O.S.V.N. never existed. The invasion of Cambodia resulted in the death of a few communist troops but otherwise had only negative results. It hardly even slowed the flow of supplies to the Viet Cong and North Vietnamese in the south. It turned Cambodia into a battleground and eventually prompted a successful insurgency, thereby making the domino theory come true.

The Cambodian invasion extended the list of nations the United States was pledged to defend, despite Nixon's solemn promise that he was not making any pledges to the Lon Nol military regime, which had recently overthrown the government of Prince Norodom Sihanouk. The invasion temporarily revived the antiwar movement at home, especially after four students were shot down by the Ohio National Guard at Kent State University, and it gave Henry Kissinger an opportunity to display his academic brilliance as he explained to the Senate why the invasion of Cambodia was not an invasion of Cambodia.*

The American people, however, were not willing to see their boys fighting in yet another country. It was not just the students at Kent State and elsewhere who screamed in protest; even the Congress of the United States passed a bill forcing Nixon to remove American ground and air forces from Cambodia by July 1970. Nixon continued to bomb Cambodia, which he had been doing secretly for more than a year—the secret, of course, was well known by the Cambodians and Hanoi but not by the American people or Congress.† He did have to pull the troops out, announcing as he did so that the operation had been a great success. In fact, he had put himself in the position of having another government to defend that could not possibly defend itself, and he had left A.R.V.N. with a new responsibility that it could not meet.

In announcing the invasion, Nixon had said, 'If, when the chips are down, the world's most powerful nation . . . acts like a pitiful, helpless giant, the forces of totalitarianism and anarchy will threaten free nations and free institutions throughout the world.' The almost totally negative

---

* According to Kissinger, the Cambodian government did not know — and did not want to know — what was going on in its border areas. The Cambodian government had not actually invited the American troops into the country, but it had not resisted either. The territory the Americans invaded was hardly 'neutral,' filled as it was with communist troops, and the Cambodians did not exercise sovereignty there. We were not making war on the Cambodian government. Therefore the invasion of Cambodia was not an invasion of Cambodia.

† Henry Kissinger had no problem justifying the deception. If the secret had been known, he later told a Senate committee, it would have led to demonstrations in the streets, thereby jeopardizing the administration's plans for peace. This was at least consistent with Nixon's position that the United States was making war to insure peace.

results of the great risk he had taken in expanding the war showed in fact that the United States — at least in a guerrilla war in Asia — was helpless.

In February 1971, six months after pulling American (but not A.R.V.N.) troops out of Cambodia, Nixon launched a strike into Laos. Because of Congressional action he could not commit U.S. ground troops, but he was under no restraints with regard to air power. So American bombers and helicopters flew mission after mission to protect the A.R.V.N. invaders, whose objective was to disrupt, and hopefully to destroy, the Ho Chi Minh Trail. Although the skies belonged to the U.S.–G.V.N. forces, and although thousands of tons of bombs fell on the communists, Hanoi's forces sent A.R.V.N. reeling. It suffered 50 per cent losses in the forty-five-day operation. As Frances Fitzgerald notes, the Laos invasion convinced the South Vietnamese that Vietnamization 'meant increased Vietnamese deaths in pursuit of the American policy objective to extract the American troops from Vietnam without peace negotiations.'

Vietnamization was revealed to be a failure. Laos, which had been relatively quiet, was now as deeply involved in the Indochinese war as Cambodia. Nixon had set up another domino for the communists to knock over, but he accomplished little more. The flow of supplies down the trail actually increased.

The Paris peace talks, set up by Johnson, went on – and on and on. Nixon, convinced that Vietnamization *had* to work, refused to make any compromise. His position was that if Hanoi pulled its troops out of South Vietnam, gave back the American P.O.W.'s, promised not to support the Viet Cong, and accepted nationwide elections administered by the Saigon regime,* the United States would stop

---

* Nixon and Hanoi both knew full well the truth of the old saying, 'In a democracy it's not who votes that counts, but who counts the votes.'

the bombing. The Viet Cong and Hanoi would accept nothing short of control in Saigon. The talks remained deadlocked. By early 1972 Nixon had most American ground troops out of Vietnam, but he had greatly increased U.S. Air Force activity in Southeast Asia and had reached new levels of daily tonnage of bombs dropped. Once again, there was no end in sight.

All of which was tremendously frustrating. Kissinger, who had emerged by 1971 as Nixon's chief foreign-policy adviser (and would soon be Secretary of State), felt the frustration, but unlike the doves, Kissinger could not abide the thought of simply putting the United States troops on ships and bringing them home, leaving the Vietnamese to fight it out among themselves. Vietnam was too important to abandon. Why? Because, according to Kissinger, 'the commitment of 500,000 Americans has settled the issue of the importance of Vietnam. For what is involved now is confidence in American promises.' He sounded a little like World War I British Field Marshal Sir Douglas Haig, sending 100,000 reinforcements to be slaughtered in Flanders Fields in order to show the enemy how determined the British were to meet their obligations.

Still, Kissinger did want peace, even though a military victory was no longer possible, if it had ever been. The Americans had thrown nearly everything they had, short of nuclear weapons, into the battle. They had exploded more bombs on Indochina than they had on Japan and Germany put together, and still they were not winning. Economic and political pressures had forced first Johnson, then Nixon, to cut back. Hanoi, undefeated on the battlefield, would never quit as long as Thieu held power in Saigon, and Nixon and Kissinger would accept no peace that removed Thieu from power. So the war went on, and Kissinger's frustration increased.

Kissinger, like Dean Rusk before him, believed that the path to peace with Hanoi led through Moscow and Peking. If the two communist superpowers would only refrain from supplying arms to the North Vietnamese, **Hanoi** would have to sue for peace. Never mind that Hanoi was getting less than half the supplies from its backers as Saigon was from the Americans (if the United States stopped supplying Saigon, there would also be an immediate peace). Kissinger repeatedly urged the Russians to let Hanoi go down the drain before the Vietnamese war escalated into a great-power confrontation. Kissinger saw the world as John Foster Dulles had seen it: a constant struggle for supremacy between the great powers.

One sees in Kissinger's writings, most especially in the expanded version of *American Foreign Policy* (1974), his view of the world. He never acknowledged – because he never understood – the suffering of the people of Indochina. He regarded North Vietnam, A.R.V.N., Saigon, Hanoi, Cambodia, the Viet Cong, and Laos as pawns to be moved around the board by the great powers. He had no sense of the economic and social struggles going on in the rice paddies, highlands, and mountains of Southeast Asia. He never realized the starkly simple nature of the war – landlords versus peasants – and therefore insisted on seeing it as a highly complex game in which the moves were made from Washington, Moscow, and Peking.

Kissinger's views led him to the capitals of the communist superpowers in his search for peace in Vietnam. He could not believe that Hanoi had its own aims and objectives, more or less unconnected to Russia's or China's. So Kissinger invented the term linkage. Everything was related – the industrial nations' oil shortage, the Vietnam war, emigration from Russia, China's military capacity, and so on. Thus, according to Kissinger, the path to peace – not just for our generation, but for our children and our children's children – was the broadest possible agreement with Russia, an all-encompassing agreement that would bring worldwide, permanent peace. Through linkage, Kissinger would out-Metternich Metternich.

The first step would be an arms-control agreement with

the U.S.S.R. From it would flow a more general détente, trade with Russia, lowered tensions in the Middle East, and peace in Indochina – with Thieu and Lon Nol still in power. For these reasons and because the Strategic Arms Limitation Talks (S.A.L.T.) were inherently the single most important issue facing the U.S. and the U.S.S.R., who between them were spending ultimately uncountable sums of money on more and more unbelievably destructive weapons, Kissinger put a mighty effort into arms control. The Johnson administration had started the talks but had given them such a low priority that Nixon and Kissinger were, in effect, starting anew.

They came to S.A.L.T. with some sobering realizations, chief of which was that the days of American unchallenged superiority were finished. The United States had 1,054 intercontinental ballistic missiles (I.C.B.M.'s), 656 submarine-launched missiles, and 540 long-range bombers, a force sufficient to kill each Russian fifty times over. The Russians, however, had built, in a crash program, 1,200 I.C.B.M.'s, 200 submarine-launched missiles, and 200 big bombers. As Morton Halperin, one of Kissinger's assistants, noted in a staff study, 'It was impossible to escape the conclusion that no conceivable American strategic program would give you the kind of superiority that you had in the 1950s.'

Halperin's conclusion was hard to take and hardly taken. Nixon did announce that sufficiency, rather than superiority, would be the new American strategic goal, Kissinger did acknowledge that 'an attempt to gain a unilateral advantage in the strategic field must be self-defeating,' and the Americans did place a high priority on S.A.L.T. Nevertheless, Nixon still hoped to keep the American lead in strategic weapons, and he succeeded.

One of Nixon's first acts as President was to send the nuclear nonproliferation treaty (which prevented the 'have nots' from getting nuclear weapons), negotiated by the Johnson administration, to the Senate for approval. The day after that approval came – supposedly clearing the way for meaningful S.A.L.T. talks – Nixon announced a new antiballistic-missile (A.B.M.) program. His purpose was to create 'bargaining chips' for S.A.L.T. In other words, like bombing in Vietnam to insure peace, Nixon was building new weapons so that the United States would not have to build new weapons. The President also endorsed the Multiple Independently Targeted Reentry Vehicle (M.I.R.V.), which could give each I.C.B.M. three to ten separately targeted nuclear warheads. Most military experts considered M.I.R.V. to be a quantum leap comparable to the switch from conventional to nuclear weaponry. Despite his talk about 'sufficiency,' Nixon still pushed on, determined to keep the United States number one. He would not allow the American negotiators at S.A.L.T. to bring up the subject of M.I.R.V.; he wanted the United States to develop, perfect, and deploy the M.I.R.V.'s before he would consider a freeze on them.

As the talks went on, Kissinger had members of his National Security Council staff prepare American position papers. Their conclusion, arrived at after painstaking work, was that nothing could be done to bring about any change in the arms race. Kissinger backed them up when he declared that 'general meaningless principles' about disarmament were no substitute for 'massive studies.' The trouble was that whenever any expert within the bureaucracy began detailed studies, he always ended up supporting the *status quo* in the arms race or some slight variation of it. So the Cold War bureaucrats on both sides continued to grind out analyses and statistics proving that the policy was correct and could not be changed.

The S.A.L.T. agreement that was finally signed in 1972 froze I.C.B.M. deployment but not M.I.R.V., which was about as meaningful as freezing the cavalry of the European nations in 1938 but not the tanks. Throughout the period of the Nixon administration the Pentagon added three new warheads per day to the M.I.R.V. arsenal, a policy the Gerald Ford administration continued. By 1973, according to the U.S. State Department, the United States had 6,000 warheads to the Russians' 2,500. By 1977 the United States would have 10,000 warheads, the Russians 4,000. It was a strange way to control the arms race. As Laurence Martin, Director of War Studies at the University of London, notes, 'So far the S.A.L.T. exercise has done more to accelerate than to restrain strategic arms procurement on both sides.'

Still, Kissinger had to fight for the ratification of the interim agreement that S.A.L.T. produced. When Dean Acheson faced the Senate Foreign Relations Committee in the late forties and early fifties, he had to answer absurd questions from Cold War Senators about why he was not doing more to stand up to the Russians. Kissinger, before the same committee, had to answer absurd questions about why he was playing fast and loose with America's security. Kissinger finally got the interim agreement through the Senate, thereby completing the first step in linkage. The next move was to bring Peking in on the game.

Since 1949 the United States had had no relations with the People's Republic of China, pretending all the while that the Nationalist Chinese on Taiwan, not the communists in Peking, represented the 'real' China. As a policy, nonrecognition had little to recommend it (aside from its value on the domestic political scene); certainly it had not made China any less communist. When Nixon and Kissinger took office, China was not an issue they had to face. Democrats were afraid to raise the subject for fear of being labeled soft on communism, and Republicans – led by Nixon himself – claimed to feel an intense loyalty to the Nationalist Chinese. Neither the public, the press, nor the Congress had the slightest hint that the new President might reexamine the old policy, with which he had been intimately associated throughout his career.

Suddenly, in July of 1971, Nixon announced that he was going to visit China at the invitation of China's leaders. Henry Kissinger had arranged the trip during a series of secret meetings with Chou En-lai; it would take place in February of 1972. There had been no public pressure to change the China policy, and no public debate had taken place on the subject in years. Why had it been done? Who stood to gain from it? Insiders seemed to feel that it was Kissinger's idea, one he had sold to Nixon. Kissinger may have simply felt that the United States could not go on forever ignoring the world's largest nation, but if so it was a new thought to him, as nothing in his previous record indicated that he disagreed with Cold War America's China policy. Commentators speculated that perhaps Kissinger wanted to use the opening to China as a way to squeeze both Moscow and Hanoi.

It appeared that Kissinger saw vast possibilities for the United States in a Sino-Soviet split. In Kissinger's view, Hanoi was a puppet with two pairs of hands manipulating it. This was a strange view for Kissinger to hold, since he (and Nixon and most American politicians) had publicly insisted for decades that Peking was a puppet on Moscow's string. Kissinger did not abandon his puppet metaphor when he recognized the existence of hostility between China and Russia; he only transferred it to Hanoi. That Hanoi was no more a puppet than China had ever been seems not to have occurred to him.

Kissinger's great problem, on which his ambitious plans to be a modern Metternich rested, was to get the United States safely out of Vietnam, with Thieu in power for at least a 'decent interval.' Since Hanoi would not accept such a deal, Kissinger had to look elsewhere. China and Russia could make Hanoi behave, if they wanted to. The way to get them to want to, Kissinger reasoned, was to keep them guessing about actual U.S. intentions. Kissinger's active pursual of détente (which was presented as a new policy but which in fact consisted of barely warmed up leftovers disguised by a few new spices, most notably direct instead of indirect American grain sales to Russia) could not help but make the Chinese worry about a possible U.S.–U.S.S.R. alliance against China. Stranger things have happened, after all. Kissinger's opening to China, meanwhile, made Russia's leaders fearful of a U.S.–China alliance directed against them. There were many nuances to Kissinger's game of keeping 'em guessing, but always a consistent aim: to get Moscow and Peking to force Hanoi to allow the United States to extract itself from South Vietnam and to refrain from toppling Thieu until a 'decent interval' had gone by (presumably until Nixon left the White House in 1977).

Ultimately, Kissinger's strategy proved dead wrong. Whatever their fears and worries, neither Moscow nor Peking changed their Vietnam policy. They continued to send supplies to their beleaguered fellow communists, but that was all. Hanoi, in sharp contrast to Saigon, neither asked for nor would have accepted Russian or Chinese troops. There is no evidence that either communist nation helped Kissinger in any way with his Vietnam problem.

If Kissinger wanted to open the door to China in order to play the global diplomacy game, what about Nixon? What were his motives? Since he did not lead a public discussion or debate beforehand and has done precious little explaining of his reasoning afterward, one has to guess. Such hypotheses are easy to come by. Nixon wanted to make history, and recognition of China – especially by one of the original and most ferocious of the Cold Warriors – would most assuredly be historic. It was the right thing to do, he may have figured, and he was the right man to do it, his anticommunist credentials being what they were, or he might have been drawn into Kissinger's game. Certainly the policy shift appealed to Nixon's love for surprises and for the dramatic.

It was also good politics. The right wing might (and to some extent did) complain, but it had no one but Nixon to cling to. The left wing could only applaud. The boldness and drama of the new policy, the basic common sense in recognizing China, and the magnificent television coverage of the trip itself, with Nixon always at the center, could not help but win him millions of votes. Just the sight of him shaking hands with Chou or chatting with Mao Tse-tung gave Nixon stature. The timing was perfect – early enough in the Presidential election year to allow Nixon to claim that he was not electioneering, but late enough to keep it in the forefront of voters' minds on election day. Kissinger later claimed that the trip came early in 1972 'because the President directed that a step of such importance for world peace and the long-term relationships between our country and the People's Republic of China should not get mixed up in the campaign,' a good example of saying the opposite of what you mean.

The trip itself was a sensation. How much that was substantial came out of it remains unclear. By August 1974, when Nixon resigned from office, the United States had not exchanged ambassadors with China, nor had such an exchange taken place during the first year of Gerald Ford's Presidency. No great trade deals had been made. The problem of Taiwan and the Nationalists remained an open sore. But however slim the immediate results, Nixon's China trip was an historic and necessary event. He did what had to be done, and it is quite probably true that no other American President could have pulled it off. Thanks to Nixon's boldness, the United States now has an opportunity to establish truly friendly relations with the world's oldest and most populous civilization.

The best year of Nixon's life was easily 1972, and not just because of the China trip or the election. Shortly after returning from China, Nixon announced (on 8 May) that in response to a major North Vietnamese offensive he was mining the North Vietnamese ports and expanding his bombing campaign. Besides giving the Pentagon a chance to prove it could do what it said it could do (in the event, it couldn't – even though the military had claimed for years that such an escalation of the war would be decisive), the action reassured any doubters who feared that Nixon had suddenly gone soft on communism. To his delight, Nixon got away with something Johnson had always feared to try. Despite the loss of a ship in Haiphong harbor, the Russians acted as if nothing had happened, and a month later Nixon visited Moscow for a summit meeting. Kissinger credited his diplomacy for this success; others attributed it to Russia's need for America's wheat and corn. Nor did Peking react, other than in verbal denunciations.

Even riding as high as he was in 1972, Nixon still had problems, and chief on the list was Vietnam. He absolutely had to have peace to be reelected, or at least some semblance of a peace at hand, but he also had to have Thieu in power, else he would become 'the first President to lose a war.' Nixon risked his own reelection (and this is one place where Nixon put his feelings first, the votes second) to avoid that outcome. He instructed Kissinger to take a hard line in his secret talks with North Vietnam's Le Duc Tho; Nixon simultaneously stepped up his military offensive against North Vietnam, Cambodia, and Laos.

It was primarily an air offensive, because by the spring of 1972, Nixon had reduced the American ground-troop level in Vietnam to 70,000, far below the 540,000 that had been there when he took office four years earlier. American combat deaths were down from three hundred to ten per week. Vietnamization was a success from Nixon's point of view — if only Hanoi would sign a peace agreement.

The secret Kissinger–Le Duc Tho talks were dragged out and terribly complex. Incredibly small points were haggled over while each side blamed the other for insincerity. There was some shifting of positions. What stands out, however, is a real consistency. Throughout, Hanoi was willing to allow the Americans to get out and to turn over the P.O.W.'s when they did. From that point on,

Hanoi insisted that what happened in Vietnam was none of America's business, which meant Hanoi would sign no binding contract as to her behavior in the future. Washington consistently argued that Hanoi had to agree to abandon the use of force in settling the problem of a divided Vietnam. Such an agreement, of course, would insure Thieu's position for some years to come, given that he controlled the army, the police, the civil service, and most importantly, the ballot boxes in South Vietnam.

Eventually, Hanoi indicated its willingness to sign an agreement, perhaps realizing that once the Americans were gone, Nixon and Kissinger would find it difficult to influence events. So on 26 October 1972, just in time for the election, a triumphant Kissinger could announce that 'peace is at hand,' and Nixon could claim that his policies had brought 'peace with honor.' The Democratic Presidential candidate, George McGovern, who had had rotten luck throughout his inept campaign, lost the only issue he still had going for him. Despite McGovern's last-minute appeal to the American people, 'Don't let this man fool you again,' 60 per cent of the voters were satisfied that Nixon had redeemed his pledge to get the United States out of Vietnam. Nixon scored the greatest victory in modern American electoral history.

Then, immediately after the election, the talks broke down again. Kissinger, at Nixon's insistence, had raised the price just when Le Duc Tho was ready to sign. Nixon would not be satisfied with anything short of an iron-clad guarantee that Thieu would remain in power. Worried that he might be 'sold out,' Thieu followed the example of Syngman Rhee in Korea twenty years earlier and threatened to ignore any cease-fire agreement the Americans might sign.

Le Duc Tho would make no further concession, however, and in fact responded to Kissinger's new demands with some new demands of his own. This is when Nixon began the last and most sordid act of this most sordid of all American wars. The Christmas 1972 bombing campaign against Hanoi quickly made it the most heavily bombed city in the history of the world and sickened the hearts of decent people everywhere.

Nixon's publicly stated reason for the air offensive was to force Hanoi to release the P.O.W.'s, but the campaign itself led to the loss of at least fifteen B-52's and eleven fighter-bombers (Hanoi claimed much higher American losses), increasing by ninety-three the number of P.O.W.'s held by Hanoi. The losses, meanwhile, were more than the U.S. Air Force could take. The generals had never liked the idea of sending costly B-52's over Hanoi, a city heavily defended against air attack, thanks to the Russians. As the losses mounted, the generals wanted out. Nixon must also have been aware of the world-wide opposition to the bombing, and Kissinger may have convinced him that the October agreement was the best the United States could get. Nixon was also informed that the new Democratic Congress, coming into office in January 1973, was going to cut off all funds for bombing. For whatever reason, Nixon called off the bombers and agreed to sign a cease-fire agreement. On 23 January 1973, Kissinger officially ended all active American participation in the war in Vietnam (but not in Cambodia or Laos).

Nixon claimed that the Christmas bombing had done the trick, but two of his own officials gave that story the lie when they were interviewed by Marvin and Bernard Kalb. 'Peanuts,' said one official when asked what difference the Christmas bombing had made. 'That enormous bombing made little critical difference. What the B-52's did was to get the margin in January pretty much back to where it was in October.' Another official explained, 'Look, we were in an embarrassing situation. Could we suddenly say we'll sign in January what we wouldn't in October? We had to do something. So the bombing began, to try to create the image of a defeated enemy crawling back to the peace table to accept terms demanded by the

United States. Maybe the bombing had some effect – there are differing perceptions on this – but the B-52's weren't critical, although the administration has been able to sell that notion.'

The cease-fire in Vietnam broke down almost immediately. Nixon rushed arms to Thieu, giving South Vietnam the fourth most powerful air force in the world and much the largest in Southeast Asia. More money poured in as the United States remained the sole support of the South Vietnamese economy. Nixon continued to bomb Cambodia and Laos. All four sides to the cease-fire agreement, so painfully negotiated over such a long period of time, violated it in every imaginable way, as everyone had known beforehand they would. All that had really been agreed to was that the United States would pull its fighting men out of Vietnam, and that Hanoi would give back the P.O.W.'s.

The war went on, bloodier than ever on the ground. In 1975 the Thieu regime collapsed when its only remaining prop, the magnificently equipped A.R.V.N., collapsed. President Gerald R. Ford, who had replaced Nixon, pleaded with Congress for more money and arms for Thieu (and for Lon Nol in Cambodia, whose regime was also collapsing). Congress refused to budge; it would sink no more money into Southeast Asia. The Vietnamese, Cambodian, and Laotian civil wars finally ended. The white man was gone from Indochina.

Except in Hong Kong and South Korea, in fact, the white man was now out of mainland Asia, the Americans being the last to leave. (This statement, of course, ignores the fact that the Russians control a huge chunk of Asia.) The process begun by the Japanese one generation earlier, when they had proclaimed that Asia should be run by Asians, was nearly complete. America's long relationship with Asia, begun with the acquisition of the Philippines three quarters of a century earlier, had reached a divide. America had been involved in war in Asia for twenty-two of the thirty-four years between 1941 and 1975. Between 1964 and 1973 the United States had nearly a million soldiers, airmen, and sailors stationed in five mainland Asian countries. By 1975 American armed forces were stationed only in South Korea, and except for Hong Kong no part of Asia or her offshore islands were controlled by any Western European nation. This was quite a different situation from 1939, when Japan and Thailand were the only truly independent nations in Asia.

By 1976, the two hundredth birthday of the United States (the first colonial nation to revolt and achieve independence), colonialism was pretty well dead everywhere. Franklin Roosevelt had once said that Rafael Trujillo was 'an s.o.b.' but that he was 'our s.o.b.' Forty years later more people than not were still ruled by 's.o.b.'s,' but at least they were their own 's.o.b.'s.' The great age of imperialism was over. Whether America and the U.S.S.R., the last and most powerful of the imperialists, continue to recognize this fact or not remains to be seen.

Much depends on what has happened to and continues to change the office of the President since Nixon's disgrace. One of the major themes in the American rise to globalism after 1938 has been the immense growth in the power of the Presidency, especially in foreign affairs. Nixon proved that the President, as Commander in Chief at the command post for the 'free world' in the Cold War, could get away with anything. No one seriously believed that he could have been impeached because of his secret bombing of Cambodia or for his invasion of that country, even though both actions were clear violations of the Constitution. Nor would he have been impeached for scandals involving unreported campaign funds, the use of public funds to improve his private homes, the use of the F.B.I. and the C.I.A. to get at his political enemies, or any other offense. Had it not been for the system of tape recordings Nixon himself established in the White House, with their proof of his criminal activity, Nixon would have stayed in office no matter what he did.

Congress did pass, in 1972, the War Powers Act, which requires the President to give an accounting of his actions within thirty days of committing troops to a foreign war. After that time Congress has to approve the Presidential action.

It was an awkward way for Congress to assert its constitutional right (and duty) to declare war. The last time the President consulted Congress over war powers was in 1964, when Johnson sent the Gulf of Tonkin Resolution through the legislature in a breeze. Congress had played absolutely no role in the major decisions of the Nixon White House: Vietnamization, the air and later the ground offensives against Cambodia and Laos, the China trip, the Moscow summit, the mining of Haiphong harbor, the Christmas bombing, or the cease-fire agreement. The War Powers Act, by starting with the assumption that the President had to be free to move quickly in a crisis, gave the game away. Once the President, acting in strict accord with the law, had troops committed, could anyone believe that the Congress would force him to pull out?

By wrapping himself in the flag and appealing to the patriotism – and the jingoism – of the public, the President could keep his war going. That the public still yearned, even after Nixon, for strong leadership, that it would still respond enthusiastically to American saber rattling, became clear in May 1975, when President Ford sent the Marines into Cambodia to rescue a captured merchant vessel. The affair revealed that the quickest path to popularity for a President remained a *successful* foreign adventure. In such situations, hopes for a less active, more cautious, less expansive foreign policy are slim.

Still, the Presidency has been at least temporarily

weakened by Watergate, which may have been a piece of undeserved good luck for America and the world. Less than a year after Nixon's fall, the South Vietnamese and Cambodian governments were on the verge of collapse. President Ford pleaded with Congress for emergency appropriations to aid them, but he dared not push too hard, so unpopular was the war by then (nor did he dare – being an unelected, accidental President). It is sobering (and frightening) to think about what Nixon might have done had he remained President. It is impossible to believe that with 60 per cent of the voters behind him and with his own determination to avoid being 'the first President to lose a war,' Nixon would have acted as Ford did and simply watch as Saigon fell to the enemy.

Despite the Vietnam debacle, the American view of the world has hardly changed. As Robert Tucker put it in 1973, 'Now as before, America would play a predominant role in the world, however that role might be redefined. . . . The nation's security and well-being would continue to be broadly equated with a world in which America occupies a preponderant position in the international hierarchy and in which change could be effected only in certain ways while certain types of change would be precluded altogether.'

How well America can control the world remains unclear, but obviously the glorious days of 1945 to 1970 are over. America can no longer give orders to the non-communist world and expect to see them immediately obeyed. Certainly it is a different world from 1938. Then, the United States had been as close to self-sufficiency as any large industrial modern nation is ever likely to get. The fantastic rise in American consumption after World War II, however, had made the American life-style dependent on foreign sources. Cheap raw materials from the so-called underdeveloped world had been the fuel for the great American economic boom. One does not have to be Marxist or a member of the New Left to see that American prosperity was geared to the continued flow of cheap raw materials, or that America's dominant world position was necessary to maintain that flow. Since the American people showed not the slightest willingness to reduce their life-style, an active American foreign policy appeared inevitable, but the most an active policy could accomplish would be to stave off, not prevent, the moment of truth.

This was revealed during the Arab oil boycott of 1973. For decades it had been axiomatic among American foreign-policy makers that the oil producers (or the tin or rubber or cocoa or coffee producers) could never get together to form a cartel. But during the 1973 Arab-Israeli war, the Organization of Petroleum Exporting Countries (O.P.E.C.) did it – and suddenly everyone realized that the Arabs had a stranglehold on the industrialized states, including America, which was importing one-third of her energy needs from the Arabs. Through brilliant personal diplomacy and unceasing labors, Henry Kissinger was able to lower the tension in the Middle East and get the oil flowing again, but the basic problems remain: Israel's occupation of Arab lands, a homeland for the Palestineans, and an Arab recognition of Israel's right to exist. Thus the West continues to live under the threat of another oil embargo. Even more ominous, the other raw-material suppliers to the West are beginning to consider forming their own cartels. The fat, happy days of the post–World War II era are coming to an end. It is, of course, unknown how America will react to these new threats to her access to cheap raw materials.

What is the United States going to make of the Vietnam experience? What is clear is that the country has decided to learn as little as possible from it. To the evident great relief of the war-weary nation, President Ford set the tone when he called for amnesia, not analysis. 'The lessons of the past in Vietnam,' Ford declared in 1975, 'have already been learned – learned by Presidents, learned by Congress, learned by the American people – and we should have our focus on the future.' The American people responded gratefully to his invitation to forget the whole nightmare.

So those who had made or supported the Vietnam policy remained in power, unquestioned about their role in the debacle, while those who had been critical since at least 1964 remained on the outside, looking in. That the doves had been right all along – their criticism was *not* based on hindsight – was ignored. No one asked why the mistakes had been made, much less what assumptions had been wrong.

There is, however, reason for cautious optimism about the future of American foreign policy. As President Ford indicated, there is general agreement to avoid foreign adventures, especially involvement in wars of national liberation.* That vague gentleman's agreement has yet to be translated into reductions in the Pentagon's budget, but it does exist as a sentiment. It is possible that it might lead to a gradual reduction in the American role of policeman of the world; tendencies in the direction of cutting back are meanwhile being reinforced by domestic economic and social requirements.

If one legacy of the Vietnam war is a less active American foreign policy, perhaps it was not all in vain, for the American people have shown again and again what prodigious bursts of energy they are capable of expending when not distracted by war. The great forward strides

---

* Yet at the beginning of 1976, Ford and Kissinger were doing all they could to get the United States involved in a civil war in Angola, claiming that it was a vital strategic spot, since it was a dagger pointed at Brazil. Congress was holding them back, with some success, but the Angolan adventure, coming so soon after the end in Vietnam, seemed an ill omen. One was reminded of the aftermath of the Korean War. Then disgruntled army officers had formed the 'Never Again Club,' dedicated to never again fighting a land war in Asia. Eight years later, in 1961, Kennedy was sending those same officers to Vietnam to fight.

in conquering the wilderness and settling the West came during periods of peace, as did the enormous industrial booms of the 1880s, 1920s, and 1950s. The great waves of reforms (as in the 1930s and early 1960s) also came during periods of peace. If the American people now turn their uncountable resources of talent, skills, energy, and intensity of concern away from the communist conspiracy and direct them instead toward the solution of the real problems of survival on this planet, the result might well be the greatest of all America's gifts to the world. As Benjamin Franklin put it in 1773, there never was a good war or a bad peace.

Suggestions for Further Reading

General

THERE are a number of good general histories of the Cold War although unfortunately most tend to begin in 1945. An exception is D. F. Fleming, *The Cold War and Its Origins, 1917–1960* (Doubleday, New York, 1961), a comprehensive two-volume study which, if poorly organized, is vigorous in its criticism of American policy. A better balanced and much shorter treatment is Walter LaFeber, *America, Russia, and the Cold War, 1945–1966* (John Wiley, New York, 1967). Louis Halle, *The Cold War as History* (Harper & Row, New York, 1967), attempts with some success to view with detachment, and has been described as the confessions of a former Cold Warrior. For a traditional interpretation of the Cold War, see John Spanier, *American Foreign Policy Since World War II* (3rd edition, Praeger, New York, 1968). One of the first, and still the most important, critical accounts of America's Cold War policies is William A. Williams, *The Tragedy of American Diplomacy* (2nd edition, Dell, New York, 1962). Herbert S. Dinerstein looks at events from the Russian point-of-view in *Fifty Years of Soviet Foreign Policy* (Johns Hopkins University, Baltimore, 1968). Walt W. Rostow explains his view of the world in *The United States in the World Arena: An Essay in Recent History* (Harper & Row, New York, 1960). A good general survey of the personalities involved is Lloyd C. Gardner, *Architects of Illusion: Men and Ideas in American Foreign Policy* (Quadrangle Books, Chicago, 1970). For this and the following sections, the interested student should consult LaFeber's excellent bibliography.

World War II

The literature on American policy in World War II is staggering in scope. One happy result is that there are a number of excellent, short, interpretative works, such as Robert A. Divine, *Roosevelt and World War II* (Johns Hopkins Univ., Baltimore, 1969), Kent

Roberts Greenfield, *American Strategy in World War II: A Reconsideration* (Johns Hopkins Univ., Baltimore, 1963), which is stronger on military than foreign policy, John L. Snell, *Illusion and Necessity: The Diplomacy of Global War* (Houghton Mifflin, Boston, 1963), and Gaddis Smith, *American Diplomacy During the Second World War* (John Wiley, New York, 1965). Stephen E. Ambrose, *The Supreme Commander: The War Years of Dwight D. Eisenhower* (Doubleday, New York, 1970), is a detailed account of American policy in Europe, while Gar Alperovitz, *Atomic Diplomacy* (Simon & Schuster, New York, 1965), examines the motives behind the use of the atomic bomb. Although long, detailed, and somewhat dated, Robert E. Sherwood's *Roosevelt and Hopkins: An Intimate History* (Revised, Harper & Row, New York, 1950) is still very much worth reading. The standard works for the wartime diplomacy are Herbert Feis, *Churchill, Roosevelt, Stalin: The War They Waged and the Peace They Sought* (Princeton Univ., Princeton, 1957), which is almost an official history, and William H. McNeill, *America, Britain, and Russia: Their Co-operation and Conflict, 1941–1946* (Oxford University Press, 1953). For a forthright revisionist account, highly critical of American policy, see Gabriel Kolko, *The Politics of War: The World and United States Foreign Policy, 1943–1945* (Random House, New York, 1968).

The Truman Years

Truman's own *Memoirs* (2 vols., Doubleday, Garden City, New York, 1955) and those of Dean Acheson, *Present at the Creation* (Norton, New York, 1969), provide a comprehensive official view, while George Kennan, *Memoirs 1925–1950* (Little, Brown, Boston, 1967), is a joy to read, not only because of Kennan's matchless style but also because he is somewhat detached, admits to mistakes, and examines the assumptions on which policy was based. All these virtues are lacking in Truman's and Acheson's works. Walter Millis, editor, *The Forrestal Diaries* (Viking, New York, 1951), and Arthur H. Vandenberg, *Private Papers* (Houghton Mifflin, Boston, 1952), are important sources. Joseph M. Jones, *The Fifteen Weeks* (Harcourt, Brace & World, New York, 1955), examines in detail, but uncritically, the events leading to the Truman Doctrine and the Marshall Plan. David Rees, *Korea: The Limited War* (St Martin's, New York, 1964), is a good general treatment that should be supplemented with I. F. Stone, *The Hidden History of the*

Korean War (Monthly Review, New York, 1952, reissued in 1969), which raises crucial questions about American policies in Korea. Robert E. Osgood, *N.A.T.O.: The Entangling Alliance* (Univ. of Chicago, Chicago, 1962), is a model study.

The Eisenhower Years

Eisenhower's memoirs, *The White House Years: A Personal Account* (2 vols., Doubleday, New York, 1963 and 1965), are primarily concerned with foreign policy. Samuel P. Huntington, *The Common Defense: Strategic Programs in National Politics* (Columbia University, New York, 1961), a truly outstanding work, is essential to any study of Eisenhower's (and Truman's) military policy. There was a multitude of critics of the New Look; perhaps the most important was Maxwell Taylor, *The Uncertain Trumpet* (Harper & Row, New York, 1959). Herman Finer, *Dulles Over Suez* (Quadrangle Books, Chicago, 1964), is a critical account of the Secretary of State's role in the 1956 crisis. Edmund Stillman and William Pfaff, *Power and Impotence: The Failure of America's Foreign Policy* (Random House, New York, 1966), while covering far more than the Eisenhower years, is a brilliant examination of the assumptions about the world of the Eisenhower administration. The most searching attack on Eisenhower's policy toward Castro is William A. Williams, *The United States, Cuba and Castro* (Monthly Review, New York, 1962). Theodore Draper, *Castro's Revolution* (Praeger, New York, 1962), expressed the view that Castro betrayed the revolution.

Kennedy and Johnson

Arthur M. Schlesinger, Jr, *A Thousand Days: John F. Kennedy in the White House* (Houghton Mifflin, Boston, 1965), and Theodore Sorensen, *Kennedy* (Harper & Row, New York, 1965), are accounts by insiders who are fully devoted to the memory of the late President. Schlesinger has more on foreign affairs than Sorensen does. Philip Geyelin, *Lyndon B. Johnson and the World* (Praeger, New York, 1966), and Rowland Evans and Robert Novak, *Lyndon B. Johnson: The Exercise of Power* (World, New York, 1966), are the most complete accounts yet available on Johnson. Elie Abel's *The Missile Crisis* (Lippincott, Philadelphia, 1966), is a first-rate account by a professional journalist; a part of the inside story is told by Robert

F. Kennedy in his *Thirteen Days: A Memoir of the Cuban Missile Crisis* (Norton, New York, 1969). The literature on Vietnam is overwhelming and growing; the best short scholarly account is probably George Kahin and John W. Lewis, *The United States in Vietnam* (Dial, New York, 1967). All of Bernard Fall's books are good; students should begin with the collection of his articles, *Vietnam Witness, 1953–1966* (Praeger, New York, 1966). Townsend Hoopes, *The Limits of Intervention* (McKay, New York, 1969), is an exceptionally good memoir by a key participant in the crucial decision to halt the bombing of North Vietnam. Robert W. Tucker, *Nation or Empire?* (Johns Hopkins Univ., Baltimore, 1968), is an excellent essay on the deeper meanings of the dove-hawk debate over Vietnam. David Kraslaw and Stuart Loory, in *The Secret Search for Peace in Vietnam* (Random House, New York, 1968), give the details of Hanoi's peace moves and Washington's reactions.

The Nixon Years

There is no up-to-date biography of Nixon, although there are many works on various stages of his career. The most thoughtful and thoroughly researched of the current biographies is Garry Wills, *Nixon Agonistes* (New American Library, New York, 1970); Wills does an outstanding job on Nixon's personality, his career, and his culture. Rowland Evans, Jr., and Robert D. Novak, *Nixon in the White House* (Random House, New York, 1971), is a quickie with little of substance on foreign policy. Dan Rather and Gary Paul Gates, *The Palace Guard* (Harper & Row, New York, 1974), is full of wonderfully interesting gossip and some insights but also weak on foreign policy. The best single work to appear so far on the foreign policy of the Nixon administration is Marvin Kalb and Bernard Kalb, *Kissinger* (Little, Brown, Boston, 1974). The Kalbs are reporters, and their work is full of insider information based on extensive interviews. They are sympathetic toward Kissinger and their work suffers from an absence of analysis, but it does have a great deal of detailed information. Kissinger's own *American Foreign Policy* (expanded ed., Norton, New York, 1974) presents the views of Nixon's Secretary of State, including some of his testimony at various times before the Senate Foreign Relations Committee. Henry Brandon's *The Retreat of American Power* (Delta, New York, 1974) and William Safire's *Before the Fall* (Doubleday, New York, 1975) are useful in any study of the Nixon administration. Much the best work I have seen on Vietnam is Frances Fitzgerald, *Fire in the Lake: The Vietnamese and the Americans in Vietnam* (Random House, New York, 1972), which is must reading for anyone who wishes to understand the Vietnam war. An outstanding summary of where America stands in the world and where she is going is Robert E. Osgood et al., *Retreat from Empire?: The First Nixon Administration* (Johns Hopkins Univ., Baltimore, 1973).

Index

CONFLICT AND TRANSFORMATION
The United States, 1844–1877

William R. Brock

This survey of the momentous period that encompassed the American Civil War is concerned not
only with that tragedy but also with the emergence
of modern American civilization from the simplicity
and confidence of earlier times. Although William
R. Brock gives politics their due weight, his uncon-
ventional approach sees political decisions in the
context of society as a whole. He therefore inter-
prets the Civil War as an ideological struggle between men who were responding to the deeper
needs of their times. Economic influences are considered, but the emphasis is on the way in which
convictions drove men to irreconcilable positions.
Thus the book's underlying theme is the perennial
problem of democratic societies: How can politics
deal with controversy when each side believes that
its opponents have betrayed the nation's faith and
traditions? William R. Brock is Professor of Modern
History at the University of Glasgow.

COMING OF AGE
The United States during the 1920's and 1930's

Donald R. McCoy

In this panoramic review of American politics, economics, and diplomacy between the two world wars, Donald R. McCoy discusses the development of big government, the rise of mass production and consumption, and the nation's new role in the international sphere. The turbulence of the interwar period is shown to have accelerated, rather than reversed, long-term trends in American history. Although the differences between the prosperity of the twenties and the depression of the thirties are covered in detail, the book's major theme is continuity, not contrast. Donald R. McCoy is Professor of History at the University of Kansas.

ON REVOLUTION

Hannah Arendt

The renowned social and political philosopher examines the phenomenon of revolution as exemplified by the archetypal uprisings in America, in France, and in Russia. 'Miss Arendt's admirers will welcome her excursion into the relatively neglected field of comparative revolution. She is never dull, enormously erudite, always imaginative, original, and full of insights' – *Sunday Times* (London). 'A brilliant tour de force as well as a drawn challenge to a generation of statistic-and-quotation-minded political scientists' — Harrison E. Salisbury, *The New York Times*.

AN INTRODUCTION TO CONTEMPORARY HISTORY

Geoffrey Barraclough

Professor Geoffrey Barraclough isolates in this volume some of the main themes of contemporary history. His purpose is to show the ways in which, since the closing years of the nineteenth century, the fundamental structure of world politics has changed. Our political vision must be adjusted accordingly. In Professor Barraclough's analysis, however, contemporary history is not confined to politics. Among the themes he pursues, in a book that boldly envisions the onset of a new epoch in the history of mankind, are the impact of science, the spread of technology, the challenge of Marxist ideology, and the reorientation, in this century, of all the arts.

THE FREE AND THE UNFREE
A New History of the United States

Peter N. Carroll and David W. Noble

Although European expansion was the driving force
that first opened up the frontier land called America,
the growth of the new nation would be forged over
the centuries by the diverse peoples who struggled
to make it their home. But not everyone who made
a home in the country that carved democracy out of
tyranny was accepted as an American, as a full citi-
zen; when the democratic, humanitarian principles
were tested by native Americans, blacks, immigrants,
religious minorities, and women, these principles
were too often found wanting. *The Free and the
Unfree* documents the dynamic relationship between these outgroups and the power-holders as it
weaves in a broad tapestry the threads of social,
cultural, political, and economic development of a
vigorous nation. The book conveys, with a keen
sense of participation, the unfolding of the United
States through four historical eras: from the country
on the eve of Columbus's discovery to the War for
Independence, from the founding of the Republic
to the upheaval of the Civil War, from Reconstruction to World War I, and from the 1920s to the
history-making Watergate scandal and the election
of President Jimmy Carter.

LATIN AMERICAN DEVELOPMENT
A Geographical Perspective

Alan Gilbert

Latin America is part and parcel of the Third World. Along with other less-developed areas, it exhibits a dependence on the industrialized world and shows a high degree of income inequality; and yet, despite these critical and continuing problems, it has experienced many beneficial changes during the past thirty years. Today, more people are engaged in secure industrial and commercial employment; improved social services have raised levels of literacy and lowered death rates; more governments have begun to accede to the demands of the deprived. Alan Gilbert examines the spatial incidence of these changes, studying in detail the modifications wrought by industrial growth, urbanization, rural development, and transport expansion. His aims are to demonstrate the uneven regional impact of economic development and to examine the practical choices confronting national and regional planners. As he shows, such choices pose many questions where there is little planning unanimity. Whether to control metropolitan expansion, where to best direct public investment, and how and when to assist declining regions still have no adequate answers. His critical summary of the extensive literature, however, encourages the reader to consider these questions and above all to ask whether current planning decisions are providing valid answers to them.

THE MAKING OF MODERN RUSSIA

Lionel Kochan

'This is a history of Russia from the earliest times up to the outbreak of the Second World War. However, in keeping with his choice of title, Mr. Kochan has concentrated on the modern period, devoting about as many pages to the eight years following the Emancipation of the Serfs in 1861 as to the preceding 800-odd years. . . . A successful balance has been held between such conflicting themes as foreign policy . . . foreign influences and native intellectual trends. . . . His book could be a valuable introduction to the general reader in search of guidance' – *Sunday Times* (London).